A COMMONWEALTH
OF GOLFERS

~

A COMMO
OF GO

Edited by Laurence Sheehan ∼ Photographs by Michael Carroll

NWEALTH
LFERS
1903-2003

A Centennial Tribute to the Game and Its Players

WITH CONTRIBUTIONS FROM

Geoffrey S. Cornish

John P. English

George Kimball

Bradley S. Klein

John P. Marquand

Francis Ouimet

John Updike

Herbert Warren Wind

The Massachusetts
Golf Association

A COMMONWEALTH OF GOLFERS
©2002 by the Massachusetts Golf Association

Photographs ©2002 by Michael Carroll

Massachusetts Golf Association
300 Arnold Palmer Blvd.
Norton, MA 02766-1365
(800) 356-2201
www.mgalinks.org

MGA Centennial Committee
Richard D. Haskell, *Chairman*
Thomas E. Landry, *Executive Director, MGA*
Becky Blaeser, *Director of Communications, MGA*
John F. Dezieck
John P. English
James F. Gaquin, Jr.
Jerry R. Green
Thomas P. Lavigne
J. Louis Newell
Anne Marie Tobin

Impress, Inc., Northampton, MA
Hans Teensma, *Design Director*
Lisa Newman, *Production Director*
Katie Craig, *Associate Designer*
Michael Nesmith, *Photo Assistant*
Kathryn Precourt, *Stylist*

Printed by Toppan Shenzhen, China

Library of Congress Cataloging-in-Publication Data
A Commonwealth of Golfers, A Tribute to the Game and Its Players/by the Massachusetts Golf Association.
    —1st ed.
Golf—Massachusetts. I. Massachusetts Golf Association

ISBN 0-971-99530-3

10 9 8 7 6 5 4 3 2 1

FIRST EDITION

PERMISSIONS
"Portrait of the Architect as a Young Man" is reprinted from the 1999 U.S. Open Championship Program, Courtesy Golf Magazine Properties.
"A Caddie's Story" is reprinted from *A Game of Golf*, copyright ©1932, by permission of the Francis Ouimet Scholarship Fund.
"Birth of the Ryder Cup" is reprinted from The 33rd Ryder Cup Matches Program. Courtesy PGA of America.
"Notes of a Native Son," originally published in *The New Yorker*, is reprinted by permission, copyright ©1971, 1972, 1978, 1983, 1984, 1985, 1987.
"Trouble in the Locker Room" from *Life at Happy Knoll* by John Marquand, copyright ©1955, 1956, 1957 by J. P. Marquand; copyright ©renewed. By permission of Little, Brown and Company.

OTHER PHOTO CREDITS
AP/Worldwide: R.T. Jones, Jr. et al (17), G. Sarazen et al (28)
Boston Globe: J. Frithsen (33), P. Bradley (47), K. Johnson (48), C. Volpone (269), E. Fletcher (272)
Boston Public Library: 1919 Open at Brae Burn (18), R.T. Jones, Jr. et al (18), F. Ouimet (20), G. Vare (21), H. Picard et al (28), H. Smith et al (28), F. Wright and E. Lowery (33), R. Ruggles (33), P. Harney (33), W. Blaney (36), C. Curtis and H. Wightman (37), F. Corcoran (42), K. Whitworth (47), G. Wright (72), A. Ross (268), B. Toski (268), J. Burke (278), H. Wind (280)
Courtesy Hyannisport Club: J. Kennedy (234)
University of Massachusetts: L. Dickinson (193)
MGA: B. Douglass (48), K. Johnson et al (267), B. Crowley (269), D. Quigley (269), L. MacDuff, J. Miller and J. Millen (270), M. Hetnick (270), F. Pitts (272), M. and B. O'Kelly (273), D. Reycroft and R. Bump (274)
Ouimet Library: F. Ouimet and E. Lowery (20), L. Martin (37)
Courtesy Milton R. Reach III: H. Vardon et al (16), men in horse cart (37), R.T. Jones, Jr. et al (199), M.R. Reach et al (199)
Brian Smith: A. Tobin (47), F. Vana (48), J. Salinetti (48), Tedesco (49), Ryder Cup (2—52-53), J. Driscoll (267), J. Ruschioni (275)
Courtesy Charles H. Sellman: F. Sellman (43)
Courtesy Edward S. Stimpson III: E. Stimpson (27)
Courtesy Spalding Worldwide: A.G. Spalding (186), R.T. Jones, Jr. (186)
Courtesy William Tarlow: R. and W. Tarlow (92)
USGA: H. Jaques, Jr. (27), T. Woods (51), Walker Cup (2—146-147), W. Hagen (204), B. Crosby (207), B. Darwin (210), B. Crenshaw (213), J. Guilford (266), L. Little (278), W. Crossley (279)
Courtesy Winged Foot Golf Club: J. Anderson (27)
Courtesy WGAM: R. Vahey (276), J. Goodwin (276)

Acknowledgments

I T WOULD NOT HAVE BEEN POSSIBLE to compile this book without the cooperation and encouragement of literally hundreds of people all across Massachusetts, and beyond, and even as we single out the following individuals for special thanks, we reluctantly omit the names of many others who came to our aid. Thanks, then, to Bill Safrin, Peter McEachern and Peter Connolly at Myopia, Walter Lankau and Karen Giles at Stow Acres, Daniel Weadock and Brian Lynch at The International, Louis Newell, Brendan Walsh and David Chag at The Country Club and Bob Donovan at the Francis Ouimet Scholarship Fund. Also we thank Bill Tarlow and Alastair Johnston for help in piecing together a picture of the historic golf-shoe manufacturing industry in Brockton, and Brian DeLacey for his insights into the early days of golf in Boston.

Our thanks go to David Mittell at Duxbury, Ted and Stephen Mingolla and Gary Young at Pleasant Valley, Steve Demmer at Kittansett, Mike Donahoe at Vesper and Paul Lazar at Worcester. Also thanks to Joe Gomes for digging into his files for materials on the early history of Acushnet.

In the western part of the state we received help from Jim Walker and Marty Salvadore at Stockbridge, Glenn Zito, Bob Bontempo and Bob Bagg at The Orchards, Robert Rulewich at Crumpin-Fox, Milton R. Reach Jr., Milton Reach III, Paul Pohl and Cary Jubinville at Longmeadow and Andy Blau at Pittsfield. Mike Milewski at UMass and Susanne Clement at the GCSAA, along with Geoffrey Cornish, Joe Troll and Mel Lucas,

helped us draw a bead on the early days of green-keeping. Jackie Beck was kind enough to let us photograph in the archive room at Spalding, with help from Michael Waite. Thanks also to Gitty Scheft for helping us obtain permission to excerpt from *The New Yorker* writings of Herbert Warren Wind.

On the Cape, we were welcomed by Jay Wick and Dan Hogberg at Oyster Harbors, Brian Silva at The Captains, Dennis Hoye at Cranberry Valley, Sandy Dowling and Rick Johnson at Hyannisport, and Brian Hamilton, Richard Davenport and Thomas Maas at Eastward Ho! Thanks to all, on Nantucket, especially Mark Heartfield and Doug Ellsworth at Sankaty Head and Mark Lucas at Nantucket. We are especially grateful for the hospitality and good humor of our golfing friends in Harwich Port, Mary and Tidal Henry.

We also would like to thank Rick Dunfey and Brian Smith at *MassGolfer* and Jim McCabe and Paul Harber at the *Boston Globe*. Also, Shirley Hatch was an immense help in organizing our photo files.

The design and production team at Impress, led by the unflappable Hans Teensma, transformed our raw materials into a feast for the eyes. Thank you Hans, Lisa and Katie.

Finally, our hats are off to Dick Haskell and the members of his centennial committee for their guidance, moral and material support and infinite patience, and, in the case of John English, for his essay on the history of the game in Massachusetts.

Larry Sheehan
Mike Carroll

Table of Contents

Massachusetts Golf House, Museum and Hall of Fame in Norton, Massachusetts

Foreword

WITH THE OPENING of our new headquarters at TPC Boston in Norton, the Massachusetts Golf Association has begun a momentous transition from the past to the future. It is only fitting, in this centennial year of the MGA, that we pay tribute to all that has come before.

A Commonwealth of Golfers celebrates the rich and diverse heritage of golf in Massachusetts, at the same time tracing the pioneering role of the MGA in the growth and development of the game over the past 100 years. In 1903 the stated mission of the MGA was "to promote the interests of golf."

Today, with 380 member clubs and some 101,500 member golfers, the organization has evolved into a professionally staffed and managed entity, but it remains firmly committed to the simply stated high purpose first set forth when the game was in its infancy in this country.

A Commonwealth of Golfers is both a journey through the past and through the infinitely varied topography of golf as it exists in Massachusetts.

The camera of nationally acclaimed photographer Michael Carroll ranged widely throughout the state, capturing not only contrasts in golfing terrain and shotmaking challenge, but unique expressions in the personality and character of the game itself. We hope you will find this book's carefully sewn quilt of beautiful images, accompanied by testimonies to the game and its players by such masters of the written word as John Updike and Herbert Warren Wind (Massachusetts citizens both), to be a fair and full representation of the Commonwealth's wonder-filled world of golf.

— Michael J. Reilly
Dedham Country & Polo Club
President, Massachusetts Golf Association, 2002–03

PAST PRESIDENTS OF THE MASSACHUSETTS GOLF ASSOCIATION

G. Herbert Windeler	The Country Club	1903–10
Herbert Jaques	The Country Club	1911–14
Harry L. Ayer	Essex County Club	1915–16
Henry W. Wilder	The Country Club	1917–18
Albert D. Locke	Brae Burn Country Club	1919
Barton K. Stephenson	Winchester Country Club	1920–21
Everett S. Litchfield	The Country Club	1922–23
William F. Garcelon	Commonwealth Country Club	1924–25
Raynor M. Gardiner	Weston Golf Club	1926–27
Harold W. Pierce	The Country Club	1928
Alvah W. Rydstrom	Norfolk Golf Club	1929–30
Talbot C. Chase	Oakley Country Club	1931–32
Charles H. Cross	Unicorn Golf Club	1933–34
Charles E. Mason	The Country Club	1935–36
Erastus B. Badger	Winchester Country Club	1937–38
C. Campbell Patterson, Jr.	The Country Club	1939–40
Melville P. Merritt	Tedesco Country Club	1941–42
William O. Blaney	Brae Burn Country Club	1943–44
Joseph H. Batchelder	Salem Country Club	1945–46
Benjamin F. Jaques	Blue Hill Country Club	1947–48
Osmund O. Keiver	Tedesco Country Club	1949
Clarence Cochrane	Bellevue Golf Club	1950–51
Clark Hodder	Framingham Country Club	1952
George O. Russell, Jr.	Weston Golf Club	1953–54
John W. Goodrich	The Country Club	1955–56
Joseph A. Galvin, Jr.	Brae Burn Country Club	1957–58
Leon S. Bishop	Thorny Lea Golf Club	1959–60
Duncan Dewar, Jr.	Worcester Country Club	1961
Edward L. Butler	Duxbury Yacht Club	1961–62
William G. Harding	Dedham Country & Polo Club	1963–64
Arthur W. Rice, Jr.	Weston Golf Club	1965–66
Charles M. Pyle, Jr.	The Country Club	1967–68
Henry F. Wischusen	Bellevue Golf Club	1969–70
John P. English	Taconic Golf Club	1971
Curtis M. Carr	Pleasant Valley Country Club	1972
Lionel MacDuff	Salem Country Club	1973–74
John Arnold	Duxbury Yacht Club	1975–76
James B. Wilcox	Winchester Country Club	1977–78
A. Dixon Sykes	Weston Golf Club	1979–80
Andrew C. Bailey	Dedham Country & Polo Club	1981
Ferdinand L. Carangelo	Tedesco Country Club	1982–83
Harry B. McCracken	Charles River Country Club	1984–85
Ray C. Bump, Jr.	Country Club of Halifax	1986–87
William C. Foley	Wollaston Golf Club	1988–89
Robert G. Dowling III	Hyannisport Club	1990–91
Paul S. Evans	Duxbury Yacht Club	1992–93
Daniel L. Hurley	Indian Ridge Country Club	1994–95
John R. Perry, Jr.	Weston Golf Club	1996–97
Oliver G. Kelley	Milton-Hoosic Club	1998–99
Cary R. Jubinville	The Orchards Golf Club	2000–01

Member Clubs of the Massachusetts Golf Association

Dates indicate year founded. Centennial clubs (100 years old or older) are designated in color.

Acoaxet Club, 1919
Acushnet River Valley Golf Course, 1998
Agawam Municipal Golf Course, 1928
Allendale Country Club, 1956
Amesbury Golf & Country Club, 1923
Amherst Golf Club, 1900
Andover Country Club, 1924
Atlantic Country Club, 1994
Ballymeade Country Club, 1990
Bas Ridge Golf Course, 1927
Bass River Golf Course, 1900
Bass Rocks Golf Club, 1896
Bay Path Golf Course, 1962
Bay Pointe Country Club, 1964
Bayberry Hills Golf Course, 1988
Bear Hill Golf Club, 1900
Beaver Brook Golf Course, 1964
Bedfordshire Golf Club, 1989
Bedrock Golf Club, 1992
Bellevue Golf Club, 1898
Belmont Country Club, 1908
Berkshire Hills Country Club, 1925
Berlin Country Club, 1957
Beverly Golf & Tennis Club, 1910
Black Rock Golf Club, 2000
Blackstone National Golf Club, 1996
Blissful Meadows Golf Course, 1992
Blue Hill Country Club, 1924
Blue Rock Golf Course, 1962
Bradford Country Club, 1990
Brae Burn Country Club, 1897
Braintree Municipal Golf Course, 1955
Brockton Country Club, 1900
Brookline Golf Club, 1931
Brookmeadow Country Club, 1967
Butternut Farm Golf Club, 1993
Cape Ann Golf Course, 1931
Cape Cod Country Club, 1928
Cape Cod National Golf Club, 1998
Cedar Glen Golf Club, 1928
Cedar Hill Golf Club, 1981
Charles River Country Club, 1921
Charter Oak Country Club, 2000
Chatham Seaside Links, 1914
Chelmsford Country Club, 1964
Chemawa Country Club, 1959
Chequessett Yacht & Country Club, 1929
Cherry Hill Golf Course, 1965
Chicopee Country Club, 1965
Clearview Country Club, 1969
Cohasse Country Club, 1916
Cohasset Golf Club, 1894
Concord Country Club, 1895
Country Club of Billerica, 1972

Country Club of Greenfield, 1896
Country Club of Halifax, 1966
Country Club of New Bedford, 1902
Country Club of New Seabury, 1962
Country Club of Pittsfield, 1897
Country Club of Wilbraham, 1927
Country View Golf Club, 1964
Cranberry Valley Golf Course, 1974
Cranwell Resort & Golf Club, 1926
Crestview Country Club, 1958
Crestwood Country Club, 1959
Crumpin-Fox Club, 1979
Crystal Springs Golf Course, 1961
Cummaquid Golf Club, 1895
Cyprian Keyes Golf Club, 1997
D.W. Field Golf Course, 1926
Dedham Country & Polo Club, 1910
Dennis Highlands Golf Course, 1984
Dennis Pines Golf Course, 1964
Dunroamin Country Club, 1966
Duxbury Yacht Club, 1895
East Mountain Country Club, 1963
Easton Country Club, 1961
Eastward Ho! Country Club, 1922
Edgartown Golf Club, 1926
Edge Hill Golf Course, 1996
Edgewood Golf Course, 1935
Egremont Country Club, 1930
Ellinwood Country Club, 1929
Elmcrest Country Club, 1965
Essex County Club, 1893
Evergreen Valley Golf Course, 1991
Falcon Golf Course, 1966
Fall River Country Club, 1895
Falmouth Country Club, 1965
Far Corner Golf Course, 1967
Farm Neck Golf Club, 1979
Ferncroft Country Club, 1969
Firefly Golf Course, 1963
Forest Park Country Club, 1900
Foxborough Country Club, 1955
Framingham Country Club, 1902
Franconia Golf Course, 1929
Franklin Country Club, 1899
Franklin Park Golf Course, 1896
Fresh Pond Golf Course, 1938
Furnace Brook Golf Club, 1947
Gardner Municipal Golf Course, 1936
General Electric Athletic Association, 1939
George Wright Golf Course, 1938
Glen Ellen Country Club, 1963
Grand View Country Club, 1963
Green Harbor Golf Club, 1971
Green Hill Municipal Golf Course, 1929

Greenock Country Club, 1895
Groton Country Club, 1925
Hampden Country Club, 1974
Hatherly Country Club, 1899
Haverhill Country Club, 1925
Hawthorne Country Club, 1961
Heather Hill Country Club, 1959
Hemlock Ridge Golf Course, 1971
Heritage Country Club, 1964
Heritage Hill Country Club, 1974
Hickory Hill Golf Course, 1968
Hickory Ridge Country Club, 1976
Highland Country Club, 1901
Highland Golf Links, 1898
Hillcrest Country Club, 1939
Hillside Country Club, 1977
Hillview Golf Course, 1956
Holden Hills Country Club, 1955
Holyoke Country Club, 1908
Hopedale Country Club, 1953
Hopkinton Country Club, 2001
Hyannis Golf Club, 1972
Hyannisport Club, 1897
Indian Meadows Golf Course, 1990
Indian Pond Country Club, 2000
Indian Ridge Country Club, 1962
Ipswich Country Club, 1989
John F. Parker Municipal Golf Course, 1980
Juniper Hill Golf Course, 1931
Kelley Greens Golf Course, 1894
Kernwood Country Club, 1914
Kettle Brook Golf Club, 1999
Kings Way Golf Club, 1988
Lakeview Golf Course, 1918
Lakeville Country Club, 1968
Larry Gannon Municipal Golf Course, 1931
LeBaron Hills Country Club, 2001
Ledgemont Country Club, 1947
Leicester Country Club, 1896
Leo J. Martin Golf Course, 1932
Lexington Golf Club, 1895
Little Harbor Country Club, 1964
Locust Valley Golf Course, 1932
Long Meadow Golf Club, 1909
Longmeadow Country Club, 1922
Lost Brook Golf Club, 1962
Ludlow Country Club, 1921
Maplegate Country Club, 1994
Maplewood Golf Course, 1960
Marion Golf Course, 1903
Marlborough Country Club, 1922
Marshfield Country Club, 1922
Maynard Country Club, 1921
Meadow Brook Golf Club, 1898

Merrimack Golf Course, 1902
Miacomet Golf Club, 1963
Middlebrook Country Club, 1954
Middleton Golf Course, 1966
Mill Valley Golf Links, 1960
Millwood Golf Course, 1968
Mink Meadows Golf Course, 1936
Mohawk Meadows Golf Course, 2001
Monoosnock Country Club, 1924
Mount Hood Golf Course, 1940
Mount Pleasant Country Club, 1956
Mount Pleasant Golf Club, 1910
Myopia Hunt Club, 1875
Nabnasset Lake Country Club, 1935
Nantucket Golf Club, 1998
Nashawtuc Country Club, 1960
Needham Golf Club, 1923
Nehoiden Golf Club, 1903
New Bedford Municipal Golf Course, 1981
New England Country Club, 1990
New Meadows Golf Club, 1977
New Sandy Burr Country Club, 1922
Newton Commonwealth Golf Course, 1897
Nonquitt Golf Club, 1962
Norfolk Golf Club, 1896
North Adams Country Club, 1903
North Andover Country Club, 1897
North Hill Country Club, 1966
Northampton Country Club, 1898
Northfield Golf Club, 1908
Norton Country Club, 1959
Norwood Country Club, 1977
Oak Hill Country Club, 1921
Oak Ridge Golf Club, 1974
Oak Ridge Golf Course, 1962
Oakley Country Club, 1898
Ocean Edge Golf Club, 1986
Olde Barnstable Fairgrounds
  Golf Course, 1992
Olde Salem Greens Golf Course, 1906
Olde Scotland Links, 1997
Ould Newbury Golf Club, 1919
Oyster Harbors Club, 1926
Pakachoag Golf Course, 1971
Patriot Golf Course, 1996
Paul Harney's Golf Club, 1967
Pembroke Country Club, 1972
Penfield's Twin Brooks Golf Course, 2001
Petersham Country Club, 1922
Pine Brook Country Club, 1924
Pine Grove Golf Club, 1957
Pine Meadows Golf Course, 1938
Pine Oaks Golf Club, 1967
Pine Ridge Country Club, 1969
Pine Valley Country Club, 1959
Pinecrest Golf Course, 1958
Pinehills Golf Club, 2001
Pleasant Valley Country Club, 1961
Plymouth Country Club, 1908

Pocasset Golf Club, 1916
Ponkapoag Golf Course, 1932
Pontoosuc Lake Country Club, 1920
Poquoy Brook Golf Course, 1963
Presidents Golf Course, 1972
Quaboag Country Club, 1899
Quail Hollow Golf & Country Club, 1991
Quashnet Valley Country Club, 1973
Red Tail Golf Club, 2001
Rehoboth Country Club, 1966
Reservation Golf Club, 1895
Ridder Farm Golf and Country Club, 1961
River Bend Country Club, 1998
Rochester Golf Course, 1968
Rockland Golf Course, 1963
Rockport Golf Club, 1915
Rolling Green Golf Course, 1969
Round Hill Golf Links, 1973
Rowley Country Club, 1971
Royal Crest Country Club, 1973
Royal Oaks Country Club, 1999
Sagamore Spring Golf Club, 1929
Salem Country Club, 1895
Sandwich Hollows Country Club, 1973
Sankaty Head Golf Club, 1923
Sassamon Trace Golf Course, 2001
Scituate Country Club, 1919
Segregansett Country Club, 1893
Shaker Farms Country Club, 1955
Shaker Hills Golf Club, 1991
Sharon Country Club, 1898
Sheraton Colonial Hotel & Golf Club, 1922
Skyline Country Club, 1963
South Shore Country Club, 1922
Southampton Country Club, 1929
Southers Marsh Golf Club, 2000
Southwick Country Club, 1928
Spring Valley Country Club, 1963
Springfield Country Club, 1897
Squirrel Run Golf & Country Club, 1992
St. Anne Country Club, 1962
St. Mark's Golf Course, 1923
Sterling Country Club, 1991
Stockbridge Golf Club, 1895
Stow Acres Country Club, 1927
Strawberry Valley Golf Course, 1961
Swansea Country Club, 1967
Taconic Golf Club, 1896
Tatnuck Country Club, 1898
Tedesco Country Club, 1903
Templewood Golf Course, 2000
Tewksbury Country Club, 1998
The Blandford Club, 1909
The Brookside Club, 1997
The Captains Golf Course, 1985
The Country Club, 1882
The Georgetown Club, 1991
The Golf Course at Cold Spring, 2000
The International Golf Club, 1901

The Kittansett Club, 1922
The Ledges Golf Club, 2001
The Meadows Golf Course, 1933
The Milton-Hoosic Club, 1891
The Orchards Golf Club, 1922
The Ranch Golf Club, 2001
The Ridge Club, 1989
The Woods of Westminster, 1998
Thomas Memorial Golf &
  Country Club, 1958
Thomson Country Club, 1963
Thorny Lea Golf Club, 1900
Touisett Country Club, 1961
Tournament Players Club of Boston, 2000
Townsend Ridge Country Club, 1996
Trull Brook Golf Course, 1963
Twin Hills Country Club, 1964
Twin Springs Golf Club, 1933
Tyngsboro Country Club, 1934
Unicorn Golf Course, 1925
Vesper Country Club, 1875
Veterans Memorial Golf Course, 1962
Wachusett Country Club, 1927
Wahconah Country Club, 1930
Walpole Country Club, 1927
Wampanoag Golf Club, 1937
Wampatuck Country Club, 1904
Waubeeka Golf Links, 1966
Waverly Oaks Golf Club, 1998
Wayland Country Club, 1946
Webster-Dudley Golf Club, 1926
Wedgewood Pines Country Club, 1997
Wellesley Country Club, 1910
Wenham Country Club, 1899
Wentworth Hills Golf & Country Club, 2000
Westborough Country Club, 1921
Westminster Country Club, 1957
Weston Golf Club, 1894
Westover Golf Course, 1957
White Cliffs Country Club, 1983
White Pines Golf Course, 1999
Whitinsville Golf Club, 1925
Wianno Club, 1916
Widow's Walk Golf Course, 1997
Willowbend Club, 1987
Winchendon Country Club, 1926
Winchester Country Club, 1902
Winthrop Golf Club, 1903
Woburn Country Club, 1923
Wollaston Golf Club, 1895
Woodbriar Golf Course, 1961
Woodland Golf Club, 1896
Woods Hole Golf Club, 1899
Worcester Country Club, 1900
Worthington Golf Club, 1904
Wyantenuck Country Club, 1896
Wyckoff Country Club, 1967

The long, colorful history of golf in Massachusetts has been shaped by people of genius, innovation, perseverance and dedication. Through its member clubs throughout the state, the Massachusetts Golf Association has played no small part in that history. For 100 years and counting, the officers, staff members and volunteers of the MGA have worked to promote the interests of golf, to better conditions of play, to provide fair and open competitions and to illuminate for all golfers the rules and customs of a game to which the word "honor" clings like a golf glove to the hand. Indeed, the remarkable growth of the game in the Bay State can be attributed in part to those men and women whose primary interest has focused on the quality of the game itself. They have given golf in Massachusetts a heritage of unity, good sportsmanship and personal integrity which distinguish it to this day. In the story of golf in the Commonwealth, their individual and collective efforts stand out in sharp relief.

COMMONWEALTH

Woodland Golf Club, Auburndale, Massachusetts

GOLF IN THE COMMONWEALTH

~

The story of golf in Massachusetts is as rich and varied as the golf courses themselves, ranging from citified to suburban, from windswept links on Cape Cod to the vertiginous layouts of the Berkshires.

BY JOHN P. ENGLISH

THE INTRODUCTION OF GOLF in Massachusetts apparently took place on July 13, 1728 (275 years ago), when Governor William Burnett arrived from England with his family, servants—and a set of golf clubs. Governor Burnett's tenure was short; he died in 1729. In the inventory of his estate, with his magic lantern, telescope, musical instruments and other treasures was listed: "9 gouffe clubs and an iron vlued at 2 pounds." The inventory constitutes the first known reference to golf in the Bay State. One can only wonder if and where the governor used those clubs—in front of the State House on Boston Common?

A century and a half elapsed before the next milestone in Massachusetts golf, and it came with the burgeoning of country clubs across the land—country clubs, not golf clubs. The Country Club in

Brookline was the first of these to achieve permanence in its site, but there was no thought of golf there at the time the club was conceived in early April of 1882, at a dinner at the home of James Murray Forbes on Commonwealth Avenue in Boston. The idea was only to provide "a comfortable clubhouse for the use of members and their families, a simple restaurant, bed rooms, a bowling alley, lawn tennis grounds, & c. ..." It would be helpful, however, for such a club to be in place as golf found a permanent home here later on. But it would be another decade before the game moved in.

There are reports of trial runs at golf in several places during that decade, most notably when George Wright, originally famous as a shortstop in professional baseball, received some golf clubs he had ordered through an English catalog for the Wright & Ditson sporting goods store he operated at 344 Washington

FIELDS OF GLORY: BELMONT Belmont Country Club, a Donald Ross design dating from 1918, has witnessed its fair share of top-flight golf over the years, hosting four Massachusetts Amateurs, four Massachusetts Opens and, in earlier years, a host of professional tournaments and exhibitions. Hole pictured: No. 8, a 376-yard dogleg par-4. *Above:* Many of the 63 golf clubs in Massachusetts that have already reached the century mark have published histories to commemorate the occasion, as have some clubs with shorter tenures.

Street in Boston. With permission from the Boston Parks Department and the aid of the Badminton Library volume *Golf*, Wright directed John Smith, a clerk, to lay out some holes at Franklin Park. On December 10, 1890, Wright then gave the game a well-publicized trial with Temple Craig, Fred Mansfield and Fred McDonald. Wright, Smith and Mansfield gave it another try on Revere Beach in March of 1891. Reports on their reactions are mixed. Wright himself was favorably impressed, but others felt the game required too much walking and would never catch on. In any event, golf was not re-established at Franklin Park for another five years. Even earlier, in what may have been only one of other less publicized ventures, Abbott Lawrence apparently was playing on three holes laid out in a meadow on Highland Street in Taunton.

Certainly golf was played earlier in nearby states—and even organized into clubs which have survived. Scots golfers living in Troy, New York, traveled over to Dorset, Vermont, and almost certainly were organized and playing there in 1886. Joseph M. Fox surely organized the Foxburg Country Club in Foxburg, Pennsylvania, in 1887. The Apple Tree Gang in Yonkers, New York, formed the St. Andrew's Golf Club in 1888. And in neighboring Newport, Rhode Island, Theodore G. Havemeyer laid out a nine-hole course on Brenton's Point and organized the Newport Country Club in 1890.

It remained for a young woman, however, to establish the game on a permanent basis in Massachusetts. Her name was Florence Boit, and she lived in Boston. In the autumn of 1892, Miss Boit, who had played the game at Pau, a resort in southern France, brought some clubs and balls to the home of her aunt and uncle, the Arthur B. Hunnewells in Wellesley, and demonstrated it on their estate and on the lands of R. G. Shaw and Hollis Hunnewell which adjoined. Among those who watched her exhibitions were members of the Cabot family of Brookline and Laurence Curtis, a neighbor in Boston. They clearly caught the fever. George and W. R. Cabot

tell of playing the game subsequently at Louis Cabot's estate on Jamaica Pond in Brookline in November of 1892, and of organizing the Warren Farms Golf Club with some 50 members exclusively for golf early in 1893, although the Warren Farms club did not survive. Happily, however, Curtis persuaded the executive committee of The Country Club on November 29, 1892, to approve the laying out of a course there "and to spend the necessary amount up to $50." In the spring of 1893 Curtis, Hunnewell and Robert Baron opened to their fellow members the first six holes of what was to become the first permanent golf course in Massachusetts.

In the same spring season, an equally significant event occurred in a humble home across the way from The Country Club at 246 Clyde Street: a boy

UNFORGETTABLE FOURSOMES Appearing in an exhibition match at Springfield Country Club in 1900 were (left to right) Harry Vardon, who would go on to win the British Open six times, still a record for that championship; Jim Toole, a fine local amateur golfer; Milton "M.B." Reach, general manager of A. G. Spalding & Bros. in Chicopee; and Ted Ray, 1912 British Open and 1920 U.S. Open champion. The British professionals, Vardon and Ray, had been hired by Spalding to tour the States to promote the game and Spalding's golf equipment. Their lengthy visit drew vast galleries by the standards of the day. During the tour, Vardon, who usually played against the better ball of two opponents, won over 50 matches, halved 2 and lost 13. He also made time to capture the 1900 U.S. Open at Chicago Golf Club.

named Francis DeSales Ouimet was born on May 8, 1893. In that same month, most appropriately, the Spalding Athletic Library in New York published *Golf*, its first volume on the game.

The game spread here as if contagious in 1893 and 1894—and it may well have been. Players on the North Shore set up in 1893 both the Essex County Club in Manchester and another golf club in Prides Crossing which did not survive. The golfers in Taunton organized themselves as the Segregansett Country Club in 1893, and the game seems to have been played in Norfolk in the same time frame.

The simple beginning on the Hunnewell estate in Wellesley had informal parallels on the Weld estate in Brookline, the Appleton farm in Ipswich and the Moraine farm on Wenham Lake. Laurence

Below: An exhibition match at Woodland Golf Club in 1928 pitted (left to right) Johnny Farrell and Robert Tyre Jones, Jr., against Walter Hagen and Gene Sarazen and raised an astounding $10,000 for the U.S. Ryder Cup team, of which Hagen was captain. Collectively, members of this foursome would go on to win 26 modern major championships, 32 if Jones' five U.S. Amateur and one British Amateur titles are included. Jones lost the match for his side when he missed a short putt on the home green. *Boston Globe* reporter W. A. Whitcomb wrote: "Putting on a canting green from a distance of eight feet is no part of a pleasant undertaking even though there is nothing more important at stake than a 10-cent cigar." Unfazed, Jones stayed on in Boston to win the U.S. Amateur at Brae Burn the following week.

Curtis, who had brought golf to The Country Club, generated a seven-hole course for the Nahant Club in 1894. Golf was given a trial in 1894, too, by Henry M. Whitney, a summer resident, and friends on a six-hole course laid out on his land in Cohasset; the Cohasset Golf Club came into being and is still right there. The Rev. William E. Russell developed nine holes on Kendall Green, also in 1894, and this became the Weston Golf Club. Myopia Hunt Club made the game available to its members in Hamilton in 1894. Joseph H. Choate, Jr., and Eliot Tuckerman laid out three holes in a Stockbridge meadow, and Katherine di Pollone later set nine holes on her estate nearby in 1894 which led to the formation of the Stockbridge Golf Club the following year. Henry C. Thacher had a nine-hole private course on his property off Strawberry Lane in Yarmouth Port and Dr. Gorham Baker was playing on his lands in adjoining Barnstable in 1894, activities which led to the formation of the Cummaquid Golf Club a year later. Golf quite probably was introduced at other places in these early years. Certainly it had spread from Brookline to the North Shore, Cape Cod and the Berkshires, and the foundation had been laid for escalation in 1895.

In 1894, too, The Country Club brought Willie Campbell from Scotland to be its first professional, and Myopia imported Robert White from Scotland as its first professional and greenkeeper. Campbell became a missionary for the game, assisting several other clubs in creating their first courses. White moved on to New York and in 1916 shared in the founding of the Professional Golfers Association of America and served until 1920 as its first president.

As golf found its first permanent home in Massachusetts at The Country Club, so it also found early homes at other clubs not originally organized for the game. Myopia had been started in Winchester in the mid-1870s for baseball, tennis, foxhounds and other sports. It re-opened in Hamilton in 1882, in part to provide better facilities for horsemen and

FIELDS OF GLORY: BRAE BURN Walter Hagen retrieves his ball after holing out in an 18-hole playoff to defeat local favorite Mike Brady, seen in white, by one stroke in the 1919 U.S. Open at Brae Burn Country Club in West Newton, this despite a week of partying in Boston with his friend, singer Al Jolson. In his long career, the Brighton-born Brady won three Massachusetts Opens and had 9 top-10 finishes in 15 national opens. Brae Burn also has hosted one U.S. Amateur, two U.S. Women's Amateurs, two Curtis Cups—and more MGA championships than any other club in Massachusetts.

Bobby Jones' U.S. Amateur win at Brae Burn in 1928 made up for a disappointing exhibition match he had played there at age 15 with Alexa Stirling, when his temper got the better of him. "I behaved very badly when my game went apart," he later recalled. "I heaved numerous clubs, and once threw the ball away. I read the pity in Alexa's soft brown eyes and finally settled down, but not before I had made a complete fool of myself."

did not add golf to its offerings until 1894—over some opposition from those horsemen. What was to become the Milton-Hoosic Club opened for social activities in 1891 and the following year displayed an interest in golf by laying out a few holes at the Houghton Farm, which it had leased, on Hoosic-Whisick Pond. Unfortunately, the Houghton Farm was soon taken to form a part of the Blue Hills Reservation, and it was not until the club purchased the Shaller Farm, a separate site in Canton, in 1895, that it was able to develop a clubhouse and golf course there. The Milton Club and Hoosic-Whisick Club merger in 1946 created the Milton-Hoosic Club.

It was autumn of 1896 before golf returned to Franklin Park, and the credit this time redounds to Willie Campbell, the same man who had come from Scotland to The Country Club two years earlier. He hoped to broaden the appeal of the game by making it available not only at private clubs but to the public, as it had been in his native Scotland. Campbell in his role as a golf missionary persuaded the Boston Parks Department to build a nine-hole public course at Franklin Park and helped lay it out. This course opened in the fall of 1896 with Campbell in charge—only one year after the nation's first public course at Van Cortland Park in New York. By the time of his premature death in 1900, it was clear that his vision would be realized. To maximize this, however, he was succeeded by his wife, Georgina, who had been assisting her husband teaching women and children. In so doing, she became our first woman professional. And the course thrived until World War I.

The growth of the game was not now to be denied, and fortunately it grew in the hands of men and women whose primary interest focused on the quality of the game itself—its rules, its honor, its courtesies. They gave it a heritage of unity, good sportsmanship and personal integrity which distinguish it to this day.

Need for coordination and uniformity in rules and championships was apparent from the start, and Laurence Curtis and Samuel Sears, representing The Country Club, joined representatives from St. Andrew's Golf Club, Newport Golf Club, Shinnecock Hills Golf Club and Chicago Golf Club in New York on December 22, 1894, to found the United States Golf Association (USGA) and to elect Theodore G. Havemeyer of the Newport club its first president. Havemeyer, like Florence Boit, had become acquainted with the game while vacationing in Pau, France. The first club to be recorded as a member of the USGA after the incorporation by the original five was the Essex County Club, which joined a month later, in January of 1895. The new association's first Amateur, Open and Women's Championships were played in the summer of 1895 on Havemeyer's nine-hole course in Newport.

The role played by Laurence Curtis and Samuel Sears in launching the USGA was prophetic of the role to be played by so many other individuals representing clubs throughout the Commonwealth in the game's formative years. It was to be a role which would place Massachusetts among the true incubators of the game of golf as it was transplanted into North America in the last decade of the 19th century and the early years of the 20th.

While the USGA had its birth in New York, the leverage exercised by Massachusetts men in developing the game as we know it today is reflected in the fact that this Commonwealth provided four of its first eight presidents—Laurence Curtis, W. B. Thomas, G. Herbert Windeler (later to become the

Brae Burn's 2nd hole is only 308 yards long (272 yards from the ladies' tees, pictured) but is rated as the No. 7 handicap hole because of the narrow landing area for the tee shot and the severely bunkered two-tiered green, only 16 yards wide and 28 yards deep.

MOMENT OF TRUTH The iconic image of Francis Ouimet and his 10-year-old caddie Eddie Lowery on their way to triumph in the 1913 U.S. Open at The Country Club in Brookline is one of many fascinating images gracing the walls of the Ouimet Library. In later years, Ouimet (top) and Lowery became major figures in amateur golf at the state and national level, both as competitors and promoters of the game. The story of Ouimet's victory in the *Boston Evening Transcript*, written by John Anderson, himself a former Massachusetts Amateur champion, was picked up by papers across the country.

OUIMET IS THE WINNER

Captures the National Open Golf Championship

Woodland Amateur Beats British Professionals

Young Golfer's Victory Was Clean and Decisive

His Score Was 72 for the Eighteen Holes

Five Up on Vardon and Six on Ray

Wonderful Work Came Following the Turn

At That Point of Game They Were All Even

COMPLETE SCORE OF PLAY-OFF

Out	1	2	3	4	5	6	7	8	9	
Ouimet	5	4	4	4	5	4	4	3	5—38
Vardon	5	4	4	4	5	3	4	4	5—38
Ray	5	4	5	4	5	4	3	3	5—38

In	10	11	12	13	14	15	16	17	18	
Ouimet	3	4	4	4	5	4	3	3	4—34—38—72
Vardon	4	4	5	3	5	4	3	5	6—39—38—77
Ray	4	4	5	4	5	6	4	5	3—40—38—78

first president of the Massachusetts Golf Association (MGA) and Herbert Jaques, Sr. All four represented The Country Club. In addition, Herbert Jaques, Jr., and Harold W. Pierce, also members of The Country Club, later served as presidents, bringing the total to six. No other club in the land has provided the USGA with so many presidents.

Nor did it stop there. No other club has given the USGA as many years of service as executive committee members. The Country Club has been represented on the roll of officers and executive committee members in 76 of the 109 years since its founding. Individuals from The Country Club and from other clubs in Massachusetts who have served as officers and executive committee members include Harry L. Ayer, Jeanne-Marie Boylan, M. Lewis Crosby and Albert D. Locke, all of Brae Burn Country Club; Azariah T. Buffington of the Country Club of Fall River; Asa P. French of Chestnut Hill Golf Club; Francis D. Ouimet of Woodland Golf Club; Herbert C. Leeds of Myopia Hunt Club; Alfred I. Ripley of Oakley Country Club; and Edward L. Emerson, Charles L. Peirson, Charles M. Pyle, Jr., Arthur W. Rice, Jr., Henry H. Wilder and G. F. Willett, all of The Country Club—15, in addition to the 6 who served as presidents. And this does not include Edward E. Lowery, Francis Ouimet's caddie during the U.S. Open at Brookline in 1913, whose later service to the USGA came after he had moved to San Francisco.

The national championships which the fledgling USGA had inaugurated at Newport in 1895 prospered under such guidance, and the sponsoring body moved them around the country in ensuing years to areas where golf had taken hold. Eastern Massachusetts was, of course, one of these, and the USGA sent the third playing of its Women's Amateur Championship to the Essex County Club in August, 1897, the first of 11 Women's Amateurs and, overall, 45 USGA championships. In addition, one PGA championship, three Walker Cup, three Curtis Cup and two Ryder Cup matches have been awarded to the Bay State through 2003, the MGA's centennial year, the latest being the Men's and Women's State Team championships at Charles River and Wellesley Country Clubs.

There were 29 entrants in that first women's tournament at Essex. Beatrix Hoyt, 17, of the Shinnecock Hills Golf Club on Long Island won the medal with 108 and defeated Nellie Sargent, an Essex member, in the final to register the second of her three successive championships. Miss Sargent had been runner-up also in the first championship at the Meadow Brook Club in New York two years earlier. The Essex event in 1897 marked, also, the debut on the national scene of Margaret Curtis, a member of the entertaining club and one of the eight qualifiers at the age of 13.

By the turn of the century, the game was growing beyond the estates and clubs of the gentry as the motor vehicle was replacing the horse and carriage, stimulating a revolution in the economy of the nation and, among many other things, making an essentially suburban game even more accessible. The Studebaker Brothers Manufacturing Company sold its first motor vehicle in 1902, and Ford put its Model A on the market in 1903. (According to *Golf*, Massachusetts led the country in number of golf clubs with "upwards of 170.")

Florence Boit's contribution ensured our debt to women in the early development of the game here, and this was enhanced within three years of that U.S. Women's Amateur at Essex County Club (and three years

before Massachusetts' male golfers organized themselves). On March 5, 1900, a small group of women golfers met on Commonwealth Avenue in Boston and founded the Women's Golf Association of Boston, re-named in 1929 the Women's Golf Association of Massachusetts (WGAM). The founding women represented four clubs: Brae Burn, Concord, The Country Club and Oakley. Mrs. Frank E. Zerrahn of The Country Club was elected

FIELDS OF GLORY: WINCHESTER Glenna Collett Vare, called "the female Bobby Jones" after winning six U.S. Women's Amateurs, poses for the camera at Salem Country Club during the 1932 national championship. Vare, who played out of the Miacomet Club in Providence, won the 1921 women's state amateur at Winchester Country Club, when she was Glenna Collett. Celebrating its centennial in 2002, Winchester has long been in the forefront of amateur golf in the state. Hole pictured: the par-3 172-yard 9th.

first president, and the group quickly arranged the schedule of inter-club team matches, starting in May, which has been a hallmark of their programs ever since. An individual championship was inaugurated in the fall of 1900 at Oakley, and Grace B. Keyes of Concord defeated Harriot Curtis in the final. Today, the WGAM speaks for a membership of 2,200 women golfers.

More swiftly than their male counterparts, also, Massachusetts women made a significant impact in national play. Pauline Mackay of Oakley was the first: in 1905 she won the state and national amateur women's championships, defeating Margaret Curtis of Essex County in an all-Massachusetts USGA final at the Morris County Club in New Jersey. In the decade following, Massachusetts women won 7 of the 10 U.S. Women's Amateur titles: sister Harriot Curtis of Essex County won at Brae Burn in 1906; Margaret finally won at Midlothian, near Chicago, in 1907, dethroning sister Harriot in the final; Katherine Harley of the Country Club of Fall River won at Chevy Chase, near Washington, D.C., in 1908; Margaret Curtis won again at Baltusrol, in New Jersey, in 1911 and a third time at her home course, Essex County, in 1912. Mrs. H. Arnold Jackson of Oakley, the former Katherine Harley, followed Francis Ouimet's 1914 victory in the U.S. Amateur by win-

The Founding Clubs of the Massachusetts Golf Association

Albemarle G. C., Newtonville*

Allston G. C.*

Alpine G. C. of Fitchburg*

Andover G. C.

Bellevue G. C. of Melrose

Braeburn Golf Club

Brockton Country Club

Chestnut Hill G. C.*

Clifton G. C.*

Commonwealth Country C. of Allston

Concord G. C.

The Country Club of Brookline

Essex County Club

Fall River G. C.

Framingham Country Club

Hoosic Whisick Club

Kenilworth G. C. of Allston*

Lexington Golf Club

Meadow Brook G. C.

Medford G. C.*

Merrimac Valley G. C. of Lawrence

Misery Island G. C.*

Merry Mount G. C.*

Myopia Hunt Club

Country Club of New Bedford

Newton Centre G. C.*

Newton Golf Club*

Newton Highlands G. C.*

Norfolk G. C. of Dedham

Oakley Country Club

Salem Country Club of Danvers/Danvers C. C.*

Salem G. C.

Segregansett G. C. of Taunton

Country Club of Springfield

Tedesco Country Club

Vesper Country Club of Lowell

Wellington Hills G. C.*

Weston G. C.

Winchester G. C.

Winthrop G. C.

Wollaston Golf Club

Woodland G. C.

*Clubs identified by asterisks are no longer in existence.

ning a second time at Nassau on Long Island in 1914, thus bringing both the men's and women's national amateur championships to Massachusetts in the same year.

The Curtis sisters, by the way, were nieces of Laurence Curtis, who had introduced golf at The Country Club and at Nahant. Margaret's dominance was not limited to golf either. After dethroning her sister in the 1907 national golf final, she switched weapons in 1908 and won the national doubles championship at lawn tennis with Evelyn Sears, marking the only time an American has held national championships in both sports simultaneously.

Considerably later, in 1927, the Curtis sisters, who continued an active interest in girls' and women's play throughout their lives, presented a silver bowl of Paul Revere design, "to stimulate friendly rivalry among the women golfers of many lands." It took another five years to activate their idea and then only the United States and Great Britain participated, but by 1932 the USGA and the Ladies Golf Union of Great Britain had agreed to regular international matches and the Curtis Cup series came into being with a match at Wentworth, England, which the United States women won. Appropriately, the USGA returned the fourth playing of the match to the Curtis sisters' home club, Essex County, in 1938, and the United

States team under the captaincy of Frances E. Stebbins of Brae Burn won 5 to 3½. The international match has been returned twice again to Massachusetts, in 1958 and 1970, both times to Brae Burn, and no other state has entertained the event as many times. Another United States team, winning at Nottinghamshire, England, in 1960, was captained by a woman from Massachusetts, Mrs. Henri F. Prunaret of Brae Burn, and Joanne Goodwin of Haverhill Country Club was a member of her team.

Massachusetts men finally made their organizational move in the fall of 1902—a year when Teddy Roosevelt was president, the Wright brothers were taking to the air at Kitty Hawk, North Carolina, and on the eve of the baseball season when the Boston Red Sox, playing on the old Huntington Avenue grounds, were to win organized baseball's first World Series, defeating the Pittsburgh Pirates five games to four.

As early as 1899 a meeting of representatives of clubs in the Greater Boston area had agreed not to organize a state association, the feeling being "strongly against anything which might lead to mug-hunting and emphatically against the cultivation of the pseudo-amateur who usually appears when rivalry becomes keen in competitions among clubs in an association." G. Herbert Windeler, then secretary of The Country Club, pressed a more positive view, however, and three years later again circularized golf clubs throughout the state with an invitation to meet at the Exchange Club in Boston on December 11, 1902. Thirty-two sent representatives, and this time it was "the sense of this

SHIELD OF GLORY Bostonian Laurence Curtis, in whose honor one of the more impressive golf trophies at The Country Club is named, helped to open the first permanent golf course in Massachusetts in Brookline in 1893.

meeting that an Association be formed of Clubs belonging to the U.S.G.A. in the state of Massachusetts." A second session was required to bring this off, for another motion directed the chair to "appoint a committee of seven, to include himself, to draw up a Constitution and By-Laws for an Association, to be submitted for adoption." This second session took place again at the Exchange Club on February 24, 1903, some 38 clubs represented this time (six separately listed under "Other Golf Clubs" because they were not at the time affiliated with the USGA), and "The Constitution and By-Laws, as approved by the committee, were taken up and adopted as amended."

Forty-two clubs were represented at one or both sessions and so became founding clubs of the MGA. Their names are listed in the box on the opposite page exactly as they appeared in the original minutes (only 28 clubs are still in existence).

The mission of this new association was simplicity itself, as embodied in the original constitution: "The object of the Association shall be to promote the interests of golf." Those by-laws and an early action by the first executive committee of nine members revealed a narrower objective, however: Section 3 provided that: "It shall be the duty of the Executive Committee to arrange dates for competitions acceptable to the clubs and to provide for an Annual State Championship," and on March 4 the executive committee directed its handicap committee to submit "a handicap list of members of clubs belonging to this Association, based on the Par system"—reflecting the association's primary interest in arranging amateur competitions, with handicaps.

The first Massachusetts Amateur, "for residents of Massachusetts who are members of clubs belonging to the Association," was conducted in September of that same year, 1903, at Myopia. It was at match

Afterthoughts on Golf

A Massachusetts girl's recollections of golf in the 1890s

Afterthoughts, **by Georgina Paine Fisher Howland, "privately published for her grandchildren" in 1955, is a memoir of growing up in the Boston area more than a century ago. The following excerpt, set largely on Weston Golf Club's original nine holes, provides a glimpse into the education of a golfer when both 'Nina' Paine and the game of golf were young.**

GOLF CAME TO WESTON when I was six or seven years old—just about the time that Papa had given up trotting and sailing and was ready for a new amusement. The Unitarian minister, a very nice Mr. Russell,* came home from a trip to Scotland one summer bringing a bag of hitherto unheard of golf clubs; and very soon a nine hole course was laid out on pasture land belonging to the Coburn family, abounding in hills, stone walls and cows. Papa caught the fever immediately; and though he was older than most of the other men who began at the same time, sixty-two in fact, he soon became one of the best players and won the first Club championship. Younger men eventually surpassed him, but for a good many years there was no one in Weston who found him easy to beat, and not until he was eighty did he give up playing entirely.

My education in the game began when I was nine, and Papa took it much more seriously than my school work. By the time I was eleven it was the accepted thing for me to play with him every afternoon while we were in Weston; and only a very rainy day, a thermometer above 88, or snow, ever kept us off the links. But—I may as well admit it—there were occasional days when we played for his pleasure rather than for mine.

I really did love golf, though; partly for itself and partly because of being with Papa. He went to Boston every morning for Directors' meetings or something of the sort, and in the afternoon I would be driven down to meet him at the Weston station—not till much later

on in an automobile, but in the beach-waggon, a two-seated open carriage with a horse who invariably disliked trains. As Papa descended from the smoking-car, I always looked to see if there were a long, slender package under his arm—for if so, it might be a new golf club for me. And often there was, for he spared no trouble in fitting me out with clubs that he hoped might improve my game.

After Papa had got into the carriage, the train had pulled out, and the horse had stopped fidgeting, we would proceed to the golf course and have our round. Once in a while Papa brought a Scotch professional out with him, and we both took lessons to the accompaniment of a genuine Scotch burr. Most of my instruction, however, came from Papa himself, and it was so good and we played so much that before a great while my game became rather creditable, considering my size and sex.

But the Weston hills were steep, and my shots not long enough to be sure of always surmounting them. One day when I seemed entirely unable to "carry" a particularly high hill, and my ball kept rolling back to my feet no matter how hard I hit, I let myself go and began to complain about my difficulties and my luck. Suddenly Papa said very quietly but very disgustedly, "Nina, can't you stop grumbling?" Never before had he reprimanded me for anything, and to have incurred his scorn was disgrace and calamity. I never grumbled on the golf course again.

By the time I was thirteen, Papa and I played even. Our afternoon's stake was supposedly an ice cream soda—which we stopped for at the old grocery store on the way home—of which we both partook and for which he paid, no matter which of us had won.

There were Saturday afternoon handicap tournaments, and sometimes he or I would win and be presented with an ugly little pewter cup. Before long the Club instituted a Ladies' Championship as well as a Men's—which I never won, in spite of Papa's firm belief that I ought to because I could hit further than the

*The Rev. William E. Russell, pastor of the First Parish Church in Weston, was instrumental in starting the Weston Golf Club in 1894. — ED.

usual winner, Mrs. Batchelder. Mrs. Batchelder was very solemn about her game and spent hours every day practicing putts and approaches, with the result that she became frighteningly good at her 'short game.' In matches against her, my longer drives and brassie shots were of no avail, and she beat me every time with accurate approaches and deadly putting.

One autumn, when I was fourteen, there had been a Ladies' Invitation Tournament, and one of the visiting players had gone around in 91—which broke the previous ladies' record for the course, a 93 made by Miss Gertrude Fiske, another Weston friend who annoyed Papa by beating me in the Championships. A few weeks later Papa and I were playing the ninth hole one afternoon, when we saw Mrs. Batchelder strolling toward us with an expression of bliss on her nice, sunburned face. As we met she said, "Well, I'm going home to throw away my clubs! I've just made a 91 to tie the Ladies' Record."

I myself had been playing better than usual, and when we added up our score cards on the putting-green we discovered that I had gone round the nine holes in 44—two strokes better than my previous best. We hadn't intended to play a second nine that day; but suddenly, instead of taking off my gloves and handing them to the caddy to put into my golf bag, I found myself saying, "Papa, I'm going to play round again and beat 91!" Since I had never yet done better than 96 for the double round, and after playing a few good holes was almost certain to do the next very badly, this was pretty brash. However, Papa approved, and we started on the second nine.

Hole after hole went by without disaster, but a crucial moment lay ahead. For flanking the last hundred yards of the long and difficult eighth hole was a rocky precipice; and if my ball were to fly or even trickle over its dizzy edge, all possibility of a good score would vanish. Rather apprehensively I started the hole—knowing that it must be accomplished in seven strokes, and then the ninth in three, if I were to get another 44. In spite of my excitement no trouble occurred at the various stone walls that crossed the fairway in inconvenient places, and after four shots I had arrived at shooting distance for the putting-green. I played a brassie shot; and watched incredulous as my ball ignored the yawning precipice and sailed straight on to the green. I holed out comfortably in seven, and wondered what would happen on the ninth hole. But the gods were with me still.

My ball settled into the final cup for a three; and there it was, a new Ladies' Record of 88!

Papa and I were pretty happy—he, I think, even more than I. But we did wonder how we were going to break the news to Mrs. Batchelder when we met her on the course next day, for of course she was not going to throw away her clubs. To our dismay, as we approached the Club House we saw that she was still there, rocking happily on the piazza, and obviously waiting to tell us all about her round....

It was a long story, and as it went on, Papa and I began to hope that perhaps she would depart without our having to confess. Finally she did get up and said good-bye. But just as she was stepping off the piazza, to go and unhitch her horse and buggy in the shed, she turned and asked me in a voice that sounded like that of some faraway goddess on Olympus, "And what score did you get today, Nina?"

~

At home that evening I couldn't decide whether to laugh or cry. But the rest of the family seemed always to be winning laurels of one sort or another to bring home to Papa, and it was gratifying to have added a small sprig myself. The only one as it turned out; for I never did anything at all remarkable again, and Mrs. Batchelder kept on beating me in the Championships. In a pigeon-hole of my secretary in Weston, however, a dilapidated old golf ball is still treasured, with the inscription:

OCT. 11 '03
44 — 44
88

RECOLLECTIONS OF AMATEUR CHAMPIONSHIP COUNTRY CLUB 1910.

play, with 38 entrants. The winner was Arthur G. Lockwood of the Allston Golf Club, using the recently developed Haskell rubber ball.

Meanwhile, six clubs of Berkshire County as early as 1900 had been sponsoring an annual championship for the Berkshire Gold Medal which led to the formation of the Allied Golf Clubs of Berkshire County. That group's first championship, in 1904, was won by Walter R. Tuckerman. And, on a lesser competitive level, the Stockbridge Golf Club started its classic amateur invitation tournament in 1897, now claimed to be the oldest such event in the country; until 1941 it was a traditional, individual-match-play affair, since then it has been at four-ball.

It was two years after its first Amateur that the MGA got around to an Open Championship to include its professionals. When it did, in 1905, it con-

ducted the event at the Vesper Country Club in June. Donald Ross, a Scot then professional at Oakley but later to become a legend among golf course architects, was the winner with 320 for 72 holes. His brother Alex, professional at Brae Burn, won the next five Opens, from 1906 through 1910. Donald won a second time in 1911, then Alex won a sixth time in 1912 so that the first eight Massachusetts Opens were the exclusive property of the Ross brothers.

It was still, however, primarily a competitive era for amateurs who were members of private clubs. Professionals were teachers and sold the tools of their trade. And the game was spreading in other, unexpected ways, even encroaching on winter. On January 1, 1907, 25 hardy amateur golfers played a competition at the original Wollaston Golf Club, in North Quincy, foreshadowing that club's long popular New Year's Day event in the years to come.

MOVERS AND SHAKERS *Opposite page:* **Caricatures of G. Herbert Windeler and Herbert Jaques, influential members of The Country Club in its early years, appear in an artist's "recollections" of the 1910 U.S. Amateur hosted by that club and now hanging in the club's men's locker room. Windeler was a driving force in the formation of the MGA and served as its first president.**

Clockwise from right: **Clinton native John G. Anderson was a four-letter athlete at Amherst College, won the Massachusetts Amateur in 1907 at the age of 16 and again in 1911. An early dean of golf writers in the United States, he proselytized for the game on the pages of the *Boston Transcript*, *New York Sun*, *Golf Illustrated* and *American Golfer*. A founder of the New England Intercollegiate Golf Association in 1903, he also participated in the formation of the Professional Golfers Association in 1920.**

In the late 1920s and early 1930s, Herbert Jaques, Jr., a president of The Country Club like his father before him, spearheaded the USGA's efforts to standardize the size of the golf ball.

Edward Stimpson, winner of the Massachusetts Amateur at his home club, Brae Burn, in 1935, invented a device for measuring the speed of putting greens in 1936. He argued for its usefulness in preparing golf courses for championship play in *Golfdom*, but it took four decades for the USGA to finally give its blessings to his now famous and invaluable "Stimpmeter."

here's the Stimp meter, which measures the putting speed of turf.

Eddie Stimpson, 1935 Massachusetts champion, herewith presents an int... the stimp meter. As for the one we have the definite idea that... because of the mechanical princ... the player actually couldn't mea... what he has learned about gree... rant use of the device.

However, there may be some... vice as an instrument for... might want to answer argumen... and uniformity of their greens

We toss Stimpson's id... into the lists for the argum...

INTRODUCING THE STIMP

By EDDIE STIMPSON

LAST March, J. W. F. MacDonald of Brae Burn asked... artificial putting green and a mechanical putter he had... The green, ten by three feet, was built on a sturdy wood... faced with heavy felt matting. The... cup was slightly undersized to make... mate the line on a... the hole look bigger when play was... judge and examine... resumed on the course. A heavy metal... surface, such as is... stand with a ball-bearing swivel held... at Brae Burn, by the... a putter securely so that any desired... in sinking a putt... direction and force in a putt could be... was harder to sink... duplicated with reasonable accuracy.... than direction... taken to send the...

MacDonald had experimented to deter-... The MacDonald... the more important factor... to any devia... the direction in... variety of putt...

While Wollaston, with its hilly, well-drained course, pioneered winter golf in Greater Boston, this colder version of an otherwise warm-weather game also caught on in the gentler seaside climate and on the sandy soil of Cape Cod, where Cummaquid, the first golf club on the Cape, and the Seapuit Golf Club had been organized in 1895 and 1896, respectively, and immediately had initiated an inter-club rivalry for the Cummaquid-Seapuit Challenge Cup.

As the MGA grew, the success of its early Amateur and Open Championships led to an array of other state championships, which now total 11 (all but the Open for amateurs): a Junior, inaugurated in 1914 (and won by Francis Ouimet's brother, Ray); a Caddie in 1919, later melded into the Junior; a Senior in 1961; a Father and Son in 1977; a Father and Daughter and a Four-Ball in 1981; a Public Links in 1982, a Mid-Amateur in 1984, a Senior Four-Ball

in 1997, and a Net Team in 2000. The Massachusetts Amateur is a stunning example, by itself, of the surging interest in competitions. Starting with 38 entrants in 1903, the entry peaked at 1,063 in 1999, and a dozen sectional qualifying sites around the state are now the norm for this event alone. While the MGA can and has since used its MGA/USGA GHIN handicap index to hold entries to more manageable proportions—the maximum is now down to 4.4—this aspect of the MGA's basic success creates two problems.

The 11 MGA championships and their qualifying sites require some 75 golf courses. The USGA, which started regional qualifying for its Open Championship back in 1924 with a site at the Worcester Country Club, now normally needs another dozen qualifying sites for its events here, placing heavy burdens on MGA member clubs to provide appropriate courses year after year and on the volunteer members of the MGA executive committee to manage responsibly so many sites all over the state. Caught up in this incipient crisis in 1991, Robert G. Dowling, as president, and Daniel L. Hurley, as chairman of the championship committee, established a body of volunteer tournament officials to work with members of the executive committee and with, first, Richard A. Crosby and later Kevin D. Patterson of the MGA staff, in managing this array of championship sites. Familiarly

STATE OPEN NOTABLES In its first half-century, the Massachusetts Open consistently attracted strong fields. *Top:* Byron Nelson, second from right, shown with Plymouth native Henry Picard and their caddies, won the 1939 Massachusetts Open at Worcester Country Club. Although Picard never won his own state open, he won the Masters in 1938 and the PGA Championship in 1939. *Middle:* Horton Smith won the 1940 Massachusetts Open at Oyster Harbors Club. *Bottom:* Gene Sarazen, left, won the 1935 state open at Oak Hill Country Club in Fitchburg. He is seen here on the first tee at Oak Hill with Dave Hackney (center) of Vesper Country Club and amateur great Jesse Guilford of Woodland Golf Club. *Opposite:* An early hand-lettered scroll of state open champions spelled all names correctly—except that of the Bay State.

called "blue coats," those who fleshed out the program by attending rules workshops and spending long days serving as starters, scorers and rules officials at qualifying and championship sites have gone a long way toward salvaging a program in danger of floundering in its own success. Unfortunately, the pressure for qualifying sites remains, dependent on the continuing goodwill of the MGA member clubs.

Although the focus back in the formative years of competitions was primarily on amateur participation, the 20th century was in its second decade before the USGA got around to sending its Amateur Championship for men to Massachusetts. When it did, in 1910, it selected The Country Club, the winner was William C. Fownes of Oakmont Country Club, in Pittsburgh, and the last Massachusetts survivor was Walter Tuckerman of Stockbridge, beaten in the semi-final round. While seemingly delayed, the event started a trend which has now seen five U.S. Amateurs played at The Country Club, the most recent in 1982. Only the Merion Golf Club, near Philadelphia, has entertained the event as many times.

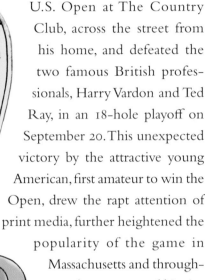

The timing of this amateur event at The Country Club may also have been a factor in the coincident development of male amateurs who attained national levels. First of these was John G. Anderson, who came out of Amherst to win the Massachusetts Amateur twice, in 1907 and 1911, and to reach the final of the U.S. Amateur twice, in 1913 and 1915. In the process, he also undertook to write about the game, and his articles for the old *Boston Evening Transcript* stamped him as perhaps our earliest golf writer and a worthy predecessor of A. Linde Fowler, also of the *Transcript*, Herbert Warren Wind of *The New Yorker*, and others. In 1915 he moved to New York and there achieved wide recognition—in golf, in the Millrose Games and beyond as a true renaissance man. His golf record includes 53 championships, including the French Amateur in 1924. Winged Foot Golf Club, in Mamaroneck, New York, named its classic invitation four-ball in his memory two months after his death in 1933.

This amateur wave crested in 1913 when Francis Ouimet, once a caddie at the club but now the 20-year-old state amateur champion playing as a junior member at Woodland, entered the U.S. Open at The Country Club, across the street from his home, and defeated the two famous British professionals, Harry Vardon and Ted Ray, in an 18-hole playoff on September 20. This unexpected victory by the attractive young American, first amateur to win the Open, drew the rapt attention of print media, further heightened the popularity of the game in Massachusetts and throughout the country, and his victory in the U.S. Amateur at the Ekwanok Country Club in Vermont the following summer enhanced his fame and that of the game he played so well. When he died on September 2, 1967, at the age of 74, after winning a U.S. Open and two U.S. Amateurs (17 years apart in 1914 and 1931), a Massachusetts Open and six Massachusetts Amateurs, participating in eight Walker Cup matches (twice as playing captain and then four more times as non-playing captain), and captaining also the Royal and Ancient Golf Club of St. Andrews (R&A), Scotland, he left a legacy of grace and good sportsmanship on two continents which matched the skill with which he had played the game.

A basic requirement for successful competitive golf among amateurs below the championship level is, of course, a centralized handicap system, and handicapping had long been an MGA preoccupation. By the time the asssociation reached its 10th birthday in 1913 it came to recognize a need for staff assistance and employed its first official handicapper in the person of Arthur G. Lockwood, who had won its first Amateur. It also formally abolished "bogey" for all clubs in the association and, instead, substituted an "allotted score" assigned to each club by the MGA's handicap committee "to be the only basis for ascertaining handicaps." Shades of the modern slope system and the handicap index!

Continuing attention to handicapping brought results, however, none more pervasive than the innovation of the handicap four-ball tournament, entirely at match play. Early club invitation tournaments had usually been played in one of two formats: a qualifying round which divided the individual players into flights according to their skills followed by match play, or progressively in the 1920s and 1930s an "open" event for all amateur comers at 18 holes stroke play, gross and net prizes, which permitted golfers to play a variety of courses. MGA tournament calendars in the 1920s commonly listed some 60 of these "open" events in a season. However, R.W. (Bunny) Estabrook and Charles W. Amory of Essex County early on conceived what became widely known as the "Essex system" of invitation four-ball match play, with handicaps to broaden the appeal and the congeniality of the event, and put it into effect in their men's invitation tournament in 1915. When 36 holes a day over a three-day weekend was seen to be costing a number of senior entrants, a round-a-day division was added in 1926. This creative form—leveling the competition through handicapping, applying handicaps

NORTH SHORE GEM With its views of Gloucester Harbor, Bass Rocks Golf Club in Gloucester is barely 6,000 yards long but the ledge rock and scrubland which impinge on most fairways reinforce the axiom that "straight is better than long." The family-oriented club is the home club of three-time Massachusetts Senior Amateur champion John Frithsen.

successfully to four-ball play, bringing together players of differing abilities and emphasizing the sociable aspects of the weekend—was quickly picked up by other clubs and resorts, stimulating a spectrum of weekend club tournaments and four-ball leagues for inter-club rivalry.

World War I brought a suspension of the game, of course, but the momentum of the first two decades of the century did regenerate in the early

1920s. The number of courses in the United States approached 2,000, and it became profitable for developers to build new courses as features of real estate developments, which they did in the booming late 1920s. Accompanying this growth of the game came, for the first but not the only time, a questioning of old rules laid down by golfing forefathers abroad and adopted by the rules-making authority here. Massachusetts had a role in the handling of this transition, and it was a responsible role. Early in 1920, the MGA executive committee, at a meeting chaired by President Barton K. Stephenson of the Winchester Country Club, responded to the questioning of several old rules by instructing delegates to a forthcoming national rules conference to vote for abolition of the stymie, to allow cleaning of the ball on the now-manicured putting greens, to allow also the lifting and cleaning of a ball embedded on a putt-

ing green, to apply the stroke-play rule for a lost ball to match play and to standardize the size and weight of the ball. At the same time, unfortunately, the Western Golf Association and some others felt so strongly about the need for rules changes that there was talk of breaking with the USGA and developing a separate code of rules. The MGA executive committee, conscious of the chaotic possibilities in two codes of rules for the game, met later in 1920, "noted with regret the dissension" and in a display of leadership expressed itself as "strongly opposed to any attempt to supplant the United States Golf Association." The storm passed and rules changes did come—but slowly.

As competition resumed after the war, also, a second Massachusetts amateur, Jesse P. Guilford, like Ouimet a member at Woodland, won the U.S. Amateur in 1921 with some of the longest hitting seen to that day (including drives up to 280 yards long). His victory at the St. Louis Country Club during a rainy week in September of 1921 highlighted another remarkable state and national career: From 1916 through 1929, Guilford also won three Massachusetts Amateurs, two Massachusetts Opens and represented the United States on three victorious Walker Cup teams. Reflecting that amateur era in Massachusetts, the honor roll of the MGA handicap committee, published in the spring of 1923, was headed by two native sons and a young student at Harvard:

SCRATCH

Francis D. Ouimet, Woodland

Jesse P. Guilford, Woodland

Robert T. Jones, Jr., Harvard

It was inevitable, of course, that the professionals who sold the amateur players their clubs and balls and taught them to play would eventually want to emerge from their shops and display their own talents. For this, however, they needed their own vehicle, and in 1921 a group of area professionals founded the New England Professional Golfers' Organization.

Its first championship took place at Myopia over 36 holes of stroke play in October of that year. Gil Nicholls of Providence won with 78-78—156, earning $100 and a gold medal. The next year the championship was extended to 72 holes and another attraction was added—a pro-am, played at Winchester and won by John Cowan and his amateur partner from Oakley. Inevitably, the pros' group became the New England section of Robert White's Professional Golfers Association (PGA).

Emerging along with professional play came senior play. More rarely now was golf referred to as "an old man's game," and older players, like professionals, increasingly sought refuge in their own kind. This led on May 2, 1922, to the organization of the New England Senior Golfers' Association for players 55 years and older by a group meeting at Woodland. The association they formed, second oldest in the nation for seniors, opened not merely a new page but a whole book of opportunities for amateur competition with social amenities. Other senior groups sprang up, notably the Bay State Senior Golfers Association in the Berkshires in 1961, and senior divisions under one name or another became popular tournament adjuncts. The USGA entered the field with its Senior Amateur Championship in 1955, an event won in its second playing by Frederick J. Wright, Jr., of Trapelo Golf Club. In 1962 the USGA added a Senior Women's Amateur Championship.

Inevitably, the search for a more perfect handicap system intensified. In the administrations of Presidents William F. Garcelon and Raynor M. Gardiner in the mid-1920s, the MGA executive committee approved a new principle of course rating, rather than par, as a basis for handicaps, and on February 15, 1925, adopted its first course rating system. This involved the addition or subtraction of decimal points from the par of each hole, depending on its difficulty. William O. Blaney of Brae Burn, a leader in efforts to refine the system, joined the MGA course rating committee in this period and

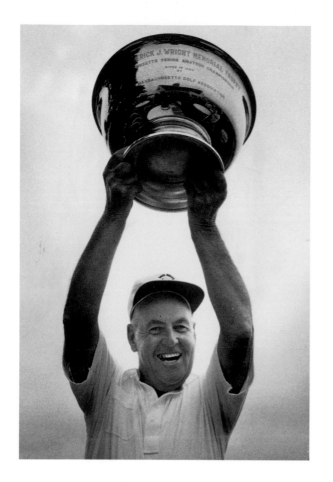

SPOILS OF VICTORY The MGA's most cherished trophies are reserved for its most venerable championships (clockwise from bottom left): the Massachusetts Amateur, won in 1931 by Fred Wright, Jr. (right), at Winchester Country Club (one of his record seven state amateur titles), with Eddie Lowery the runner-up; the Massachusetts Senior Amateur, won in 1984 by John Frithsen at Eastward Ho! Country Club (one of his three state senior amateurs); the Massachusetts Junior Amateur, won in 1932 by Richard Ruggles at Wollaston Golf Club; the Massachusetts Open, won in 1968 by Paul Harney at The International Golf Club (one of his five state open titles). After compiling a 52-4 record in intercollegiate golf matches at Holy Cross, Harney, a native of Worcester, won seven times on the pro tour, including victories in the 1965 and 1966 Los Angeles Open. At 42, Harney overcame front-running Hale Irwin on the closing holes at Torrey Pines to win the 1972 San Diego Open. (In photo, he holds the permanent Massachusetts Open trophy in his left hand.)

CAPE COD GEM The oldest organized golf club on the Cape, Cummaquid Golf Club began as a 9-hole course in 1895 and was expanded to
18 holes by golf course architect Henry Mitchell in the late 1960s. An
early member was John Reid, one of the founders of St. Andrew's Golf
Club in Yonkers, New York. The inland layout is characterized by
rolling fairways and stoutly defended greens. The club's 18th tee is
pictured in the foreground.

later became president of the association. After World
War II, the USGA, searching for an improved handicap system of its own, appointed Blaney to its handicap committee and in 1948 adopted its first system
of course rating for nationwide use, patterned on the
system which had been developed at the MGA.

As the affairs of the MGA multiplied with more
than 100 member clubs, expanding tournament
play and more demanding handicapping proce-
dures in the mid-1920s, the association came to
require a home of its own and leased Room 810 at
60 State Street in downtown Boston. In April, 1927,
Fred Corcoran, who had caddied at Belmont Spring
but made no pretense of being a skilled golfer himself, was appointed official handicapper, succeeding
Dan Horan, and began operations from the new
headquarters. The appointment, significant in the
progress of the MGA, was made by Harold W. Pierce
of The Country Club, then MGA secretary. Pierce
went on to become president of the MGA the fol-

vate the status of the Massachusetts Open by bringing in professional players of national stature, and the events of his era began to draw galleries attracted by the star power of visiting celebrities. Johnny Farrell, Leo Diegel, Joe Turnesa, Wiffy Cox, Gene Sarazen, Byron Nelson and Horton Smith came, were seen, and conquered in the late 1920s and 1930s, along with Francis Ouimet and Harold (Jug) McSpaden, representing the home forces. Walter Hagen, Henri Ciuci, Willie Macfarlane, Herman Barron, Lloyd Mangrum, Jimmy Thomson and Paul Runyan, among others, came, were seen but did not conquer here.

The 1920s, significant in so many ways, were also the heyday of Bobby Jones. In September of 1928, Jones came to Brae Burn, survived the tightest of matches in the early rounds and then overwhelmed T. Philip Perkins, the British Amateur champion, in the final to win his fourth victory in the U.S. Amateur. Jones completed his Grand Slam by winning the U.S. and British Amateur and Open championships and then retired in 1930, leaving the world of golf to find a new focus.

It soon found one in the ball itself. Until 1921, no standards had governed the size, weight or characteristics of the ball through its transformation from feathery to gutta-percha to rubber; but by 1915, when patents on the Haskell rubber ball expired and competition among manufacturers to develop a longer ball increased, popular demand had tended to stabilize the ball's size at 1.63 inches in diameter and its weight at 1.62 ounces. As of 1921, the USGA and the R&A, fearing the effect of a longer ball on current golf courses, first sought to control distance by establishing that the ball henceforth should measure no less than 1.62 inches and weigh no more than 1.62 ounces—but the matter did not end so simply. Controversy developed. Within a decade,

lowing year and served as president of the USGA in 1940 and 1941. Fred was the first of three Corcoran brothers who served the MGA successively for 42 years, originally under the title of official handicapper and later as executive secretary. Fred left in 1936 to exercise his notable promotional skills on a national scale as tournament manager for the emerging tours of the PGA and the Ladies Professional Golf Association (LPGA). He was succeeded at the MGA by brother John, who in turn was succeeded by brother Bill in 1945. Bill, third and last of the Corcorans, was taken by death in 1969.

One of Fred Corcoran's contributions was to ele-

WORLD WAR II TRUMPS GOLF *Clockwise from above:* William Blaney, seen here competing at Kernwood Country Club in Salem, was an accomplished golfer and the 1934 winner of the Massachusetts Amateur. Wearing a different hat, as MGA president, Blaney published an article in the April, 1943, issue of *Golfdom* which addressed the problem of keeping golf clubs afloat during the war in spite of drastic shortages in fuel and other supplies and materials.

In 1942, Margaret Curtis, the legendary golfer from Essex County Club who won three U.S. Women's Amateurs and four women's state amateur titles, teamed up with Hazel Wightman, 32 times a national champion in tennis, "to lead Bay State women in saving kitchen fats for explosives and in tin can salvage."

With gas rationing limiting the use of automobiles, Longmeadow Country Club began the use of a horse-drawn "taxi" to take members from a downtown location to the club. The photograph is inscribed, "First trip from Mill Rd. & Longmeadow St., May 22, 1943."

Inset: After winning the Massachusetts Amateur at Longmeadow in 1941, Watertown's Leo J. Martin enlisted in the Navy. He died in 1943 when his convoy ship struck an unidentified object in the North Atlantic. Riverside Golf Club in Weston was re-named in his honor in 1945. In 1948, Leo's twin brother, Eddie, beat Clarence Early at Worcester Country Club to win the Massachusetts Amateur. Years later he told *Boston Globe* reporter Jim McCabe he had a spot already lined up for the trophy: "On the piano next to Leo's picture."

the controversy came before a Massachusetts man serving the USGA for a solution.

Herbert Jaques, Jr., of The Country Club was a member of a veritable First Family of Massachusetts Golf. His father, Herbert Jaques, had been the eighth president of the USGA, in 1909 and 1910. Herbert

Jaques, Jr., at the time of this controversy was chairman of the USGA implements and ball committee, en route to serving as president of the USGA in 1933 and 1934. (The third Herbert Jaques, son of Herbert Jaques, Jr., would later serve as president of the Francis Ouimet Caddie Scholarship Fund from

1963 through 1965.) The controversy over the ball fell squarely in the lap of Herbert Jaques, Jr. In his role with the USGA implements and ball committee in the late 1920s, he had guided experiments with various sizes and weights of the ball on both sides of the Atlantic. At one point, the R&A and the USGA agreed that the ball best suited for all-around conditions on both continents should be not less than 1.68 inches and not more than 1.55 ounces—both larger and lighter than the current standard. The R&A later backed off, but the 1.68-1.55 ball became standard in the United States in 1931.

Unhappily, it was denigrated as a "balloon ball" and evoked a firestorm of protest. Jaques went right

back to the drawing board. Effective in 1932, the USGA left the minimum diameter the same but increased the maximum weight back to 1.62 ounces. The controversy subsided, the new weight was accepted in the United States, and the 1.68-1.62 ball remains not only the standard but a testimonial to Herbert Jaques, Jr. Agreement in Great Britain did not come quickly, but in 1990 the R&A adopted the same standard.

Like the questioning of the size and weight of the ball, the challenging of other old rules was not quickly resolved either. This was especially true of the stymie, an archaic vestige of codes based on the ancient principle that a golfer ideally put his ball in play on the tee and did not

touch it again until he lifted it out of the hole. Here again the MGA played a leadership role in a rules matter with national implications as more and more young amateurs, particularly exponents of match play, expressed objections to the practice, continuing in the USGA code, which allowed one ball to block another on the putting green in match play. The intervening ball had to be lofted over with a niblick or putted around. Responsive to this rebellious sentiment but still loyal to the national rules-making authority, the MGA set up a stymie study committee which presented to the MGA's annual meeting in 1935 a recommendation that the stymie rule be eliminated in its own championships but that the USGA still sanction the rule for states "so minded." In the following season, 1936, the Massachusetts Amateur at Charles River was conducted under a "waiver" of the stymie rule. Two years later, the USGA took the

A YEAR TO REMEMBER In 1946, fresh from service in World War II, Ted Bishop, 1941 New England Amateur champion, picked up where he had left off. He beat Eddie Martin, 7 and 6, for the Massachusetts Amateur with a 3-under-par effort at Charles River Country Club in Newton, then successfully defended his New England title at Brae Burn. He journeyed to Baltusrol Golf Club in New Jersey for the U.S. Amateur and won a series of tough matches to reach the title round with Smiley Quick, the National Public Links champion from California, whom Bishop dispatched on the 37th hole.

FIELDS OF GLORY: CHARLES RIVER With a membership boasting nearly 100 single-figure handicap golfers, it is no surprise that Charles River has a long and distinguished history as a championship site, beginning with the Massachusetts Open in 1925, won by Tom Lally with an aggregate score of 306. The course is unusual in that it has five par-5 holes and five par-3s. Hole pictured: the narrow par-4 13th, 351 yards, with a green sharply sloping from back to front.

Newton Golf Club, Newton, Mass.

Gone But Not Forgotten

The ghost clubs and bygone courses of Massachusetts

It was a century of growth — yet Massachusetts lost golf clubs at the rate of almost one a year. More were built than lost, of course, and the number now has risen to 380 — yet clubs were lost at a remarkable pace to the economics of competition, consolidation, war and depression.

In an unfortunate number of cases, clubs which contributed to the strength, color and flavor of the game in its early years have simply disappeared.

We are, for example, the poorer for having lost clubs with names like Misery Island Golf and Country Club, on an island off Manchester, and Labor-in-Vain Country Club, in Ipswich. Misery Island, reached by launch over rough water, opened for play in 1900 and was one of the clubs which founded the MGA in 1903, but by the time World War I broke out, it was no more. Labor-in-Vain came along in 1925, developed by Richard Crane, Jr., who had come from Chicago to create the Castle Hill estate on Ipswich Bay, but it, in turn, failed to survive World War II.

Misery Island, by the way, was not the only golf course situated on an island. There were two in the Merrimack River, both founding clubs of the MGA. Vesper Golf Club, off Lowell, has survived and flourished, but the Island Golf Club, off Haverhill, followed the Misery Island pattern and closed in 1925 with the

LABOR-IN-VAIN
COUNTRY CLUB
EST. 1925

opening of the Haverhill Country Club.

Then there was the old nine-hole Dugmar Golf Course, built in the town of Greenwich in the late 1920s and reachable by train from Springfield. Neither the course nor the town exist anymore. Both were flooded, along with much of the Swift River valley, in the early 1940s to create the Quabbin Reservoir and provide the water which Bostonians now drink. Still standing in heavy overgrowth, however, is the roofless but beautiful stone clubhouse, spared because it stood above the projected waterline on what has become Curtis Hill Island, now uninhabited and off limits.

It was a significant loss, too, when the Cedar Bank Links in Eastham on Cape Cod surrendered after World War II. The Cedar Bank course was the plaything of Quincy A. Shaw, a private 18 holes built in the late 1920s around his vacation home on the Salt Pond off Nauset Marsh on land which also offered duck hunting in season, glorious ocean views all year and limitless entertainment possibilities. These he exploited to the full, especially with an autumn "clambake" which included in its day both Bobby Jones and Francis Ouimet. The links was reduced to nine holes in the late 1930s, Shaw's interest declined after World War II, and it is now part of the Cape Cod National Seashore.

Then there was that breeder of champions in that

hotbed of golf: the City of Newton, which has been home to nine golf clubs. Eight were listed in 1903 as founders of the the MGA: Albemarle Golf Club, Brae Burn Country Club, Chestnut Hill Golf Club, Commonwealth Country Club, Newton Centre Golf Club, Newton Golf Club (*postcard*), Newton Highlands Golf Club and Woodland Golf Club. (Charles River Country Club came later.) Richard D. Haskell, long-time executive director of the MGA, has uncovered the startling statistic that, of the first 36 Massachusetts Amateur championships before World War II, 25, or two-thirds, were won by players representing Newton clubs.

Albemarle Golf Club in West Newton, one of those founders which did not survive, is a special case because in its lively lifetime it maintained a leading professional, George Aulbach, and attracted strong amateur players, none stronger than Fred Wright, who won the Massachusetts Junior at Albemarle in 1915 and then represented the club while winning six of his seven Massachusetts Amateurs and in United States Walker Cup play abroad. In his first state amateur victory, in 1920 at The Country Club, Wright's opponent in the final was his Albemarle clubmate, P. J. Schofield. According to MGA yearbooks of the era, Albemarle was reached by: "B. & A. R. R. to Newtonville, and by electric car line which passes clubhouse. Visitors must be introduced. 50 cents half day." Albemarle closed in 1977 and became part of the extended campus of the Fessenden School.

The Allston Golf Club, another of the founding clubs no longer with us, attained stature in golf history, too, as the home club of the winner of the first Massachusetts Amateur in 1903, two more in 1905 and 1906, and runner-up in the 1905 Massachusetts Open – Arthur G. Lockwood. Allston Golf Club closed in 1914 to become Braves Field, home of the old National League Boston Braves, and eventually the Boston University stadium.

— *John P. English*

first step toward elimination of the stymie with a new "experimental" rule under which the ball nearer the hole in match play could be lifted when the balls were within six inches of each other. The stymie was on its way out.

In almost parallel circumstances two decades later, the MGA became prominent among those pressing for change in another of the old rules, that which provided a ball could not under normal circumstances be cleaned on a putting green even though it may have acquired a lump of mud en route. With the advent of watering systems and vastly improved putting-green turf, the USGA finally agreed in 1960 and adopted a revision which permitted cleaning the ball on the putting green under any and all conditions.

In Massachusetts as elsewhere, amateur play continued to overshadow the professional side in media attention through the Bob Jones era and into the early 1930s. Joe Lloyd, Willie Anderson and Alex Ross all had won early U.S. Opens representing Bay State clubs, but they had been imported from Scotland. There had been relatively few important professional and open events beyond the national and state opens and the local Monday pro-amateurs to develop skills of homebred professionals.

The first homebred Massachusetts professional to succeed on the national level was Mike Brady, born in Brighton. As a player, he thrice won the Massachusetts Open, in 1914, 1916 and 1923, and rose to challenge the greats of his era. Although major titles slipped out of his grasp, notably in the 1911 and 1919 U.S. Opens, he enjoyed a full share of successes, too. In 1924, Brady moved to Winged Foot in New York, and served as the revered professional there for 15 years. In the 1930s, as opportunities for professional play progressed, Henry Picard came to the fore as another homebred professional with real playing talent.

Picard came into the game through the caddie ranks and golf shop at the Plymouth Country Club, although his golfing career took him to

AT THE MGA HELM *Clockwise from above:* **Cambridge-born Fred Corcoran was one of three Corcoran brothers to serve the MGA, originally under the title of official handicapper and later as executive secretary. A tireless promoter of the game, he was responsible for bringing many of the top names in golf into Massachusetts to compete. Departing in 1936 to work as PGA tournament director, Corcoran helped to make the fledgling pro tour a viable entity by raising annual prize money to $750,000. He organized the LPGA in 1948, helped formulate the World Cup competition, managed two Ryder Cup teams (and the careers of two early superstars, Ted Williams and Sam Snead) and founded the Golf Writers Association of America.**

In his 29 years as executive director, Richard D. Haskell "grew" the MGA from 172 to 318 member clubs and from 19,215 to 88,251 member golfers, introduced six new MGA championships, created the MGA Player of the Year point ranking system and introduced the MGA/GHIN handicap and USGA slope system to the state. In addition, he ushered in *The Massachusetts Golfer*, the official magazine of the MGA, and helped lead the fight for tax relief for golf facilities.

Succeeding Dick Haskell in 1998, Tom Landry has overseen perhaps the most momentous development in the 100-year history of the MGA: the funding and building of a new headquarters for the organization, to include the new Massachusetts Museum and Hall of Fame, at the Tournament Players Club of Boston in Norton. In addition, he has planned new programs and additional staffing to serve, as of 2002, 380 member clubs and 101,500 member golfers.

Charleston, South Carolina, and later Hershey, Pennsylvania. His consistent play on the earliest professional tours earned him places on the U.S. Ryder Cup teams of 1935 and 1937. He won the Masters Tournament in 1938, the PGA Championship in 1939 and was leading money winner on the 1939 tour (with $10,303). World War II intervened before Bob

Toski appeared to claim similar distinction among homebred professional players. Toski came from Haydenville, outside Northampton in Hampshire County, and was one of a family of professional golfers. He joined the pro tour in the early 1950s, won his first tournament in 1953 and became dominant in 1954 with five victories including the

$150,000 World Championship at Tam O'Shanter in Chicago in 1954 (his first prize alone was an unprecedented $50,000). Lean years followed, due to the heavy exhibition series he played, but he returned home to win the Massachusetts Open at the Hyannisport Club in 1958. "I always wanted to win the state open," he said. "I learned to play golf here and I wanted my name on the cup." Toski thereafter turned his attention to instruction in several mediums and became one of the foremost teachers of his day.

In the 1930s, Brae Burn employed Denny Shute, Winchester installed Harold (Jug) McSpaden, and Salem brought in Tony Manero, after his victory in the U.S. Open at Baltusrol in 1936, as their professionals. The first two continued to compete with notable success on the national level. Shute won the PGA Championship in 1936 and defended his title in 1937, beating McSpaden at the 37th hole in a tightly contested all-Massachusetts final at the Pittsburgh Field Club.

As the game developed, so did the art, or science, of greenkeeping. Competitions, especially those with significant money prizes, created a need for standards in day-to-day course maintenance and most especially in preparing courses for championship play. These standards were slow in coming, but one aspect of the problem came to a head at the U.S. Open at the Oakmont Country Club, near Pittsburgh, in 1935. William C. Fownes, the same who had won the 1910 U.S. Amateur at The Country Club, loved Oakmont as his own child and in preparing the course for the Open had the putting greens rolled and shaved and the bunkers furrowed with the apparent goal of insuring that no one would break 300 on "his" course. Only one did: the eventual champion Sam Parks, Jr., with a total score of 299. The greens intolerably "fast," the tournament became the Little Bighorn of putting. In the final round, none of the 20 leaders was able to break 75!

Edward S. Stimpson, a ranking amateur at Brae Burn, had won the Massachusetts Amateur on his home course that same summer. Echoes from the infamous Oakmont greens triggered his analytical mind; the problem of establishing quantitative measures for putting-green conditions intrigued him. Before putting-green conditions could be controlled, of course, they had to be measured. To this end he produced in 1936 the first elementary form of what became known throughout the country as the "Stimpmeter," a device for measuring the speed of putting greens. The first was a stick 30 inches long, painted silver, with a channel on one side and a notch for a golf ball 12 inches from the base. A ball was placed in the notch, the end was raised to the angle of release, and the ball ran down the channel and

Frank H. Sellman Distinguished Service Award

This award is presented by the MGA to the individual whose efforts have contributed to the general betterment of golf in Massachusetts. It is named in honor of Frank H. Sellman, secretary-treasurer of the MGA from 1961 to 1969 and a member of the MGA executive committee from 1959 to 1960. He was an active member of Brae Burn Country Club, the Bay State Seniors and the New England Seniors.

Frank H. Sellman

1988	Leon S. Bishop
1989	Andrew C. Bailey
1990	Charles M. Pyle, Jr.
1991	Roger Barry
1992	John Arnold
1994	Harry B. McCracken
1995	John P. English
1996	William Flynn
1998	George M. Cohen
1999	Richard A. Crosby

FIELDS OF GLORY: TEDESCO Another centennial club of the MGA, Tedesco Country Club in Marblehead has hosted 10 state championships over the years. In addition it has furnished three MGA presidents, Melville Merritt, Osmund Keiver, and Ferdinand Carangelo, and nine members of the MGA executive committee. *Opposite:* The yardage markers on Tedesco's practice range.

rolled a distance which could be measured. Stimpson argued his case for four decades, and it was not until 1976 that agronomists of the USGA green section formally requested their parent body to develop an instrument to measure the speed of putting greens. Four relatively complex designs were developed, all with built-in potential for operator error. Finally, the USGA looked again at the Stimpmeter and, with some engineering modifications, including an increase in length and a formula for its use, adopted it, with Stimpson's blessing. At first the USGA called it the "Speedstick," but the name was shortly changed to "Stimpmeter" in appropriate recognition of its origin at Brae Burn and the persistence of its inventor in getting his idea finally accepted.

War clouds were gathering again in Europe in the late 1930s as still another amateur moved up to join the legends of earlier years. Frederick J. Wright, Jr., representing Trapelo, won his seventh and last Massachusetts Amateur at the Essex County course in July of 1938. Wright, who played originally at Albemarle, had won his first Amateur in 1920 and four in succession from 1928 through 1931. He won the second New England Amateur in 1927. In perhaps his finest hour, he went abroad in 1923 with the second U.S. Walker Cup team to play the British at St. Andrews; two down with three to play, he birdied the last three holes to defeat Ernest E. W. Holderness, 1 up, as the United States won, 6 to 5. Wright had also played in the informal match between United States and British amateur teams at Hoylake, England, in 1921 which led to the official Walker Cup series. In the years to follow, the Walker Cup match was played more often in Massachusetts than in any other state—twice at The Country Club, in 1932 and 1973, and once at The Kittansett Club, in 1953—and in addition to Guilford, Ouimet and Wright, the state has been represented on United States teams by Bobby Knowles in 1951, Kevin Johnson in 1989, Allen Doyle in 1991 and 1993 and James Driscoll in 2001.

Also, one of the most memorable holes-in-one in the annals of golf—Massachusetts or beyond—occurred as the pre-war decade was ending. The leading role was played by William O. Blaney at Brae Burn, his home course. Blaney already had carved a prominent place for himself as an amateur player and by his contributions to the formulation of the game's handicap system. In the summer of 1940, Blaney was playing again the kind of golf which had won him the New England Amateur in 1928, taken him to the quarter-finals of the U.S. Amateur in 1932 and earned him the Massachusetts Amateur in 1934. As he, John Cole, Merrill Delano and Bob Meier came out for what became an epic, if informal, weekend round, they were assigned to start at the seventh hole. The round began inauspiciously for Blaney with a 1-over-par 5; the next three or four holes were uneventful. Then, as golfers mysteriously do, Blaney caught fire. When they came to the 160-yard sixth —the last of their round—he needed a par 3 for a 69. Even better, a birdie 2 would tie the amateur course record of 68. The blue markers were set on the upper, back tee. The flagstick stood in the right front quarter of the green, just beyond the brook which guards the front. Blaney pulled out his six-iron. The shot was on line all the way. The ball took two bounces on the green and dropped solidly into the final cup for a 1 and a new amateur course record of 67.

World War II was now just over the horizon for the United States, and the amateur who won the state's crown jewel in the summer of 1941 lost his life in the combat soon to come. The Massachusetts Amateur was moved westward for the first time, to the Longmeadow Country Club, and there in July Leo J. Martin, representing Trapelo, started to fulfill his early promise by defeating in the final the young home-club player, Milton B. Reach, Jr., whose father had pioneered the development of implements of the game with the Spalding company. During the following winter, Martin joined the Navy and, serving in a gun crew on a merchant ship in the Atlantic, was killed at sea in 1943. The Metropolitan District Commission public course at Riverside was renamed as a memorial to him after the war. In the first summer of war, 1942, only the Massachusetts Open was staged, and Ben Loving, the promising young professional at Longmeadow, won it after a playoff with Les Kennedy. Here, too, there was a tragic sequel. Loving also gave up his life in the war.

Championship play was not to resume under MGA auspices until a year after the ending of hostilities. When Massachusetts golfers finally came together, it was again a new golfing generation with many new faces, new styles and new standards in their approach to the game. The first of these to emerge to the national level after the war was Stanley E. (Ted) Bishop, who had worked briefly as a professional before the war but had regained his amateur status. Like Ouimet and Guilford before him, he joined Woodland and won the first of his three Massachusetts Amateurs just before the United States entered the war. After hostilities ceased, Bishop brought to Massachusetts his own version of a Slam by winning the U.S. Amateur at Baltusrol in September of 1946, after earlier victories the same season in the Massachusetts and New England Amateurs. In the national final, Bishop defeated Smiley Quick at the 37th hole. Over his career, Bishop won one U.S. Amateur, two New England

LADIES FIRST A tribute to Margaret and Harriot Curtis at Essex County Club includes a poster for the inaugural Curtis Cup in 1932. Lifelong supporters of the WGAM, the Curtis sisters donated the cup for the biennial contest between U.S. and British women golfers conducted by the USGA and the Ladies Golf Union.

1930 and then retired from competitive play, made one of his periodic treks to western Massachusetts to visit his son and played there, at the Wahconah Country Club on August 15, 1948, what proved to be the last game of his life, nine holes only because of his failing health. He died on December 19, 1971.

As senior golf grew in popularity in the post–World War II period, the golfer left out increasingly became the fellow who had yet to cross the age threshold for senior play but could no longer compete successfully with the young lions. The movement to solve this problem started during a lunch at the Commonwealth Country Club between rounds of the Massachusetts Amateur in July of 1947. Three fine but no-longer-young amateur golfers—Joe Batchelder, Bill Blaney and John Chew—lamented their dilemma and conceived a new competitive level for players in the in-between years of 40 through 54. (Chew's self-evaluation proved flawed; at the end of the week he found himself the state amateur champion. But their concept survived.) An informal gathering took place at Charles River that autumn which led to a membership organization originally called the Pre-Seniors Golf Association, formalized on March 31, 1948. The first president was Joe Batchelder, and their first "championship" followed at Charles River in September, won by Frank Pfaelzer. While the original members were distinguished by their strong competitive records in amateur play, they soon brought in others who had furthered the interests of the game through organizational contributions. In 1954 the maximum age limit was eliminated and the organization adopted

Amateurs, three Massachusetts Amateurs and played on the U.S. Walker Cup teams of 1947 and 1949. He later won the Massachusetts Senior Amateur at Tedesco Country Club in 1969.

In this period, too, another legend passed. Bob Jones, who had won the incredible Grand Slam in

a more appropriate name: The Hickory Shafts (the president called meetings to order with a gavel made from a club of the hickory-shaft era).

The idea of providing a vehicle for the fellow-in-the-middle was sound. The USGA eventually came to the same conclusion and generated its Mid-Amateur Championship in 1981, designed to meet the needs of amateurs who had reached the age of 25 and played the game as an avocation. The MGA offered its own Mid-Amateur Championship for players at least 35 years of age in 1984, lowering the threshold to 30 in 1999.

It was also time to recognize another fact of modern life—the status of women. While the MGA executive committee had grown by 1983 to 24 members, it remained a bastion of males—but women had gradually become full, influential partners in most of their clubs. Their status deserved

Left to right: Gallery reacts to a rare missed putt by Texan Kathy Whitworth at Pleasant Valley Country Club. The winningest pro on any tour with 88 victories, Whitworth almost always played well in Sutton, and captured two of the seven LPGA Championships played there in the late 1960s and early 1970s.

Anne Marie Tobin, a practicing attorney playing out of Bellevue Golf Club in Melrose, won the Massachusetts women's amateur, known as the Association Championship, a record seven times, in 1988, consecutively from 1991 to 1995 and again in 2000.

Pat Bradley, a native of Arlington, now of Westford, is regarded as the finest female player in Massachusetts history and a perennial superstar in the world of international golf. Her amateur career peaked in 1972 when she reigned as the Massachusetts, New England and Endicott Cup champion. During her LPGA Hall of Fame career, which began in 1974, Bradley earned more money than any New England golfer in history. Among her 31 tour victories were the 1981 U.S. Women's Open and the 1986 LPGA Championship.

Amateur Player of the Year

Following each championship season, the MGA crowns the Richard D. Haskell Amateur Player of the Year. This honor is given to the amateur player who has accumulated the most points throughout the championship schedule. Eligible players earn points through competition at all MGA championship events, USGA qualifying (U.S. Open, U.S. Amateur, U.S. Amateur Public Links and U.S. Mid-Amateur) and championship events and a select number of invitational and regional tournaments. The final decision on the Richard D. Haskell Amateur Player of the Year rests with the MGA Executive Committee.

PAST AMATEUR PLAYERS OF THE YEAR

Year	Player	Home Club
1976	Bruce Douglass	Thorny Lea Golf Club
1977	Peter Teravainen	Duxbury Yacht Club
1978	David Brilliant	Belmont Country Club
1979	David Lane	Vesper Country Club
1980	Bruce Chalas	Thorny Lea Golf Club
1981	Steven Tasho	Thorny Lea Golf Club
1982	James Hallet	Bass River Golf Course
1983	James Hallet	Bass River Golf Course
1984	Geoffrey Sisk	Marshfield Country Club
1985	Kevin Johnson	Country Club of Halifax
1986	Kevin Johnson	Country Club of Halifax
1987	Kevin Johnson	North Hill Country Club
1988	Kevin Johnson	North Hill Country Club
1989	James McDermott	Fall River Country Club
1990	Ted Rockwell, Jr.	Oak Hill Country Club
1991	John Salamone	Framingham Country Club
1992	Jack Kearney	Elmcrest Country Club
1993	Joe Keller	Oyster Harbors Club
1994	Frank Vana, Jr.	Marlborough Country Club
1995	Frank Vana, Jr.	Marlborough Country Club
1996	James Driscoll	Charles River Country Club
1997	Jim Salinetti	Stockbridge Golf Club
1998	Justin Peters	Pembroke Country Club
1999	Jim Salinetti	Stockbridge Golf Club
2000	Jim Salinetti	Stockbridge Golf Club
2001	Frank Vana, Jr.	Marlborough Country Club

The MGA's first Player of the Year award winner was Bruce Douglass of Thorny Lea Golf Club. The two-time state amateur winner also finished as runner-up in the 1984 and 1985 state opens.

In the same years that Jim Salinetti captured the Massachusetts Amateur, 1997, 1999 and 2000, he also teamed up with his father, Dick, to win the Father and Son Championship. Before turning professional, Salinetti also won the New England Amateur twice.

Frank Vana, Jr., the winner of three consecutive Mid-Amateur championships from 1999 to 2001, scored near the top in the Richard D. Haskell standings for more than a decade due to his consistently high finishes in important competitions. Frank, Sr., seen here helping line up a putt, served as his son's caddie in most of those events.

recognition, and they got it. The first decision was to make the president of the WGAM a full working member of the MGA executive committee during her term of office. In 1983 Mrs. William Schefft of Belmont Country Club, sister of the *The New Yorker* golf writer Herbert Warren Wind, became the first woman to so serve. For good measure, the action also included the president of the Golf Course Superintendents Association of New England, and Brian Cowan of the Eastward Ho! Country Club became the first to serve in that capacity. In 1996 Anne Marie Tobin of the Bellevue Golf Club, a practicing attorney and seven-time WGAM champion, was elected to the executive committee in her own right, not because of another office she held.

The concept of the caddie—epitomized for all time by the photograph of Francis Ouimet in the 1913 U.S. Open at The Country Club with his 10-year-old caddie, Eddie Lowery—remained a golfing icon, but the golf cart was becoming more and more common and caddie numbers were in steep decline. So the post–World War II period became a time, too, when golfers started to give back something more than small change to the boys who had carried their clubs and to encourage the boys', and eventually girls', continuing interest in the occupation. On January 15, 1949, Osmond O. Keiver of Tedesco Country Club, MGA president, offered at a luncheon for golf club presidents a plan he had developed with Ralph Bonnell of Winchester to establish a college scholarship fund for Massachusetts caddies. The plan envisaged funding by increasing the charge for MGA handicap cards then being issued to individual golfers from $1 to $2. The response was enthusiastic. In April, Francis Ouimet agreed to lend his name to the program, and the Francis Ouimet Caddie Scholarship Fund came into being under MGA sponsorship. In the first year $4,605 was raised

and thirteen college scholarships were awarded to the first class of Ouimet Scholars, which was graduated from several colleges in 1953—numbers which have grown over the half-century since to more than $9 million in scholarships and 3,500 in Ouimet Scholars.

At first, the MGA provided space and administrative support in its office on Milk Street in downtown Boston, and not until 1963 did the Fund, burdened with the problems of candidate selection and fundraising, employ its first executive director.

CHAMPIONSHIP CIRCLE Spectators surround the 18th green at Tedesco Country Club during the 1993 Massachusetts Open, one of eight MGA championships the club has hosted.

In 1975 the two organizations moved into a new, suburban building, with increased space and a more appropriate ambience for the Ouimet Fund's Museum and Library, at the Leo J. Martin Memorial Golf Course in Weston, a facility of the Metropolitan District Commission. There they created a replica of Ouimet's study and displays of his golfing memorabilia which he had bequeathed to the Fund. In time new demands on both organizations would dictate different office arrangements. After 20 years in Weston, the MGA, with its staff of six, needed more space and moved in 1995 to an office building at 175 Highland Avenue, in Needham. The WGAM, the women's amateur golf organization which had come to share quarters with the MGA in Weston, followed the MGA to Needham two years later.

Substantially then on its own, the Fund came to recognize the need for another significant change. It had been known from the beginning as the Francis Ouimet Caddie Scholarship Fund, but for years carts had been replacing caddies and the Fund had been awarding grants additionally to young people working in golf shops and course maintenance. In 1991, a marketing survey demonstrated that many clubs no longer had caddies at all and failed to see the need for supporting a "caddie" fund. The word "caddie" was therefore dropped from the official name and seal, and it became the Francis Ouimet Scholarship Fund.

Clearly, the venture into pro bono activity for Massachusetts caddies had been both a public good and a material success. Golfing eyes had been opened to new directions for service to the game and to the member clubs which also served the game. Soon other opportunities presented themselves, first in the political sphere. In the late 1960s, forces in the state legislature proposed the imposition of an excise tax on dues individual members paid to private clubs—a target group long on political vulnerability but short on political expertise and weaponry. President of the MGA at the time was Arthur W. Rice, Jr.; he saw the opportunity and stepped into the vacuum. Employing a Beacon Hill lobbyist for expertise and organizing an effective mail campaign through its member clubs, the MGA provided the leadership which defeated the tax proposal—and in the process developed a taste to accept a similar challenge soon to appear.

VOICE OF THE MGA The quarterly magazine, *MassGolfer*, began publication in 1990 "to capture the amateur spirit," and now reaches some 60,000 households.

Early in the 1970s, Andrew C. Bailey, as MGA counsel responding to cries of member clubs for relief in the area of real estate taxes, found that, in fact, golf course property was being valued increasingly at its "highest and best use," which in most cases was residential development. A danger was that this tax policy would tend over time to force golf clubs into residential real estate development, overburden communities with increasing needs for schools, police and fire protection and eliminate desirable green belt areas. The solution, in Bailey's opinion, would require an amendment to the Massachusetts constitution, and he took his case to the Speaker of the House, Tom McGee, who agreed. The campaign started in 1977, the MGA again organized its member clubs to get out the vote, and the amendment was carried by a substantial margin in the general election of 1978. Following this approval by the voters, Bailey sat down with the Commissioner of Revenue and drafted the basic provisions of what became Chapter 61B of the Massachusetts General Laws. With the assistance of McGee, the implementing legislation sailed through House and Senate and was enacted in 1979 as Chapter 713 of the 1979 Massachusetts Acts, adding Chapter 61B to the General Laws, effective July 1, 1980. While there have been amendments, 61B's key provision has survived: golf courses may elect to be assessed at no more than 25 percent of fair market value.

The core business of the golf association had continued, of course, while these sorties into charitable and political fields were taking place. It even grew. A proposal to calculate handicaps for its member clubs through a central computer had been studied and endorsed by the MGA executive committee back in June of 1964, and the MGA then contracted with the Boston Safe Deposit & Trust Co. to perform the calculations. In so doing it opened a new area of service to its member clubs, with salutary effect on its income, too. Only five years later, in 1969, the MGA, trying to service handicaps by computer for nearly 200 member clubs and thousands of individual golfers, recognized its need for a specialist and employed Richard D. Haskell as handicap coordinator. Within a short time, Bill Corcoran, last of the three brothers who had served as executive directors, died. In April Haskell was appointed to succeed in a role which he then occupied for three decades until his retirement in December of 1997.

Emphasis in the new Haskell administration turned naturally to consolidating the venture into electronic handicapping while continuing and expanding all the other championships and member services of the MGA—a mission which Haskell carried out so effectively that the MGA grew in club membership from 172 to 318, in individual member golfers from 19,215 to 88,251, and in staff from two persons to six during his tenure. The driving forces in this growth were the introduction of the MGA-USGA/GHIN computerized handicap service in 1981 (one of the first two states to adopt it) and the USGA slope system for indexing handicaps in 1984.

Haskell's contributions carried far beyond this, too. The vital area of communication provides a significant example: he first delivered in 1970 an MGA annual report, replaced in 1988 by a quarterly newsletter and in 1990 by a quarterly magazine, *The Massachusetts Golfer* (later re-named

MassGolfer), designed to communicate at all levels of the game and "to capture the amateur golfer's spirit—the competition, the camaraderie, the sportsmanship." The magazine now goes to some 60,000 households. In another aspect of good communication, he brought the MGA out of an inner circle of Greater Boston clubs and carried it effectively to clubs and golfers westward throughout the state.

On the business side of the ledger, Haskell worked with Andrew C. Bailey, the MGA counsel, to win two campaigns for excise and local property tax relief for golf facilities. He and a succeeding counsel, Robert W. Holmes, Jr., joined to achieve Section 501(c)(3) Federal tax status for the MGA as an exempt organization so that contributions to it are now deductible for income, gift and estate tax purposes (in addition, the MGA itself became exempt from local sales and property taxes and eligible to receive grants from a broad range of foundations and agencies).

WHEN TIGER WAS A CUB After Tiger Woods won his second of three consecutive U.S. Junior Amateurs at Wollaston Golf Club in 1992, the official magazine of the MGA featured him on its cover—the first of many golf magazine covers in a brilliant career.

On the playing side, Haskell oversaw the addition of six championships to broaden the levels of the MGA's competitive offerings. He developed the MGA Amateur Player of the Year point-ranking system, leading to an annual award which has been named in his honor. He increased the purse in the Massachusetts Open to the $60,000 level and coped successfully with the huge increase in championship entries.

Beyond Massachusetts, he was deeply involved in the International Association of Golf Administrators (IAGA), serving as president in 1981–82 and receiving its Distinguished Service Award in 2000. The IAGA brings together the professional administrators of 145 state, regional and national golf associations which cultivate golf worldwide.

Add to this a smiling personality. At the time of his retirement, he had this comment on Massachusetts golfers: "They don't smile as much as they should."

Tom Landry, a left-handed golfer with New England roots and education, came up from the Georgia State Golf Association to the MGA staff in June of 1993, was elevated to assistant executive director in 1996 and succeeded Haskell in January of 1998, inheriting immediately the problems of funding, building and moving into new headquarters, developing a museum and library, and celebrating the MGA centennial, all the while keeping its myriad of regular and expanding activities going and servicing its 380 member clubs and 101,500 individual member golfers. The world he entered was vastly different from the worlds of his predecessors, from Arthur Lockwood through Fred Corcoran to Dick Haskell.

According to an economic report prepared by the National Golf Foundation in 2000, golf in Massachusetts was being played by 700,000 residents of all demographic segments. More than 400 golf facilities and ranges employed some 19,000 persons, attracted upward of 500,000 visitors each year, and include an additional 234 companies and organizations involved in the business of golf. Golf-related revenue in the state was estimated to be $1.6 billion.

The move of the MGA offices to larger quarters in Needham in 1995 surely had been overdue. The original executive committee of 9 had grown to 26; the staff numbered 6. The roll of member clubs had grown to 350, two-thirds of them daily-fee clubs and municipal courses and one-tenth clubs not own-

ing real estate on which to play. (Recent member-club growth has occurred principally in upscale daily fee facilities. Growth in the private-club sector, once dominant, has slowed.) The MGA was conducting nine championships at the time involving a multiplicity of sectional qualifying rounds. It had enrolled 67,000 individual member golfers. It had in 1998 set up its own Website at www.MGAlinks.org. It had become, in fact, the seventh largest state/regional golf association in the country. And it was sharing space with the WGAM to their mutual advantage. The move to the Needham offices, while necessary, had been only a first, not a final, step.

The attractive option for the MGA had long been a home of its own. Opportunity came appropriately hand in hand with the millennium and plans being developed jointly by the PGA Tour, FleetBoston Financial Corporation and Connell Limited Partnership to build a Tournament Players Club of Boston in Norton, just off Interstate 495—that asphalt/concrete ribbon circling Greater Boston, booming with high-tech companies and the new focal point of its industrial face. The TPC of Boston

was to be one of a chain of 30-odd such clubs nationwide which operate on the corporate-member concept and from time to time entertain PGA Tour events. Specifically, opportunity came in the form of an offer of four acres of land on the entrance drive and adjacent to the ninth green to serve as the site for Massachusetts Golf House, the headquarters of the MGA with its museum, library and hall of fame. Cary R. Jubinville, then the MGA president, had no hesitation in accepting. Jubinville and his executive committee, like many of their predecessors, had long sought a home of its own for the MGA as well as space for 10 other state-based golf organizations: the WGAM, the Francis Ouimet Scholarship Fund, the New England Golf Association, the New England Senior Golfers' Association, The Hickory Shafts, the New England

MOMENT OF TRUTH Before enormous galleries, Justin Leonard and his caddie react simultaneously as Leonard's 45-foot putt rolls into the cup on No. 17 during the 1999 Ryder Cup matches at The Country Club in Brookline. The birdie putt effectively closed out the match with Jose Maria Olazabal (emerging from shadows), sealing victory for the United States side.

Intercollegiate Golf Association, the Golf Course Superintendents Association of New England, the New England Club Managers Association, the New England chapter of the Golf Course Owners Association and the Alliance of Massachusetts Golf Organizations. The MGA's vision for bringing together like-minded golf groups was being realized.

In retrospect, it often seems that the game which was nurtured on the estates of the gentry had been adopted by "the people" rather quickly, especially after Francis Ouimet's victory in the 1913 U.S. Open and the golf offerings at Franklin Park. In fact it was a long time before the game's organizational structure and its public-course players really came together. The MGA, in the mold of the USGA, had started as an organization of private golf clubs which owned or controlled the courses on which they played. Entry into their championships was in the beginning a privilege reserved for those who belonged to their member clubs. In 1922, the USGA did establish an Amateur Public Links Championship as an alternative to its Amateur Championship, but this did not, nor was it intended to, bring public-course players into full equality with private-club members.

In the late 1930s, however, USGA policy governing club membership underwent a significant and liberalizing change. By interpretation, membership qualification was broadened to recognize that a regularly organized club of golfers could exist without owning or controlling the course where it played. (The precedent had been established long before by the R&A in Scotland, the authority of British golf, which operates adjacent to the public course in St. Andrews which it in no way controls.)

SUMMER RULES As at most clubs, the job of the starter at Winchester Country Club is to get players off the 1st tee in a timely fashion and positive frame of mind.

The MGA followed the lead of the USGA in broadening its own membership qualification. The effect was to permit clubs of golfers, regularly organized to conduct their own affairs but operating at a public course, to join the USGA and the MGA as regular member clubs and thus make their individual members eligible to compete in USGA and MGA championships. After World War II, public-links players in Massachusetts began to form into so-called "inner clubs," more recently designated "non-real estate clubs," and to appear in the Massachusetts Amateur. George Curley, who played at the Riverside public course, actually was runner-up as early as 1947. While the USGA continued to offer both its Amateur and Amateur Public Links Championships, the MGA let its Amateur suffice for the aspirations of both private-club and public-course players.

In 1982, however, the MGA finally turned full-front to the special interests and aspirations of public-course players, launching the first Massachusetts Public Links Championship under the enlightened leadership of Ray C. Bump, Jr., who later served as president. The initial playing was set up for the Metropolitan District Commission's Leo J. Martin course in Weston at 36 holes, stroke play, with a gross division competing for the John Sears Trophy. Entry was open to amateur golfers who had been residents of Massachusetts for a minimum of one year, were bona fide public-course players and did not hold privileges at any course from which the public was excluded. There were 71 entries, 24 of whom were entered also in the concurrent U.S. Amateur Public Links Championship, for which sectional qualifying rounds had been re-instituted in Massachusetts in 1979. Don Reycroft and Bob Bradley, both of

Ponkapoag Golf Course, tied at 149, and Reycroft won the playoff. Neither had entered the sectional qualifying for the national championship.

From these modest beginnings came a predictable but nevertheless remarkable advance in both the activity of amateurs who played at public courses and in the public and semi-public courses which sought membership in the MGA. Two-thirds of the once all-private MGA members now are daily fee courses. Jim Hallet, a municipal-course player from the Bass River links on Cape Cod, won the Massachusetts Amateur in both 1982 and 1983, and then launched a professional career from which he returned to win the Massachusetts Open in 1985. Two years later, in 1987, Kevin Johnson, a public-course player from the Country Club of Halifax, topped Hallet's back-to-back amateur achievement by winning in successive weeks the Massachusetts Amateur at The Country Club and then the U.S. Amateur Public Links in Cincinnati. Johnson, who turned professional in 1989, had flashed early warning by winning the Massachusetts Open as an amateur in 1986 at the Country Club of New Scabury, the first amateur

A MAN AND A WOMAN A pair of golfers in full stride at Charles River Country Club, a bastion of low-handicap players in Newton.

to win since Don Hoenig—an amateur when he won for the first time in 1954—and only the second since Francis Ouimet in 1932. Johnson's triumph in the U.S. Amateur Public Links in 1987 earned him a place on the World Amateur Team in 1988 and brought Massachusetts its first national title since the immediate post-war years when Ted Bishop won the U.S. Amateur in 1946 and Wilfred Crossley, a private-club golfer from Norfolk playing public-links golf while living in Atlanta, won both the qualifying medal and the U.S. Amateur Public Links in 1947.

The MGA's strong promotion of public links golf finally brought the U.S. Amateur Public Links Championship to Stow Acres Country Club in

1995, its first visit to the Bay State, and the effect was electric. Within five years, the entry in the Massachusetts Public Links Championship rose to the 600 range, with six qualifying sites the rule, and the entry for sectional qualifying for the U.S. Amateur Public Links Championship in this region is approaching 200, one of the largest in the nation.

The emergence of top-flight players in the post–World War II period came hand in hand with the maturing of playing professionals (in contrast to club/teaching professionals), the attractiveness of the playing profession and the refinement of their circuits—the men first under the auspices of the PGA, then under the PGA Tour as an independent entity, the women under the LPGA. In fact, the last Massachusetts amateur to win a championship on the national level is Marion Maney-McInerney of Charles River, who won the U.S. Women's Mid-Amateur at Palm Beach Gardens, Florida, a decade ago in 1992. James Driscoll, also of Charles River, almost did it twice; he gained the finals in the U.S. Junior Amateur in 1995 and in the U.S. Amateur in 2000, resulting in his selection for the 2001 Walker Cup team. Driscoll had distinguished himself when he won his first Massachusetts Amateur in 1996 at the age of 18, second youngest to win that event, and he won it again in 1998. After playing in the 2001 Walker Cup match and U.S. Amateur, he, too, turned professional. Allen Doyle, who moved to Atlanta in the 1970s, earned places on three World Cup and three Walker Cup teams between 1989 and 1994, and Kevin Johnson played on the 1988 Amateur World and 1989 Walker Cup teams before turning professional. Later, on the senior tour, Doyle achieved great success; in 1999 he won the Senior PGA Championship and in 2001 the Senior Players Championship.

Television adopted golf as an entertainment and marketing medium in the 1950s (the U.S. Open was first telecast in 1951), and the charisma of Arnold Palmer and later Jack Nicklaus came onto screens nationwide. Purse money escalated (to $180 million for the men in 2000 when some 20 individual events carried prize money in the $4 million range). Endorsement money more than kept pace. For young golfers with skill, both men and women and especially players on the college circuit, the decision whether or not to turn professional after a

strong collegiate career and one or two amateur achievements became in their lexicon a "no-brainer." The era of lifelong amateur careers as enjoyed here notably by Ouimet, Guilford, Wright, Bishop and the Curtis sisters was passing—even as interest in amateur competitions, as evidenced by entries in MGA and USGA championships, continued to grow with new incentive for many young players.

The golf talent of young men and women in Massachusetts remains strong. It simply has come to be displayed, for the most part, in the financially rewarding professional field. In no case has this been displayed more brightly than by the young lady from Westford, Pat Bradley, whose promise had been evident from the beginning when she won the WGAM championship in 1972 and turned professional. Her career brought her the U.S. Women's Open in 1981, the LPGA Championship in 1986, 31 tour victories, captaincy of the 2000 U.S. Solheim Cup team and entry into the Golf Hall of Fame.

While no Massachusetts male has yet quite matched her achievements, Paul Harney came out of Worcester and Holy Cross to win four times on the tour in 1957 and 1958, then settled into the role of a club professional, returning to Pleasant Valley Country Club in 1965 after winning the Los Angeles Open in two successive years. On home turf, he won five Massachusetts Opens from 1967 to 1977.

This evolution from an avocation for amateurs toward a medium of spectator sport and entertainment, with substantial rewards for its most expert practitioners, is reflected in the careers of the star players of our day and in the events in which they participate and which we watch. Arguably, the golf event in Massachusetts with the greatest public impact in modern times has been the international match in 1999 between professional teams representing the United States and Europe for the Ryder Cup. All tickets had been sold a year in advance. Galleries on each of the three days were estimated up to 50,000. Even those who made it to the golf course found vantage points at a premium. The whole world watched—television carried the play worldwide. And executing a script which might have been written for television, Justin Leonard's 45-foot putt on the 17th green on Sunday afternoon brought victory over Jose Maria Olazabal and a comeback win for the United States side, 14½ to 13½. It is surely emblematic of this transformation as we enter a new millennium that this professional match, with its accompanying edge of incivility, was welcomed at The Country Club, long a bastion of the simple and gracious amateur spirit.

John P. English, early in his career a golf writer for the Boston Herald, *served successively as assistant executive director of the USGA, director of public relations at Williams College and president of both the Taconic Golf Club and the MGA.*

BERKSHIRES GEM Opposite: Youngsters wait for the fairway to clear on the par-4 17th hole at Wyantenuck Country Club, which plays to an elevated green, seen at left. One of the oldest golf clubs in America, Wyantenuck was founded in 1896.

By the year 1900, there were 29 golf clubs within a 12-mile radius of Boston's city hall. Like New York, Philadelphia and Chicago, Boston nurtured and protected the game as if it were its very own, and not some curious import from abroad. The experience of the founders and early members of those pioneering clubs provided a template for others to follow in organizing the game in their own locations. Golf was not a particularly democratic game in the beginning, although there were notable efforts by Bostonians to make it accessible to the general public. The truth is, most Americans worked six days a week and had no time for golf even if they could afford it. But members of America's "industrial aristocracy" had both time and money. Just as the wealth created by the Industrial Revolution in Great Britain led to a massive expansion of golf in England, so did the mighty capitalist engine of Massachusetts indirectly underwrite the new pastime. George C. Caner, Jr., eloquently summed up this connection in his history of Essex County Club. "Profits yielded by textile mills harnessing the Merrimack River," Caner wrote, "shoe and shoe machinery plants in Haverhill and Beverly, watches from Waltham, furniture from Gardner, guns from Springfield, whaling out of New Bedford and Nantucket, the China trade and its clipper ships out of Salem, cranberry bogs on the South Shore and Cape Cod, high finance trustee management, insurance, commercial real estate and manufacture of razor blades in Boston, and investment of local earnings countrywide in railroads, mining and other such enterprises, gave rise to potential membership material in the Greater Boston area with means and leisure time to devote to sports." The golf and country clubs thus formed became the foundation for all that was to come.

II. BOSTON:

OF

INCUBATOR

GOLF IN AMERICA

MYOPIA: VISION
OF A WORLD APART

~

*This inland links course of surpassing natural beauty
was shaped by the magnificent obsession
of a New England original named Herbert C. Leeds.*

IT WAS CONSIDERED the best golf course in America at the beginning of the 20th century, chosen to host the U.S. Open Championship four times in 10 years. All four Opens in that early era were high-scoring affairs, prompting one respected journal to label the course "the Alcatraz of U.S. Open venues."

Yet Myopia started as the outgrowth of the craze for another sport, baseball, sweeping the nation beginning in the 1870s. W. Delano Sanborn of Winchester, Massachusetts, had been a substitute pitcher, umpire and scorer on the baseball team at Harvard and so loved the game that, following graduation, he formed a team that took on other teams, amateur and professional, across the country. He named the squad "the Myopia Nine" or "the Myopia Club" because five of his teammates were nearsighted and wore glasses.

"The enterprising gentlemen were in reality very far-sighted," wrote H. B. Martin, the author of

Clubhouse entry is lined with individually owned liquor lockers dating from Prohibition. *Opposite:* Myopia's rolling terrain, scarcity of trees and waist-high fescue grasses along fairways impart a distinctive links character to the inland course.

Fifty Years of American Golf, "because they had formed here at this picturesque town the first country club in America; at least they planted the seed for such an institution, although they had neglected to call it the Myopia Country Club, preferring at that time the name Myopia Club."

The town in question had been Winchester, but in 1883 the club began renting quarters at a farm in South Hamilton, north of Boston, and eventually relocated to this site permanently. In its earliest days, the club sponsored baseball, tennis, water sports and equestrian pursuits such as flat racing and steeplechase. Golf was introduced with the establishment of nine holes in 1894, but only on the condition laid down by the club's horsey set that the frivolous new game not interfere with the smooth running of the foxhunt.

Enter Herbert C. Leeds, one of those larger-than-life figures found in the annals of amateur sport, whose dominating personality and golfing skills

A Myopia moment: looking for an errant drive in the tall grass along No. 1, at 274 yards one of the shortest par-4s on the course.

made Myopia what it is today.

For more than three decades he ruled over all golfing matters at the club with an iron fist. As the first vice-president of the fledgling MGA, his influence extended well beyond Myopia's borders.

"Thick-set and very strong, Leeds was a natural athlete," recounted *Atlantic Monthly* editor and Myopia member Edward Weeks in his history of the club published in 1975. "At Harvard, from which he graduated in 1877, he was a star shortstop and in football the first player ever to score a touchdown against Yale. Like most of his generation, he took up golf in his late thirties, was self-taught, and in two years had mastered the game."

After joining Myopia in 1896, Leeds was charged with upgrading the layout already in place and, using Shinnecock Hills on Long Island as one of his models, he created an inland links measuring 2,928 yards and offering, in the era of the gutta-percha ball, a formidable test. Such was the challenge offered by its tight tee boxes, chocolate-drop mounds, bunkers and perversely sloped greens and fairways that the USGA selected Myopia in 1898 to host the first Open requiring medal play of 72 holes.

Upon persuading Myopia's members to purchase an adjoining parcel of 51 acres, Leeds laid out a second nine at the club in 1901. He took advantage of the virgin land's generous elevations to add blind shots and uneven stances to the ordinary rigors of the game. "To eliminate

Opposite, clockwise from top left: Myopia's recently refurbished men's locker room; the par-4 12th hole, No. 1 handicap hole on the course, 446 yards long (from the yellow ladies' tees, it plays as a par-5); dining room with tributes to the club's past presidents, including the first, Marshall K. Abbott, pictured in foxhunt garb; with two deep bunkers guarding the front of the 18th green, the best miss on the approach is over the green, where the ground is level and free of hazards.

The 16th hole is a 192-yard downhill par-3. Behind the green, the pre-Revolutionary farmhouse that became Myopia's clubhouse was remodeled so that the two oldest rooms with the original big fireplaces were converted into a library and a dining room, without altering the Colonial character of the building.

One of the most treacherous holes at Myopia is the short par-4 13th. The front-sloping green rejects approach shots that are too short; some members elect to play to the right of the green, then chip on in hopes of one-putting for their par.

The elevated green at No.13 offers a view of the adjacent par-5 2nd hole, lined with some of Myopia's famous 'chocolate drops.'

chance from any game is to spoil it," he once penned in a scrapbook.

Thus, the average golfer found the new nine at least two strokes harder than the old nine. Subsequently, with the introduction of the livelier rubber-core ball, and inspired by an inspection tour of the links of the British Isles, Leeds fortified his design for Myopia with longer tees and new hazards. Walter Travis, the reigning U.S. and British Amateur champion at the time, called Myopia, "the best in the country…the creation largely of one man…with putting greens, mostly undulating, which are equal to the best anywhere in the world."

For Leeds himself, the course was always a work in progress. When the club hosted distinguished visitors like Harry Vardon or Bobby Jones, Leeds carefully followed their progress around his links. It was not unlike him to mark the spot where a good player's poor drive came to rest, then build a bunker on that spot after the visitor left.

The June, 1900, issue of the periodical *Golf* spoke of Leeds' indispensable role in the early years of the club as follows:

"In the spring and early summer, Mr. Herbert C. Leeds looks after things, and has a way of getting them done. Later, when he takes to yachting [Leeds was also an America's Cup crewman.—Ed.], the course cracks with inattention, and the revelry of worms is apparent on the putting-greens."

Myopia historian Weeks described the man as "a perfectionist, a martinet who took sadistic pleasure in watching the duffer suffer." A case in point was President William Howard Taft, a visitor to Myopia from 1909 to 1911, when the Summer White House was located in Beverly. A cavernous bunker on what is now the 10th hole at Myopia is named after him. It is said that every time Taft successfully escaped from this bunker, Leeds ordered

Four U. S. Opens in Ten Years

After the Myopia Hunt Club had re-established itself in Hamilton, its master of foxhounds, R. M. (Bud) Hamilton, staked out in the spring of 1894 its first simple nine holes — despite derision and even stiff opposition from horsemen. The club was still more concerned with hunts and polo than golf when Herbert C. Leeds joined in 1896. Leeds had been the first club champion at The Country Club, in 1893, and was dissatisfied with the rudimentary holes he found at Myopia. The result of his dissatisfaction became an early landmark in the development of thoughtful golf-course architecture in the United States. Leeds laid out what became the Long Nine in 1896 to take advantage of natural terrain. He heaped stone walls into mounds, grassed them over, and created the "Myopia chocolate drops." Bunkers were added only on holes not otherwise sufficiently challenging. He took pains with the location of putting greens and gave them undulating surfaces. His product influenced the state of the art throughout North America. A more immediate consequence was the bringing of the fourth U.S. Open Championship to his revised course at Myopia in 1898. It was the first of nine U.S. Opens to be played in Massachusetts, the most recent at The Country Club in 1988. The 49 players at Myopia used gutta balls, and Fred Herd, a Scot and professional at the Washington Park course in Chicago, won with a 72-hole score of 328. Leeds was leading amateur, tied for eighth at 347. The event was clearly successful, and the next three U.S. Opens to be held in Massachusetts also were played at Myopia — in 1901, 1905 and 1908. The 1905 championship went to Willie Anderson, one of the first Scots professionals to come to this country, on a score of 314, and it was his third straight and fourth win overall. No one since has won three straight U.S. Opens, although Bobby Jones, Ben Hogan and Jack Nicklaus later matched his total of four national championships.

A framed newspaper account of one of the four U.S. Opens hosted by Myopia hangs in the men's bar.
Top of page: Bridle paths still in use on the golf course are reminders of Myopia's equestrian heritage.

—John P. English

Clockwise from top left: The par-3 9th Pond Hole, only 136 yards long, with a green so narrow—12 to 15 paces across—that careless shotmaking will land the golfer in sand; Myopia's distinctive golf shop; walking up the 18th fairway; the rambling porch overlooking the practice putting green and finishing hole.

The paneled bar at Myopia is every golfer's dream of a 19th hole. *Below:* A tribute to the hard-working caddie stands among club trophies in the bar.

the bunker dug deeper, until it became so deep caddies had to assist the commander-in-chief out of the hazard by pulling him with a rope tied around his waist.

"'Papa' Leeds, as he came to be known to the younger generation, was a fascinating character," Weeks writes. "An angry birthmark covering the left side of his face made him highly sensitive. He was always photographed in profile and evidently supposed that the disfigurement committed him to a man's world." Indeed, the bachelor Leeds resided at his beloved club for most of the year in his later years, and from his usual perch on the Men's Porch, as a great-nephew attests, "it was his custom to terrify the young people…with the magnitude of the rough and the lightning qualities of the greens."

Leeds died in 1930 but the magnitude of his rough and the lightning speed of his greens live on.

Framed scorecards document amateur and professional course records set, respectively, by Bobby Knowles with a 67 on July 30, 1954, and by Jim Browning with a 64 on September 21, 1959.

MYOPIA
CLUB
CHAMPIONSHIP

1895	M. J. HENRY
1896	H. C. LEEDS
1905	L. C. FENNO
1906	H. R. JOHNSTONE
1907	H. R. JOHNSTONE
1908	H. R. JOHNSTONE
1909	P. W. WHITTEMORE
1910	P. W. WHITTEMORE
1911	P. W. WHITTEMORE
1912	P. W. WHITTEMORE
1913	T. G. STEVENSON
1914	D. L. PICKMAN, JR.
1915	C. M. AMORY
1916	D. L. PICKMAN, JR.
1917 – 1918	NO EVENT
1919	R. W. BROWN
1920	P. W. WHITTEMORE
1921	R. F. CUTTING
1922	T. FROTHINGHAM, JR.
1923	F. I. AMORY
1924	J. J. MINOT, JR.
1925	R. D. SEARS, JR.
1926	J. A. L. BLAKE
1927	F. I. AMORY
1928	R. D. SEARS, JR.
1929	R. D. SEARS, JR.
1930	J. T. NIGHTINGALE
1931	W. K. LAUGHLIN
1932	R. D. SEARS, JR.
1933	T. D. BOARDMAN
1934	T. D. BOARDMAN
1935	J. J. MINOT, JR.
1936	R. D. SEARS, JR.
1937	NO EVENT
1938	H. P. McKEAN
1939	R. D. SEARS, JR.
1940	J. T. NIGHTINGALE
1941	B. A. GOODALE
1942 TO 1945	NO EVENT
1946	E. M. BEALS
1947	G. W. SHERRILL
1948	G. W. SHERRILL
1949	R. D. SEARS III
1950	L. S. SHAW
1951	R. W. KNOWLES, JR.
1952	T. D. BOARDMAN
1953	R. W. KNOWLES, JR.
1954	R. W. KNOWLES, JR.
1955	R. D. SEARS III
1956	R. W. KNOWLES JR.
1957	L. S. SHAW

DREAMS COME TRUE:
GOLF FOR THE PEOPLE

~

*The roller-coaster sagas of Franklin Park in Dorchester
and George Wright G.C. in Hyde Park demonstrate the ongoing challenge
of making first-rate golf available to the public.* BY JOHN P. ENGLISH

GOLF WAS FIRST PLAYED in Franklin Park by George Wright and his friends in 1890, but—while a significant moment in the history of the game in Massachusetts and richly publicized—it did not represent either the foundation of golf in Franklin Park or on public courses generally.

Actually, six years elapsed before another divot was cut in Franklin Park, and credit for the establishment of the game there really redounds to Willie Campbell, who had come here in 1894 from Musselburgh, Scotland, to provide professional services to The Country Club, in Brookline. Here he extended the first rudimentary six holes to nine and, in a match dedicating the layout, defeated Willie Davis, professional at the Newport Country Club, in what one member declared to be "the first real golf any of us had ever seen."

Campbell came with a mission broader than simply serving one private club, however. He wanted to bring the game to the public. He thought it should be played by the people in open parks, as it was in his native Scotland. He took his dream

straight to the Boston Parks Department, where Frederick Law Olmsted was engaged in carrying out his own dream for a system of parks. Both Campbell and Olmsted were successful. In Campbell's case, he won authorization to create a nine-hole course in part of Olmsted's 334-acre Country Meadow section at Franklin Park. It opened for play in October of 1896. The greenkeeper was, of course, Willie Campbell, whose business card, by the way, billed him as "the most experienced player in the country." By 1900, when premature death took Campbell at 38, his vision for Franklin Park had certainly been realized: 40,000 rounds of golf were recorded.

In 1922, at the urging of MGA president Barton Stephenson, Mayor James M. Curley and the City of Boston polished their lustre by persuading Donald Ross to come in and extend the nine holes at Franklin Park to a first-class, 18-hole course.

Above: **George Wright, who died in 1937 at the age of 90, founded one of the first sporting goods companies in New England, Wright and Ditson, in 1871, among many other accomplishments in the world of sports.**
Opposite: **A view of Franklin Park's 6th green, 11th tee, 14th green, and, farthest back, the par-3 15th green.**

The 7th and 16th greens are tucked into one corner of the Franklin Park Golf Course, designed by Scotsman Willie Campbell and opened for play in October, 1896. *Inset:* Red-tailed hawk adds note of wild beauty to an urban layout.

The Ross course opened in the spring of 1923, and 36,505 rounds were played in that first year, demonstrating impressively the demand for public golf facilities and sounding the call for further expansion. So, a decade later, Boston called on Donald Ross again and he delivered again, this time the 18-hole course in Hyde Park, which opened in 1938—but not without difficulty.

"No course Ross ever did required more work to get it to fit the land," stated Bradley S. Klein in his monumental study of the architect's career, *Discovering Donald Ross.* The project was plagued by cost overruns. "Initial budget estimates of $225,000 quickly doubled when the full extent of the rocky site became apparent to engineers," Klein reported. Streams had to be culverted under fairways. Thirty tons of TNT were used to remove 10,000 cubic yards of ledge. The handsome Norman-style clubhouse alone cost $200,000. Yet as Klein describes the end result, "The golf course was notorious for both its raw beauty and terror, with sharp falloffs, rocky outcrops, and marshlands presenting dangers to every golfer."

The course was named in honor of George Wright, whose career in sports spanned eight decades. Both courses thrived until the social upheavals of the 1960s, when city funding and maintenance waned. By the mid-1970s, both had fallen into disrepair and become an embarrassment which cried for action.

Franklin Park's spacious new
clubhouse overlooks a generous
practice putting green, one of
many amenities bringing the facility in line with the needs and
desires of a growing golfing public.

While slow in arriving, renewal started, finally, in 1982 when, various other approaches having failed, Boston came to the MGA, as a non-profit organization, with a proposal that it lease the George Wright course for $1 a year and try to manage it back to respectability. It was an offer the MGA and its president, Ted Carangelo, in the end could hardly refuse—the rescue of a Donald Ross golf course. A lease was signed, and Bill Flynn, a former Massachusetts Open champion and successful public-course owner/manager, was retained. He embarked on a 20-year tour of maintenance and management which fully restored the original lustre of the George Wright course. At the same time, he also, on his own, contributed mightily to restoration of the public course in Franklin Park—efforts which earned him the MGA's Frank Sellman Distinguished Service Award in 1996.

Effort toward a greater good beyond the simple playing of the game was only beginning, however. In the summer of 1992, Tiger Woods, then 16, came to the Wollaston Golf Club in Milton in successful search of the second of his three U.S. Junior Amateur Championships, and Wollaston officials persuaded him to conduct an instructional clinic at Franklin Park to help develop interest in the game among urban youth. Some 100 disadvantaged youngsters from the neighborhood came, many of them unfamiliar with the game but attracted by Woods' fame. From their interest and presence came an inspiration for the MGA, nurtured especially by Michael I. Reilly, then a member of the MGA executive committee and in this centennial year its president.

Envisioning the potential in that start at Franklin Park, the MGA took over the clinic and expanded it to three days the next year and to five days in 1994.

So was born the Inner City Junior Golf Program and what is now a year-round ForeKids Program, benefiting some 3,000 boys and girls aged 7 to 17 state-wide each year—and with enormous potential for the game the MGA was organized in 1903 to "promote." The mission of the program was to provide inner city kids with an enjoyable, no-cost introduction to the basic fundamentals and values of golf through lessons not only on stance, grip and swing but importantly also on rules, honor, etiquette and all the virtues of the game. Instruction was to be provided on a volunteer basis by professionals assisted by leading amateurs and knowledgeable college students.

After two years at Franklin Park, the inner city clinic program began its expansion: first in 1995 to serve kids in the Lowell area at Bill Flynn's Windham Country Club, then in 1996 to benefit Springfield youngsters at the Veterans Golf Course (later at the Franconia Golf Course and at Blunt Park), in 1997 to develop young people in the Worcester area at Green Hill Municipal Golf Course—and still more recently to Brockton, Maynard and Pittsfield. These clinics accommodated 150 to 650 boys and girls each day, depending on the site. Local parks and recreation departments usually offered golfing privileges to graduating participants in return for minor labor, including caddieing, golf shop assistance and course maintenance.

Success does not necessarily eliminate problems, however. Its nature is often to create new ones. The initial success of the inner city clinics presented the MGA with the problem of how to feed year-round, youthful appetites for golf stimulated by only a brief summer introduction to the game. A recent study by the National Golf Foundation has estimated that only 10 percent of all youngsters

Opposite, counterclockwise from top left: **A men's afternoon league gets under way at George Wright; putting for dough; steps from the Norman-style clubhouse lead to 1st tee and practice area; stream running through fairway, one of many features making George Wright "notorious for both its raw beauty and terror."**

Everybody Loves Ponky

Canton's Ponkapoag Golf Club is the quintessential muni for Massachusetts golfers of all ages and abilities.

While Franklin Park and George Wright have their fans, no public golf course in the Boston area, or indeed in the entire state, can match the support that Ponkapoag Golf Club in Canton has mustered over the years. "Ponky," as it is universally called, is particularly well known as a haven for junior golf, having hosted the New England Junior Championship and the Massachusetts CYO Junior Championship for more than 40 years. The long-time Ponkapoag golf professional, Ken Campbell, is widely respected as a veritable Pied Piper of junior golf.

"To Ziggy, Socks, Bluto and the rest of the addicts at Ponkapogue Golf Club, Canton, Mass., where golf is way too much fun," reads the dedication to the 1996 comic novel, *Missing Links*, authored by *Sports Illustrated* senior writer Rick Reilly. The book thinly fictionalizes Ponky as "Ponkaquogue Municipal Golf Links and Deli, named by *Golf Illustrated* as 'possibly the worst golf course in America.' Ponky is to great golf courses what Spam is to the great chefs of Europe, but it had 18 holes most days, which was all we needed to contest our friendly golfing wagers."

Of course, course condition is not easy to maintain when a club averages 60,000 rounds a year. But this Donald Ross layout still commands respect. In a *Boston Herald* poll taken some years ago of 60 amateurs and professionals, Ponky was rated the seventh toughest course in the state, after Kittansett, Salem, Winchester, Oyster Harbors, Brae Burn and Tedesco. Not bad for a course that until recently could be played for under $10.

"We drank at Ponky, ate at Ponky, argued at Ponky, napped at Ponky, lied about sex at Ponky, rolled Serious Dice at Ponky, schemed at Ponky, got depressed at Ponky, and played golf at Ponky," writes the young narrator of *Missing Links*. "It was hell, but it was home."

Though simply furnished, the clubhouse at George Wright has an imposing architectural style. It was built in the late 1930s at a cost of $200,000, considered astronomical at the time.

introduced to golf pursue it; in the particular case of inner city boys and girls with limited access to golf courses, this estimate is most probably high. It also presents, fortunately, the kind of challenge the MGA now traditionally accepts. So, in 1997 the MGA employed Derek I. Breau as director of junior development and brought its continuing education program into being in 1998, offering to the inner cities year-round, no-cost golf instruction through cooperative arrangements worked out as the program developed, first in Chelsea with the Louis H. Latimer Society, a youth agency (later with the Chelsea Boys and Girls Club), and in Springfield with Springfield College. Its beneficial reach was extended the next year to Cambridge in cooperation with Harvard University (later with MIT), to Worcester through the Bayard DeMallie Memorial Golf Foundation, to Boston in cooperation with CityGolf, and to Lowell and New Bedford through the Boys and Girls Clubs there. It may be indicative of the response, generally, to this program that by 2001, when Salem was added, the Salem Boys and Girls Club built the first indoor golf room of its kind to accommodate it.

Fun and Games at Franklin Park

Scenes from the MGA's ForeKids Program, July 14, 2000

Inspired by a clinic the young Tiger Woods gave following his U.S. Junior Amateur triumph at Wollaston in 1992, the Massachusetts Golf Association started a series of clinics for inner city children that has turned a new generation on to the joys (and frustrations) of the game of golf.

PORTRAIT OF
THE ARCHITECT AS
A YOUNG MAN

~

*Donald Ross came to Massachusetts a greenkeeper in overalls
and practically flat broke, but after serving at Oakley and Essex, he went on
to create the greatest golf course empire on earth.* BY BRADLEY S. KLEIN

G OLF HAD BEEN introduced to the United States only six years before Donald Ross arrived here, yet he'd long been confident it would be huge. "When I was a young man in Scotland," he later wrote, "I read about America and the American businessman absorbed in making money. I knew the day would come when the American businessman would relax and want some game to play, and I knew that game would be golf. I read about the start of golf in the United States, and knew there would be a great future in it, so I

learned all I could about the game: teaching, playing, clubmaking, greenkeeping and course construction. And then I came to America to grow up with a game in which I had complete confidence."

However, it took an American to persuade him to move. Robert Wilson, a Harvard professor of astronomy who was a guest at Dornoch in 1898, invited Ross to come to his own club, Oakley Country Club in Watertown, Massachusetts. Ross set sail for New York the next April, then took the train to Boston. He walked the four miles from South Station to Wilson's home in Cambridge. The next day, Ross went over to see Oakley, where he was to be golf professional and greenkeeper.

Ross quickly set to work on rebuilding what was an 11-hole course into an 18-hole layout. The 5,901-yard, par-72 course was a bit cramped, and some holes had to be shoehorned in. From the second green, golfers walked along a 200-

Opposite at top: Oakley's 4th hole is a 513-yard par-5. Below: Between No. 4 and No. 5, a mound, originally created to dispose of rocks plucked from fairway locations, has become a striking visual element. Inset: The oil painting of Donald Ross in the Oakley clubhouse, by J. Michael Carter, is based on what is believed to be the earliest photograph taken of Ross in the United States.

yard wooded path through adjoining property that brought them to the third tee. The sixth hole featured a deep punch-bowl green set in a hollow that was six feet below the surrounding playing surface. To protect players on the green from players on the fairway who couldn't see them, club officials planted a 30-foot-high flagpole on a mound behind the green. The pole served as a semaphore that players re-set once they'd holed out, and a directional aid.

Some changes in the routing of the new course were made in 1909-1910, presumably by Ross. Other changes were made to the golf course in 1915, five years after Ross last worked there. Still, a visitor today to the 6,029-yard, par-70 Oakley layout can experience some 11 holes that are basically attributable to Ross. Holes 1 to 5 and 10 to 15 owe most of their current shape to his handiwork, as do the present 6th, 8th and 17th greens. As in all such cases, much change has intervened. How much of it is "natural" and how much is due to human intervention cannot be easily answered, owing to the character of such transformations.

There are, for example, far more trees, and taller ones too, than in Ross' day.

The club's reputation grew steadily. In 1903, the club became a founding member of the Massachusetts Golf Association, and in 1905, Donald Ross, representing Oakley, won the inaugural Massachusetts Open. In 1909, the club hosted that event.

Ross returned to Scotland in November of 1904. A month later he married Janet Conchie, to whom he had been engaged for seven years, and she returned with him to the U.S. Now comfortably ensconced in his post at Oakley, he was able to free himself each winter and spend November through April at a new property then under development in the Sandhills of

Opposite: Oakley's first clubhouse, originally a private residence designed by master architect Charles Bulfinch, is commemorated in a 40-foot mural inside the present clubhouse, seen (below) from the 16th tee, a 334-yard uphill par-4. Above: Trophies capture some of Oakley's storied past.

Donald Ross on "Pay-As-You-Play" Golf

The following is from Golf Has Never Failed Me,
a collection of writings completed by Ross while working
at Oakley and Essex, but not published until the 1990s.

THERE IS NO GOOD REASON why the label "a rich man's game" should be hung on golf. The game had its origin with the shepherd, who used his crook and a ball to while away the time while the sheep grazed. In my own native country, the shop workers and mill workers throng the links, for which their annual dues amount to about 50 cents, and their total annual expenditures to no more than $5. On account of climatic conditions and greater initial expense, it could hardly be expected that the average cost would be quite so small in this country, but it need not be made greater than the purse of any man could afford.

The development of municipal golf courses is the outstanding feature of the game in America today. It is the greatest step ever taken to make it the game of the people, as it should be. The municipal courses are all moneymakers, and big moneymakers. I am naturally conservative, yet I am certain that in a few years we will see golf played much more generally than is even played now.

I also see a brilliant future for the pay-as-you-enter golf courses of America, a tremendously big new industry. There is such a course down in Brockton, Massachusetts, and it could not begin to handle all those who wished to play this past season ... One in Providence has done very well indeed.

Miniature golf courses have made many thousands eager to play golf who never have played it before. Driving ranges have helped create a demand for the public pay-as-you-play golf courses of regulation length of which I speak.

The pay-as-you-play golf courses all over the east are doing remarkably big business.

Clockwise from top: The sharp dogleg par-4 18th at Essex, 408 yards, a classic finishing hole for either stroke or match play, with a green falling off on three sides to test the approach shot; No. 7, a 140-yard par-3, its green protected by water and bunkers; the crest of Essex County Club as seen over the entrance.

Although the sequence of holes has been altered, the shape of the holes remains consistent with Donald Ross' original vision, making Essex County Club "one of the few pure untouched Ross gems to be found in all of golf."

central North Carolina.

This, of course, was Pinehurst, founded several years earlier by James W. Tufts. At this time, Tufts had a summer home in Medford, Massachusetts—as did a few members at Oakley. When he told them of his quest to find someone to run his new golf operation, they recommended Ross. Tufts met with Ross at his Medford home and the deal was done. The affiliation boosted Ross' reputation considerably.

Perhaps it was the financial burden of having to support a child—daughter Lillian having been born in October 1909—or simply could have been that 11 seasons at Oakley had begun to wear thin and it was time, as the saying goes, to change the scenery. Whatever the motive, Ross made a big decision late in 1909. He left Oakley and signed on as head professional at the Essex County Club, 30 miles to the

northeast in a Currier & Ives–looking town called Manchester-by-the-Sea. There he took up residence in a home adjacent to the golf course, just behind what would become the 15th tee.

Essex had been founded in 1893 as a summer retreat for wealthy Bostonians. It was a fascinating tract, what with its heavily wooded areas interspersed with exposed ledge and vast deposits of sandy soil. A three-story Shinnecock-style roofed clubhouse stood at the center of the property. Ross had first seen the site in 1908, when a member, George Willett, had brought him there to oversee a complete redesign of the club's existing golf course.

Construction was bone-crushing work for the Irish laborers who rebuilt Essex. Rocks had to be blasted, then harnessed by derricks or pulley and rope, finally to be dragged away on horse-drawn sleds. Blind holes were less a strategic choice than a matter of adapting to the topography and to the

Donald Ross Golf Courses in Massachusetts

Dates indicate year design completed. Compiled by Bradley S. Klein.

Bass River Country Club	1914
Brae Burn Country Club	1912
Belmont Country Club	1918
Concord Country Club	1915
Cohasse Country Club	1916
Charles River Country Club	1921
Commonwealth Golf Club	1921
Cohasset Golf Club	1922
Essex County Club	1909
Ellinwood Country Club	1920
Franklin Park Golf Club	1922
George Wright Golf Club	1938
Greenock Golf Club	1927
Hyannisport Club	1936
Island Golf Club*	1913
Kernwood Country Club	1914
Ludlow Country Club	1920
Longmeadow Country Club	1921
Merrimack Valley Golf Club	1906
Nantucket Golf Links*	1917
Country Club of New Bedford	1924
North Andover Country Club	1920
Oakley Country Club	1900

Oak Hill Country Club	1921	Toy Town Tavern Golf Club*	1924
Oyster Harbors Club	1927	Vesper Country Club	1919
Pocasset Golf Club	1916	Wachusett Country Club	1911
Country Club of Pittsfield	1921	Wellesley Golf Club	1911
Petersham Country Club	1922	Wianno Golf Club	1913
Plymouth Country Club	1929	Worcester Country Club	1913
Ponkapoag Golf Club (No. 1)	1931	Winchester Country Club	1916
Ponkapoag Golf Club (No. 2)	1939	Weston Golf Club	1916
Springfield Country Club	1924	Whaling City Golf Course	1920
Salem Country Club	1925	Waltham Golf Club*	1921
Sandy Burr Country Club	1925	Wyckoff Park Golf Course	1923
Tatnuck Country Club	1930	Whitinsville Golf Club	1925
Tedesco Country Club	1937	Woodland Golf Club	1928
The Orchards Golf Club	1922	*No longer in existence	

Left: The house where Donald Ross lived while serving as golf professional at Essex is still in its original location behind the 15th tee. **Above:** A stereopticon now in the collection of the Francis Ouimet Library allowed students of golf to observe Ross' exemplary swing in three dimensions.

limits of human engineering.

By necessity as much as by choice, Ross relied upon the native contours to give Essex its otherworldly character. Perhaps another routing might have avoided blind shots, although it is impossible to imagine how. In any case, Ross' new layout incorporated those features. Consistent with the thinking of the day, such holes were never considered to be "unfair." Indeed, for a devout, God-fearing Presbyterian, there was no such thing as unfair. There was life, and golf was no small part of it, so that a golfer simply accepted the fate that luck—or grace—bestowed.

The work dragged on, with Ross and the club completing a few holes each year. Though Ross himself left as golf professional after the 1913 season—his home remains to this day—he made

Club champions and other winners have a place of honor in the grill room at Essex. *Top:* Plaques honoring winners of the famous Essex Four-Ball; after the happy idea of consolation events was conceived for this four-ball in 1915, the format caught on at clubs throughout the state and beyond. *Opposite:* The men's locker room at Essex County Club is a relaxed retreat infused with tradition.

several return visits before finally completing the redesign in 1917.

The Ross course, 6,308 yards long, is to an unusual degree intact today. There have been a few changes, including the relocation of one green and the shifting of several tees. And the sequence of holes has also been substantially altered—to create two loops of returning nines, rather than the truncated links-style ordering that Ross planned. But the shape of the holes is for all intents and purposes identical, thereby making Essex one of the few pure untouched Ross gems—along with Pinehurst No. 2—to be found in all of golf.

By now Ross was making his mark upon the golf world. The former greenkeeper in overalls from Dornoch had come a very long way. He was well established as a head professional, first at Oakley, then at Essex, with a winter affiliation at Pinehurst that helped further spread his name. At each job, he also got to try his hand at course design. In 1913, he made the biggest decision of his life. He gave up the life of a golf professional and greenkeeper, and went full time into golf course design, wintering still in Pinehurst but summering in New England. It was to be the pattern of life as he went on to create the greatest golf course empire on earth.

Bradley S. Klein is founding editor of Superintendent News *and architecture editor of* Golfweek. *His book,* Discovering Donald Ross, *was published in 2001 by Sleeping Bear Press. This article originally appeared in the 1999 U.S. Open Championship Program.*

Opposite: A glass positive in the office of Essex County Club superintendent Patrick Kriksceonaitis shows Beatrix Hoyt driving on the 7th hole at Essex during the final of the Women's National Amateur in 1897. *Above:* A contemporary Essex member successfully gets off the 1st tee, his Labrador retriever mimicking his every move.

If the Golf Shoe Fits...

...it must have been made in Brockton, in its glory days the shoe capital of the world.

AMERICA'S SHOEMAKING INDUSTRY began in Massachusetts, and by the late 1800s was the state's largest employer. Brockton and surrounding towns specialized in men's shoes, while the area north of Boston was known for women's shoes.

Brockton alone had 75 factories that made shoes and another 60 factories that made items related to shoes. No wonder they called it "Shoe City."

Burt & Packard, a Brockton shoemaking firm founded in 1857, was taken over in the early 1900s by an avid golfer named Perley Flint, who re-named the company Field & Flint. Besides continuing to produce men's dress shoes, Flint expanded into spiked shoes for golfers. In 1923 he conducted a contest among his employees to find a name for his fledgling golf shoe line. The winning entry was "Foot-Joy." The brand name has survived to this day, albeit without the hyphen, a recent change.

The first U.S. Ryder Cup team in 1927 wore FootJoy shoes. Field & Flint continued to build brand recognition in the late 1920s and 1930s by enticing young touring pros, including Ben

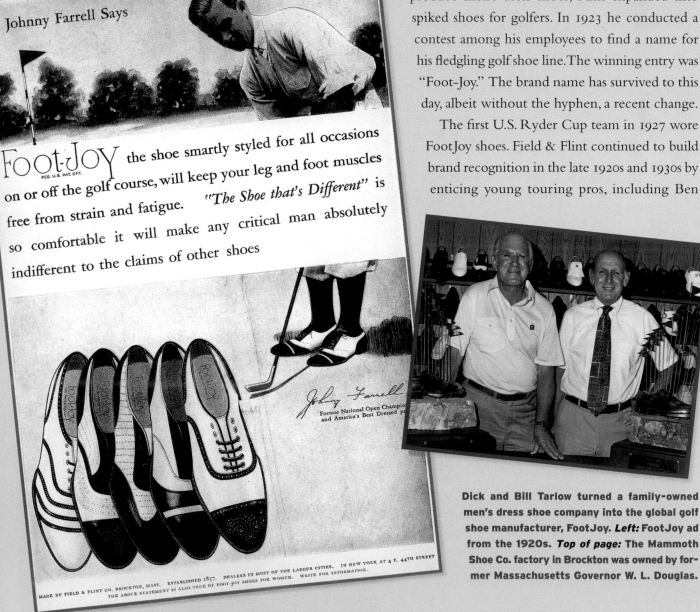

Johnny Farrell Says

FOOT-JOY *the shoe smartly styled for all occasions on or off the golf course,* will keep your leg and foot muscles free from strain and fatigue. *"The Shoe that's Different"* is so comfortable it will make any critical man absolutely indifferent to the claims of other shoes

Johnny Farrell
Former National Open Champion
and America's Best Dressed pro

MADE BY FIELD & FLINT CO., BROCKTON, MASS. ESTABLISHED 1857. DEALERS IN MOST OF THE LARGER CITIES. IN NEW YORK AT 4 E. 44TH STREET
THE ABOVE STATEMENT IS ALSO TRUE OF FOOT-JOY SHOES FOR WOMEN. WRITE FOR INFORMATION.

Dick and Bill Tarlow turned a family-owned men's dress shoe company into the global golf shoe manufacturer, FootJoy. *Left:* FootJoy ad from the 1920s. *Top of page:* The Mammoth Shoe Co. factory in Brockton was owned by former Massachusetts Governor W. L. Douglas.

Hogan, Sam Snead, Byron Nelson and Jug McSpaden, to wear FootJoys. In the early 1950s, the Charles A. Eaton Company of Brockton successfully promoted a line of golf shoes using the Etonic brand name.

In 1957, Field & Flint was sold to the Stone & Tarlow Company, yet another Brockton shoe manufacturer. At that time Stone & Tarlow produced 275,000 pairs of dress shoes annually. The much smaller Field & Flint produced 80,000 pairs of shoes, evenly split between dress and golf. Key executives of the newly merged entity, Dick and Bill Tarlow, both avid golfers (Bill captained the Dartmouth golf team), decided the future of the combined firms was in golf and devoted their efforts exclusively to developing the golf shoe business. With Ike in the White House and Arnie on tour, this turned out to be a brilliantly timed strategy.

When Julius Boros won the U.S. Open at The Country Club in 1963, he was wearing FootJoys, as were the vast majority of golfers in the field, and the company has continued to claim market dominance, through the thick and thin of corporate takeovers and global economics, just as the sprawling old factory building on Field Street in Brockton continues to turn out its high-end footwear for golfers, one pair at a time.

Golf shoe ads from the 1920s (top) and the 1960s had in common the endorsement of well-known touring pros.

NEW LIFE
FOR OLD COURSES

~

While some Massachusetts golf clubs have been lost to neglect,
adversity or just plain bad luck over the years, others have demonstrated
a remarkable capacity for growth and rejuvenation.

ONE CLUB was a mecca for black golfers in the age of Jim Crow and segregation, the other a weekend think tank for high-powered corporate executives. Both clubs have more twists and turns in their history than a course full of doglegs, but they have survived and prospered, and today they are thriving centers of golf with new owners, fresh images and loyal followings. In fact Stow Acres Country Club in Stow and The International Golf Club in Bolton, both of which started as rustic 9-hole layouts nearly a century ago, now each boast two outstanding 18-hole courses. Their very existence is proof of the inherent resilience and comeback-kid personality of golf in the Commonwealth.

The story of Stow Acres is as diverse as the architectural styles of its clubhouse, an edifice dating back to around 1800 and containing elements from

The oldest parts of the clubhouse at Stow Acres date from 1800. *Opposite:* This 425-yard par-4 on the North Course at Stow Acres requires an approach shot over water.

the Federal, Greek Revival, Italianate and French Second Empire periods. The house was built by John Randall, a prominent Boston physician, shortly after marrying Elizabeth Wells, the granddaughter of American Revolution hero Samuel Adams, and was used primarily as a country retreat. The house and the land remained in the Randall family for several generations.

Fast-forward to the year 1926, when an African-American entrepreneur named Robert H. Hawkins put together $6,000 and assumed a pre-existing $10,000 mortgage in purchasing the 190-acre estate of Dr. John Witt Randall. He turned the Stow site into Mapledale Country Club, a club featuring nine holes of golf, tennis courts and horseback riding trails. Black golfers and their families flocked to the club, some from great distances.

An avid golfer himself, Hawkins had been a caddie growing up in Massachusetts and later in Vermont, after his family moved there in 1902. As

former *Boston Globe* reporter John H. Kennedy tells the story in his book, *A Course of Their Own:*

"After high school he went to work at several country clubs in Vermont before he became general manager of Sandy Burr Country Club, the first black to reach that position in New England. At Sandy Burr, he got the idea of owning his own country club for Negroes."

With Mapledale, Hawkins realized his dream. And starting in 1926, through the organizing skills of two black physicians who were avid golfers from Washington, D.C., Mapledale hosted the first national golf tournaments held for blacks, sponsored by a brand-new organization called the United Golfers Association.

"The fledgling organization was an attempt to gather supporters of golf together, to play tournaments, to have a social center for their love for the game," recounted Kennedy. "Golf was predominantly a game for whites—in large part because of segregation and economic demands —but it was no longer their exclusive preserve."

The third Negro National staged at Mapledale in 1928 included both a professional and amateur division. Hawkins wanted to make sure that all the participants enjoyed themselves, and that year's National offered, in addition to the purse for professionals, prizes for the longest drive, the best dressed golfer and the "best looking set of golf clubs," as well as a dinner dance. The winner was Stow Acres' own golf professional, Paul Washington, who went on to win the Negro National three more times. (In 1953, Washington founded the Boston Pro-Am Golf Association, a multi-ethnic group of golf enthusiasts who played primarily at Franklin Park.)

Unfortunately, with the Depression Hawkins couldn't keep Mapledale afloat. "He was forced to relinquish all but a

Opposite, clockwise from top: Not a slicer's hole, the 417-yard par-4 15th hole on Stow Acres North, a sharp dogleg left; readying the fleet for action; blasting from sand on the 415-yard par-4 17th, another dogleg left; finishing hole rituals.
Inset: Stow Acres owner Walter Lankau has long been active in Massachusetts Golf Association affairs.

small interest in it," reported Pete McDaniel in his book *Uneven Lies, The Heroic Story of African-Americans in Golf.* "In 1929, Mapledale became Stow Golf and Country Club, a public facility which blacks still frequented but could no longer call their own."

The International Golf Club in the rolling hills of Bolton first entered the spotlight in the 1950s as the longest golf course in the world, measuring 8,040 yards from its "super championship" or "tiger" tees. The monster was the brainchild of Albert H. Surprenant of Boston and Clinton, who had made his fortune in the manufacture of plastic insulated wire and cable for guided missiles and aircraft. In 1953 he had purchased a 500-acre tract of land in Bolton, Lancaster and Clinton that included the nine-hole Runaway Brook Golf Club, first organized in 1901 and now all but abandoned.

Surprenant hired Geoffrey Cornish to design the new course and it opened for play in 1957. The tee-ing areas alone averaged 8,000 square feet—as big or bigger than the average green at many clubs. Two holes, the 5th and the 12th, measured more than 650 yards. (In 1972, after Robert Trent Jones, Sr., re-designed the course, the layout measured 8,325 yards.)

The new course was christened Surprenant National Golf and Country Club, but Francis Ouimet reportedly convinced the owner to change it to something simpler, and it was re-named Runaway Brook, in honor of the first golf course on the site. In 1961, when International Telephone & Telegraph acquired Surprenant's manufacturing plant in Clinton, ownership of the club passed to ITT. At that time Runaway Brook was re-named The International. Through its Sheraton hotel division, ITT developed a business conference center

No. 3 on The International's Oaks course, designed by Tom Fazio, is an uphill 352-yard par-4 with bunkers on the right side. *Opposite:* No. 4, with its magnificent view toward western Massachusetts, is a 172-yard one-shotter, severely downhill. *Inset:* Tee marker with symbol of The Oaks.

and 53-room lodge on the grounds which continues operation to this day albeit under new ownership. Club president and co-owner Daniel Weadock, a former ITT executive, along with his partner and general manager, Brian Lynch, bought the club in 1999.

Shepherding in an exciting new phase at The International, the partners opened a second 18-hole course in 2001. The 6,900-yard, par-72 Oaks, as it is called, is the first layout in New England to be designed by the acclaimed golf course architect Tom Fazio (although he put in one other professional stint in Massachusetts in the mid-1970s, helping his uncle and mentor, George Fazio, develop Wollaston Golf Club in Milton).

Over the years Stow Acres also changed ownership several times. In 1954, the Pages, three brothers from Waltham, bought the property and expanded the course from 9 holes to its present 36-hole layout. The course was again sold in 1986 to Walter Lankau and Roger Kane, Jr. Lankau became sole owner in 2002. An extensive renovation of the clubhouse took place in the meantime, restoring the old Randall homestead to its former grandeur.

In 1995, Stow Acres hosted the 70th staging of the U.S. Amateur Public Links Championship on its North Course, the first Massachusetts club to do so, and an appropriate choice. History—of the sort Mapledale golfers especially would appreciate—had been made in this event in 1959, when William A. Wright became the first African-American winner of a USGA title.

Old Enough to Drive

*Scenes from the Massachusetts Junior Amateur
Championship, 13-and-under division*

DEDHAM COUNTRY AND POLO CLUB, AUGUST 8, 2000

The 2000 championship was the fourth Junior Amateur that Dedham hosted, the others taking place in 1965, 1983 and 1990. The club itself dates back to the first decade of the 20th century. It came into existence on May 19, 1910, as a result of a merger between the Norfolk Country Club and the Dedham Polo Club. The Dedham club was devoted exclusively to polo and was located near the center of Dedham. Although it had three polo fields, there was no room for expansion as land in this area became more and more scarce. Meanwhile, the Norfolk club owned 83 acres near the Dedham/Westwood town line and offered nine holes of golf, tennis, polo and a clubhouse. Donald Ross had designed the nine holes in 1902. In 1920 the club reorganized and purchased more land. Seth Raynor was hired to design 10 new holes on this land; he also revised the original nine into a new layout of eight holes. By 1925, the new 10 holes were ready to play and Dedham had a challenging 18-hole course. Since that time some changes were made to various holes. In 1996 the club decided to create a master plan for restoring the course to Raynor's original 1920 design.

CHAMPIONSHIP VENUE
FOR THE AGES

~

*The "honored old holes" of The Country Club have tested golfers
of every stripe for more than a century.*

THERE'S SOMETHING both quiet-ening and ceremonial about the long, winding drive onto the grounds of The Country Club in leafy, suburban Brookline. In the time it takes a visitor to pass the guard house with its drowsy sentry (a mannequin in uni-form), traverse the 15th fairway and arrive at the club's central compound of yellow-painted clapboard buildings, the golf course itself radiating beyond them in park-like vistas, the day's cares seem to recede. Feeling almost obligated to relax, the visitor slows down mentally and emotionally. He may even reach to turn off his cell phone, and that's a good idea, too. Cell phones are for-bidden here as an intolerable breach of the peace.

Not that serenity always pre-vails. In fact there have been historic moments of high raucousness on this golf course, as when Francis Ouimet triumphed over the British superstars, Vardon and Ray, in the famous rainswept playoff for the U.S.

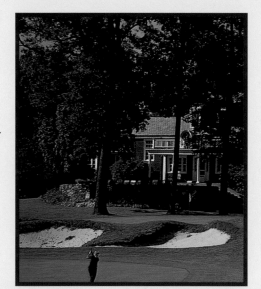

The 418-yard 18th hole finishes in front of a classically facaded locker building, built in 1915 for $45,000. *Opposite:* Trophies on a fireplace mantel in the clubhouse include one with the figure of a squirrel, the club's emblem.

Open in 1913, prompting "excited women to tear bunches of flowers from their bodies and hurl them at the youthful winner," reported the *New York Times.*

Ouimet all but sealed his victory with a birdie on the 17th hole. Reporting for the *Times* of London, Bernard Darwin conveyed this transcendent moment in golf history as follows:

"The long line of specta-tors stretched the whole length of the hole. The green looked like a black ampitheater. There was an agonizing moment or two of waiting while the crowd was cleared away. Then Mr. Ouimet hit a grand drive straight down the middle of the course while Vardon hooked his into the rough grass. [In those days, amateurs were accorded the respectful "Mr." by journalists, while pro-fessionals were not. —*Ed.*] Then Vardon made a desperate effort, but the ball plunged into the bunker. Then came another dramatic pause while the referee through his megaphone besought everyone to be quiet. Mr. Ouimet took a practice swing with his

iron, then hit the ball true as steel straight for the pin ... Mr. Ouimet laid his third stone dead, tapped the next one into the hole, and was straightaway whirled off his feet and carried shoulder high by the crowd, who cared nothing for the state of the last putting green."

In circumstances of eerie similarity 86 years later, pandemonium again broke out on the 17th at Brookline when Justin Leonard holed a 45-foot putt to assure victory for the U.S. side in the 1999 Ryder Cup. The spontaneous celebration by the American team and galleries, nearly 50,000 strong, did not sit well with some Europeans,

particularly as it forced Leonard's opponent, Jose Maria Olazabal, to wait an undue amount of time for the green to clear so that he could attempt his match-tying putt, which he narrowly missed. Afterwards one English columnist went so far as to call the Americans "repulsive people, charmless, rude, cocky, mercenary, humorless, ugly ... as odious in victory as they are unsporting in defeat."

U.S. team captain Ben Crenshaw begged to differ, later describing what had happened both in 1913 and 1999 as "two improbable events celebrated with unbelievable passion and emotion," and adding, "Ouimet didn't need to spend the rest of his life apologizing. Neither should I. Neither should my team."

Few golf clubs can lay claim to hosting so many major golf events as The Country Club—a total of 13 national championships in the 20th century, plus two Walker Cup matches (in 1932 and 1973) and the aforementioned Ryder Cup. The "honored

Counterclockwise from top left: The yellow-painted clapboard clubhouse, affectionately known as "the old lady of Clyde Street"; a downhill par-4 on the club's Primrose Nine, added in 1927 and from which holes are borrowed to strengthen the layout for major events; a caddie wearing club bib replaces flagstick; and the library, adjacent to the club's grill room.

The lounge in the men's locker room is filled with memorabilia of the major golf events held at The Country Club. *Below right:* Luis Garcia serves up a cold apres-golf beverage for club member Bill Cornish.

old holes" of the Brookline layout, in Herbert Warren Wind's felicitous phrase, seem especially suitable for match play, for as he pointed out, "their rugged fairways and their amazing variety of perched, canted and contoured greens demand shotmaking that is both full-blooded and tidy every step of the way."

The string began in 1902 with the U. S. Women's Amateur, or the National Women's Tournament as it was then called. Genevieve Hecker of the Apawamis Club in Rye, New York, the 1901 champion, defeated The Country Club's own Louisa Wells in the final, 4 and 3. Coverage of women's golf was slightly condescending in those early days. "It was an excellent drive for a woman," wrote one reporter. "She proceeded practically to throw away the match," noted another. Since that time two Women's Amateur championships have been held here, one in 1941, won by Elizabeth Hicks Newell,

the other in 1995, won by Kelli Kuehne.

In 1910 the club hosted its first U.S. Amateur Championship. It was won by William C. Fownes, Jr., who happened to be co-designer, with his father, Henry, of another early American landmark course, Oakmont Country Club in Pittsburgh. Other National Amateurs at Brookline were won by Jess Sweetser in 1922, Lawson Little, Jr., in 1934, Hillman Robbins, Jr., in 1957, and Jay Sigel in 1982. On the way to his victory, Sweetser, from the Siwanoy Country Club in Bronxville, New York,

defeated all the established players of the day, including defending Amateur champion Jesse Guilford, Chick Evans, Jr. and Bobby Jones. In 1926 he also became the first American-born to win the British Amateur. Little won both the U.S. and British Amateur in 1934, and repeated as champion in both events in 1935—a back-to-back sweep that not even Jones attained. Robbins was on active duty in the Air Force when he won over a field at Brookline that included the entire U.S. and British Walker Cup teams. Sigel followed his win with another Amateur title in 1983, the first player since Harvie Ward to win the U.S. Amateur in successive years.

In addition, two national junior championships were played at Brookline: the 1953 Girls' Junior, won by Millie Meyerson of Los Angeles, and the 1968 Junior, won by Eddie Pearce of Temple Terrace, Florida. Pearce had uncanny command of the par-5s at The Country Club; playing 17 of them in the course of the championship, he was 15 under par.

Two U.S. Open Championships followed the historic Ouimet win of 1913 at Brookline. The 1963 Open, plagued by high winds and high scores, was decided in a three-man playoff, in a reprise of 1913, this time among Julius Boros, Arnold Palmer and Jacky Cupit. Boros prevailed with a seamless round of 70. Growing up in Bridgeport, Connecticut, he had started his winning ways in professional golf by capturing the 1951 Massachusetts Open at Salem Country Club.

When the U.S. Open returned to The Country Club in 1988, marking the 75th anniversary of Ouimet's 1913 championship, the course was ripe for the taking, with perfect weather conditions, soft greens and in prime condition overall, having been recently refurbished to much acclaim by architect Rees Jones. Eleven players broke par for 72 holes, then a record for the championship, including Curtis

AMPIONSHIP

1913 Miss ANNE NASON	1973
1914 Miss H.S. CVRTIS	1974
1915 Miss H.S. CVRTIS	1975
1916 Miss F.C. OSGOOD	1976
1917 Miss E. STEVENS	1977
1918 Miss F.C. OSGOOD	1978
1919 Miss F.C. OSGOOD	1979
1920 Miss H.S. CVRTIS	1980
1921 Miss H.S. CVRTIS	1981
1922 Miss H.S. CVRTIS	1982
1923 Miss R. BATCHELDER	1983
1924 Miss H.S. CURTIS	1984
1925 Miss E. STEVENS	1985
1926 Miss R. BATCHELDER	1986
1927 Mrs. W.C. QUINBY	1987
1928 Mrs. W.C. QUINBY	1988
	1990
1955 Mrs. W. HOWARD	
1956 Mrs. M.M. GLEASON	
1957 Mrs. H.B. JACKSON	
1958 Mrs. W. HOWARD	
1959 Mrs. H.B. JACKSON	
1960 Mrs. H.B. JACKSON	199
1961 Mrs. H.B. JAC	99
1962 Mrs. H	99
1963 M	99

Opposite: **The extensive Roster of Champions at The Country Club occupies wall space on the main floor of the clubhouse, all the way up the stairs and all along the hallways on the second floor.** *Above:* **Master engraver John Kobos of Lawrence has been updating the club's main trophies annually since 1955.**

The 451-yard par-4 3rd hole plays from an elevated tee to a contoured fairway, then past mounds and over bunkers to the green. *Opposite:* The practice putting green near the 1st tee at The Country Club. *Inset:* An ivied clock on one of the nearby buildings.

Strange and Nick Faldo, the reigning British Open champion, who had finished in a tie for the lead at 278. Even though he hit only six greens in regulation, to Faldo's four, Strange ground out a 71 in the playoff on the following day, outscrambling Faldo who shot 75.

Throughout its unrivaled history as a championship site, The Country Club has pursued a parallel mission as a private club in service to its member families. In some ways the prototype for country clubs across America, Brookline pioneered the idea of a club as a place where not just golf but other sports and related social and recreational activities could be enjoyed—a kind of cruise ship marooned in a field of green.

For its Millennium Day Brunch on January 1, 2000, the club published a list of the outstanding events that had occurred over the previous 100 years, among them:

1903 – first tennis championship

1920 – completion of indoor curling rink

1937 – siting of skeet-shooting field

1950 – opening of first swimming pool

1966 – first platform tennis courts

1994 – renovation of clubhouse

And one year there was the new amenity that really turned heads:

1941 – introduction of free cocktails after annual meeting

So while great golfers and memorable shots may come and go at Brookline, the daily privileges and satisfactions of club life carry on, and foster with them an intense loyalty and affection. As Francis Ouimet himself declared during a banquet marking the club's 50th anniversary, in 1932, "There is something about The Country Club that just gets into one's heart."

Memorabilia at the Ouimet Library include a poster signed by the first 13 caddies to receive college scholarships from the Francis Ouimet Scholarship Fund, started in 1949, and a cartoon extolling Ouimet as "easily one of the most popular men of his time [who] did more for golf in the U.S. in his era than anyone before or since." The ballot box on the table came from a golf club in Scotland, where it was used to vote on new applicants for membership.

A Caddie's Story

~ BY FRANCIS OUIMET ~

BORN in a rather thinly populated section of Brookline, Massachusetts, I have often wondered what my golfing activities would have amounted to if my father had not bought a home bordering on The Country Club. Of one thing I am quite certain and that is I should never have had the opportunity of developing an interest in the game of golf to the same extent that was made possible by close proximity to a fine course. As it was, daily trips from home to a little schoolhouse, built in 1768 and known as the Putterham School, carried me back and forth across the fairways. Not that I was granted any such privileges, but in the role of a trespasser I discovered that this route saved many footsteps, got me to school on time, and, more important, enabled me to get home with the least possible delay.

There was a more intriguing motive, however. Frequently on one of my excursions I ran across a lost ball, of the gutta-percha variety. At the age of seven I had a collection of Silvertowns, Ocobos,

Vardon Flyers, Henleys, and other brands popular among golfers in 1900 that would do full credit to the professional's shop.

Long before I ever had a club, I had golf balls enough to last me for years. But the balls without a club were not very useful. Golf was so new to America in 1900 that it was difficult to get clubs. They never got lost, and were rarely discarded. The balls, however, seemed to have plenty of life in them, their varied markings held some sort of fascination for me, and it was fun watching them bound from rocks and other solid substances.

After I had hoarded golf balls enthusiastically for two years, someone gave my brother Wilfred a club. When Wilfred was busy caddieing, I helped myself to that club and used it to knock some of my hoard around the back yard. I was careful to put Wilfred's club back in its place before he put in an appearance. Otherwise, I felt, there might have been a family riot. Occasionally a tournament was held at The Country Club and on those days and after school, I would stand on the edge of a fairway and watch the golfers go by. If I saw some-

---

THE ACCOMPANYING EXCERPT is from Francis Ouimet's memoir, *A Game of Golf*, first published in 1932. Born in 1893, Ouimet grew up a poor boy of French-Canadian descent, across the street from the Brookline golf course that would first nurture then launch his career as America's first genuine golf hero. He went on to win the U.S. Amateur twice, the Massachusetts Amateur six times and the most Walker Cups ever, competing as a player eight times and as non-playing captain four more. Ouimet never turned professional. He worked in finance and sports administration as president of the Boston Bruins, vice president of the Boston Braves baseball team and chairman of the Boston Arena Authority.

In addition to *A Game of Golf*, here adorned with some of Ouimet's golf medals, the 1913 U.S. Open champion authored *Golf Facts for Young People*, in which he cautioned young golfers, "Don't give your mind time to consider any other matter than the correct playing of each shot."

one play an exceptional stroke, I watched how he did it and hastened home to take Wilfred's club and set about trying to put into practice what I had seen. Those efforts must have been funny, but they were, after all, the beginnings of my game, such as it is.

I can remember vividly the first Haskell ball I ever found. It was in the fall of 1902, and I was nine years old. Wilfred was a caddie boy at The Country Club, and the ladies were having their national championship. On the way home from school, I picked up a nice new ball. It was unlike any other I had ever seen and seemed much livelier. I showed it to Wilfred and he told me it was one of the new rubber-cored balls. Few had them, and Big Brother tried his best to talk me into parting with it. Nothing doing. I played with it, bounced it, and used it until

the paint wore off. I got some white paint and painted it. Mother was baking some bread in a hot oven and I sneaked my repainted Haskell into the oven, thinking the heat would dry the ball.

Mother smelled something burning and went all through the house trying to discover the cause. She found nothing, but the odor was so strong, and she was so worried that the house was burning up, that she kept on searching. Finally she opened the oven door and the most awful smell in the world came out of the newly made batch of bread. It was ruined—and so was my prize, the Haskell. The heat had melted the gutta-percha shell and there was nothing left of the thing but a shriveled-up mass of elastic bands. I learned then and there how Doctor Haskell made his golf balls and why it was that the rubber-cored ball was vastly superior to the solid gutta.

The Haskell crowded the gutta off the courses and made the game much more enjoyable to play. At any rate, I could play the rubber-cored better than the hard ones, and my interest in the game increased. Behind our house was a cow pasture, and here Wilfred, with the mind of a golf architect, built three holes. The first was about a hundred and fifty yards long, with a carry over a brook. The brook was a hundred yards or so from where we drove. When he hit a shot well, Wilfred could drive close to the green, but it was far beyond my reach. As a matter of fact, the very best I could do was to drive into the brook. The second hole was very short, hardly more than fifty yards. The last was a combination of the first two, and brought the player back to the starting point. We used tomato cans for hole rims. As I visualize that old course of ours, it was the most difficult one I have ever played because it contained a gravel pit, swamps, brooks, and patches of long grass. We—or rather Wilfred—had selected only the high and dry pieces of land, which were few and far between, to play over. A shot that traveled three yards off line meant a lost ball, and it was well we had plenty!

Wilfred made trips to Boston from time to time and discovered that Wright and Ditson had a golf department with a man named Alex Findlay in charge. He discovered also that a good club could be got in exchange for used golf balls, and that three dozen would be a fair exchange for the best club made. From one of these visits Wilfred brought me home a mashie, and for the first time in my young life I was independent so far as playing golf was con-

"Wilfred made trips to Boston from time to time and discovered that Wright and Ditson had a golf department with a man named Alex Findlay in charge … and that a good club could be got in exchange for used golf balls."

cerned. I had my own club, balls, and a place to play. What more could anyone ask!

A lawnmower kept two of the greens in fair condition, but the one near our house was used so much it was worn bare and had no grass whatsoever on it. You see, while we were waiting for a meal we fiddled around the hole and the grass never had a chance to grow. One advantage, from Mother's point of view, was that she always knew where to look, and it was a simple matter for her to call us into the house. We fooled around that particular spot early in the morning and long after dark, and it was small wonder that my interest in golf increased because, with all this practice, it was natural enough that I should notice some improvement in my play. Mother thought I had gone crazy because golf was the only thing I seemed interested in.

I had more time to devote to the game than Wilfred. He had chores to do around the house and barn and being older, he was the one called upon to go on errands. They say practice makes perfect, and I believe it. After striving for weeks and months to hit a ball over the brook, and losing many, I finally succeeded. A solid year of practice had enabled me to drive accurately, if not far, and one Saturday morning, after trying for an hour, I drove a ball as clean as a whistle beyond the brook.

When I told Wilfred of my accomplishment, he received my story with a good deal of doubt. I had now acquired a brassie to go with the mashie, and I invited my brother out to the pasture to see what I could do with it. Whether I was tired out from my earlier efforts or not, I do not know, but I failed utterly, and Wilfred naturally was more skeptical than ever. The next day was Sunday, and after I returned from Sunday School, I went at it again. This time Wilfred was with me, and I definitely convinced him by hitting two balls out of three over the brook. It soon got to be a habit.

A good many tournaments were held at The Country Club and the best golfers gathered to play in them. Soon I was old enough to caddie, and as a youngster of eleven I saw in action such great golfers as Arthur Lockwood, Chandler Egan, Fred Herreshoff, Jerry Travers, and Walter J. Travis among the amateurs, and Alex Campbell, The Country Club professional, Alex Smith, Tom McNamara, Willie Anderson, and many of the prominent professional players. If I noticed anything particularly successful in the play of any of these golfers, I made a mental note of it, and when opportunity afforded, I set out to my private course and practiced the things I had noted.

Therefore, you see, I was brought up in a golfing environment and learned to love the game. I read in magazines or newspapers anything I could find relating to golf, got a few of the boys in the neighborhood interested in the game, and jumped into it head over heels. One day I caddied for a dear old gentleman named Samuel Carr. Mr. Carr was a golfing enthusiast and, furthermore, always most considerate of the boy who carried his clubs. All the boys liked him. Playing the eighteenth or last hole one day, he asked me if I played golf. I told him I did.

He asked me if I had any clubs. I replied that I had two, a brassie and mashie. "When we finish, I wish you would come to the locker room with me; I may have a few clubs for you," he said.

I took Mr. Carr's clubs downstairs to the caddie shop and hustled back. He came out with four clubs under his arm, a driver with a leather face, a lofter, a mid-iron, and a putter. I think it was the biggest thrill I had ever got up to that time.

Early mornings—and when I say early I mean around four-thirty or five o'clock—I abandoned my own course and played a few holes on that of The Country Club, until a greenkeeper drove me away. Rainy days, when I was sure no one would be around, I would do the same thing. Complaints concerning my activities arrived home, and Mother warned me to keep off the course, usually ending her reprimand by saying that the game of golf was bound to get me into trouble.

I was so wrapped up in the game, however, I just couldn't leave it alone. One summer, tired of my own layout, I talked a companion, Frank Mahan, into going to Franklin Park with me. Franklin Park was a public course and we could go there and play unmolested. We set out one Saturday morning. To get to Franklin Park, we had to walk a mile and a half with our clubs to the car line. Then we rode to Brookline Village, transferred there to a Roxbury Crossing car, arrived at Roxbury Crossing and changed again to a Franklin Park car. After getting out of the last street car, we walked about three quarters of a mile to the clubhouse, checked our coats—that is all we had to check—and then played six full rounds of the nine holes, a total of fifty-four holes.

Then we went home the way we had come, completely exhausted. All this at the age of thirteen!

> "Complaints concerning my activities arrived home, and Mother warned me to keep off the course, usually ending her reprimand by saying that the game of golf was bound to get me into trouble."

The Ouimet Library houses a diverse collection of objects reflecting a long, distinguished career in golf. A framed letter from President Eisenhower, on wall next to fireplace, congratulates Ouimet on being elected captain of the Royal and Ancient Golf Club of St. Andrews, the first American so honored, in 1951. The portrait over the mantel shows "Francis," as he was universally known in golf, dressed in his captain's regalia.

III. NORTH SHORE,

Until Francis Ouimet's victory in the 1913 U.S. Open, it was possible to dismiss golf as something of a fad. In that year, there were only about 350,000 golfers in the country. Ten years later, largely inspired by Ouimet, there were 2 million. As golf grew in popularity, and radiated north, west and south from Boston, new clubs formed and early 6-hole clubs like Bass Rocks Golf Club, Grafton Country Club and the Country Club of New Bedford expanded to 18 holes. Simple demographics made outlying areas more susceptible to the siren song of golf. Worcester, a sleepy, landlocked county seat of less than 3,000 people in 1820 became, by the end of the century, an industrial metropolis of almost 100,000 inhabitants, the third-largest city in New England. Worcester's burgeoning wealth spawned a remarkable number of educational institutions, museums, learned societies and clubs, including the Worcester Country Club and Tatnuck Country Club. The same pattern was followed in other towns and cities far enough from Boston to recognize and act upon the fact that, like politics, all golf is local.

SOUTH SHORE,
& BEYOND

Whitinsville Golf Club, Whitinsville, Massachusetts

Salem's 4th hole is a 399-yard dog-leg-right par-4. Hollis Stacy made a shot for the ages here en route to winning her third U.S. Women's Open in 1984. With the nines reversed, she eagled the 13th in the final round, sending a low-flying 7-iron from the right rough into the cup.

CALL IT WITCHCRAFT,
TEE TO GREEN

~

*Salem Country Club, virtually unchanged since it was
designed and built by Donald Ross in 1926, remains a daunting yet eminently
fair test of golf for every class of player.*

THE COURSE PAUL HARNEY once called "a work of art" has appeared on every best-courses list in the golf world, and its high ranking has been borne out in the heat of competition on countless occasions. Men, women, juniors, seniors, amateurs or professionals, club players or world champions, all have been put to the test at Salem Country Club. Like the architect who created the course, Donald Ross, Salem goes about its business quietly but never fails to put through its challenge in decisive terms.

"Salem remains one of the least touched, best preserved Ross courses," noted Ben Crenshaw, a self-taught expert on the work of Donald Ross. "It is among the best works done in the 1920s, with superb routing, outstanding contours of the fairways and marvelous greens — with their extreme undulations, you have to think through a strategy on every hole."

Judy Bell, a past president of the USGA, called Salem a "grand old course which will never grow out of style," adding, "For example, your shortest par-4 just may be the most difficult I've ever seen."

**Helping hand: a golf glove
awaits being called into service
on the 1st tee at Salem.**

On that hole, the 352-yard uphill 13th, a bunker on the right side forces the golfer to drive to the rolling terrain along the left side of the fairway, where another bunker lurks, then make a precise approach to a perched, three-level green. Legend has it that Ross once described this as "the finest green I ever designed."

The club was founded in 1895 as the Salem Golf Club and its first course was laid out on farmland in North Salem; it moved to its present site in the town of Peabody in 1925 and reorganized under the name Salem Country Club. Recognized at once as an appealing venue, Salem hosted its first national championship in 1932, the U.S. Women's Amateur, which happened to turn into one of the biggest sports stories of the year.

Virginia Van Wie, a 23-year-old Chicagoan, had already been defeated three times in this event by the legendary Glenna Collett Vare. This time, meeting Vare in the 36-hole final, she turned the tables on her tormentor with "the most devastating golf ever witnessed in the women's national championship," to quote *New York Times* golf correspondent William

Clockwise from top left: Levitating leaves, a familiar sight in the fall at Salem Country Club; inside the club, a tribute to Babe Zaharias, the 1954 U.S. Women's Open champion; a club function room built like a ship in honor of the region's nautical traditions; the famous three-level green at No. 13, Salem's signature hole; a moonlit practice range; a Salem green protected by one of 54 bunkers on the course, relatively few compared to other Ross classics.

Salem's Colonial-style clubhouse was built in 1926 after a design by one of its members, architect Gordon Robb; standing on a hill 200 feet above sea level, it afforded views of the ocean before trees grew up to block them.

Richardson. Van Wie's "great exhibition of shot-making" occurred in the morning 18, when she fired a 73, an astonishing four strokes below women's par, which staked her to an 8-up cushion at the lunch break. She went on to win, 10 and 8.

Since that time, Salem has hosted more than 20 state, regional and national championships, most recently the 2001 U.S. Senior Open, won by Bruce Fleisher. Along with a substantial check, the title-winner of this event has been privileged to hold up the Francis D. Ouimet Memorial Trophy. Originally called the Tuxedo Cup, this two-handled, sterling silver trophy had been gathering dust at The Country Club for practically a century.

It dated back to the nation's first interclub event, a competition in 1894 between The Country Club, Shinnecock Hills, two teams from the Tuxedo Club in Tuxedo Park, New York, and two others from St. Andrew's in Yonkers, New York. In any event, when the Senior Open came into being in 1980, members of The Country Club donated the handsome trophy to the USGA in the name of their favorite golfing son, Francis Ouimet.

Perhaps the most emotional victory witnessed at Salem was when Mildred Didrickson Zaharias won the U.S. Women's Open in 1954. Making her first Open appearance in three years, "Babe" not only won her third U.S. Open title only 15 months after undergoing surgery for cancer, she won by a mind-boggling 12 strokes with a

291 total, shooting 73-75 on the grueling 36-hole final day. Zaharias' stirring performance (at the age of 40), hailed by *Golf World* as "the greatest sustained golf in a women's championship," made front-page headlines across the country.

"Babe was in top form in the last round," Herbert Warren Wind of *The New Yorker* recalled. "On the last nine holes she chatted with the members of the large gallery following her around. She told them the type of shot she would be playing on her approaches and then stepped up to the ball and hit precisely the shot she had described."

Salem has been a popular venue for the Massachusetts Amateur, beginning in 1930 when Fred Wright took his third of four state titles in a row and fifth of a record seven overall with a 7 and 5 win over Brae Burn's Bill Blaney. Other Massachusetts Amateur champions at Salem have been Ted Bishop in 1940, Ernie Doherty in 1953, Joe Carr in 1962 and Jim McDermott in 1980.

Connecticut native Julius Boros won the Massachusetts Open at Salem in 1951, his first victory as a professional. In 1970, also at Salem, Paul Harney won his fourth straight Massachusetts Open after defeating Jim Browning in an 18-hole playoff with a course record 65. When the state open returned to Salem in 1991, Mount Snow teaching pro John Elliott, using his prodigious length, broke away from a pack of top-ranked contenders over the final nine holes, shooting a closing 67, the low round of the week.

Ever since *Golf Digest* initiated its biennial "America's Greatest Courses" rankings in 1966, Salem Country Club has been one of only 44 clubs to be included on the list of 100 courses every time. Salem's exalted status among golfers in the know is not likely to change anytime soon.

Golf Begins at 50

Scenes from the practice round at the
U.S. Senior Open, Salem Country Club,
June 27th, 2001

This page, clockwise from top right: Gary Player, pitching onto the 18th green; Salem's distinctive logo, surrounded by even more distinctive autographs; golf galleries in motion; calling it a day on 18. **Inset:** An errant shot, marked for all to see.

Opposite page, clockwise from top left: Arnold Palmer, marking on 18; competitors making multiple chips and putts in preparation for next day's first round; new arrival looking for the best groups to follow; ball drop area on No. 18; Bob Murphy, in the foreground, among the competitors evaluating their options on Donald Ross's test of golf at Salem; Dave Stockton after his practice round, swamped by autograph seekers of all ages.

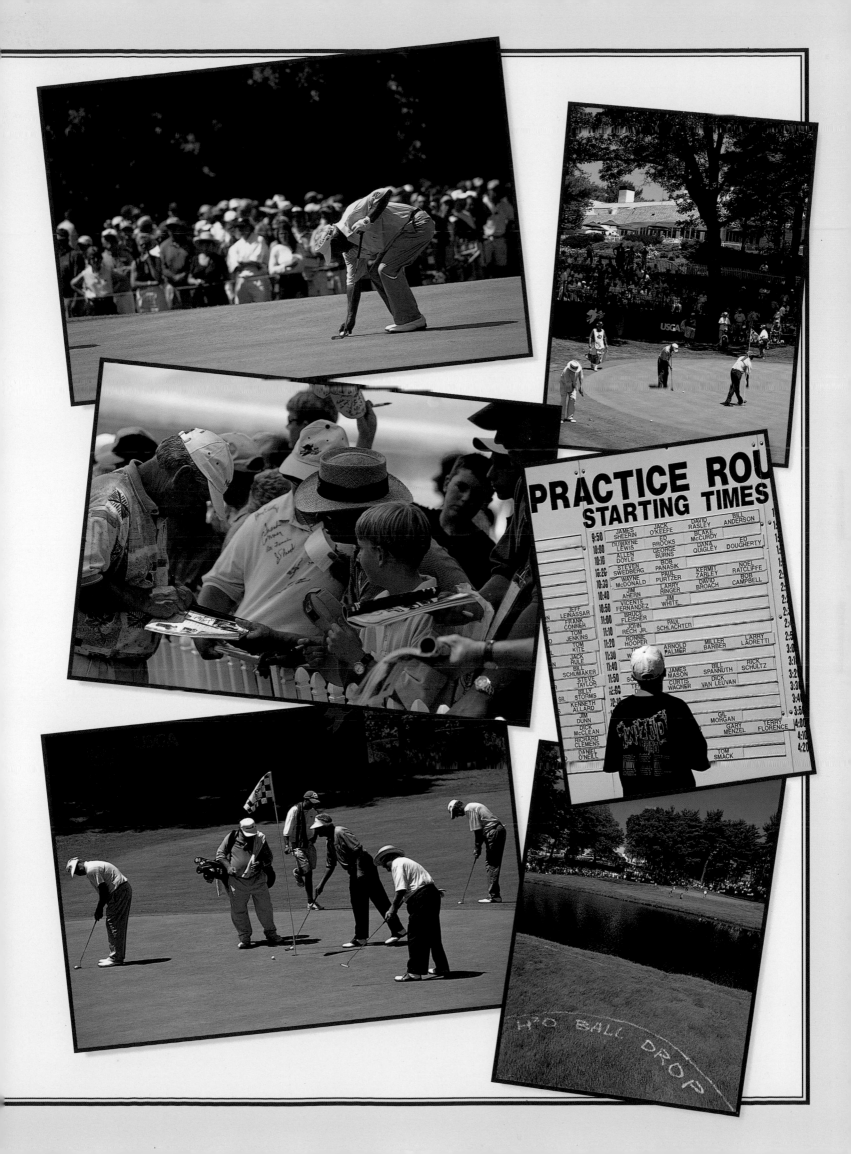

PRACTICE ROU
STARTING TIMES

9:50	JAMES SHEERIN	JACK O'KEEFE	DAVID RASLEY	BILL ANDERSON
10:00	N. WAYNE LEWIS	ED BROOKS	BLAKE McCURDY	
10:10	ALLEN DOYLE	GEORGE BURNS	DANA QUIGLEY	ED DOUGHERTY
10:20	STEVEN SWEDBERG	BOB PANASIK		
10:30	WAYNE McDONALD	PAUL PURTZER	KERMIT ZARLEY	NOEL RATCLIFFE
10:40	JIM AHERN	LARRY RINGER	DAVID BROACH	BOB CAMPBELL
	JEFF LEINASSAR	VICENTE FERNANDEZ	JIM WHITE	
10:50	FRANK CONNER	BRUCE FLEISHER		
11:00	TOM JENKINS	JOHN RECH JR.	PAUL SCHLACHTER	
11:10	TOM KITE	RONNIE HOOPER		
11:20	JACK RULE		ARNOLD PALMER	MILLER BARBER	LARRY LAORETTI
11:30	BILL SCHUMAKER			
11:40	STEVE TAYLOR		JAMES MASON	BILL SPANNUTH	RICK SCHULTZ
11:50	BILLY STORMS		CURTIS WAGNER	DICK VAN LEUVAN	
12:00	KENNETH ALLARD			
12:10	JIM DUNN			
	DICK McCLEAN			GIL MORGAN	
	RICHARD CLEMENS			GARY MENZEL	TERRY FLORENCE	14:00
	DANIEL O'NEIL				4:10
				TOM SMACK	4:20

H²O BALL DROP

"THE BEST DAY CAMP
IN THE WORLD"

~

In the historic Pilgrim settlement of Duxbury,
golf and sailing came together under one proud flag.

WITH A NAME LIKE Duxbury Yacht Club, it is not surprising to learn that this club began as an institution not for golfers, but for "blue water people," as yachtsmen like to call themselves, and this has influenced the way the club and its members have behaved ever since. Located on Duxbury Bay on the north shore of Plymouth Harbor, Duxbury Yacht Club was founded in 1875, re-organized under different colors in 1895, and by the 1930s was the second largest yachting center in the state (after Marblehead) with a fleet of 150 boats. To this day, even though the club now offers golf, tennis, paddle tennis and swimming as well as sailing and cruising, it has preserved the governance structure of a typical yacht club. People elected as club officers are called commodores, vice commodores and rear commodores, and they show up for special events in naval-style regalia.

Early club members tried their hand at the then novel game of golf as early as 1900—perhaps when

The yacht club colors, dating from 1895, hang prominently in the golf clubhouse. *Opposite:* **The clubhouse seen from across the 18th fairway.**

the tide was out or on days unsuited for sailing on Duxbury Bay. They played on makeshift holes laid out on what was known as Parker's Pasture, "some care being necessary," according to one early account, "to avoid the cows." More formal play began in 1913, when the old yacht clubhouse was moved a half-mile inland, a rough road built to it, and a six-hole course laid out in the meadows. More land was purchased in 1926 so that some new greens could be created and the nine-hole course could be brought up to speed generally by Boston golf architect Wayne Stiles. The addition of nine more holes was realized in 1971, this time with the help of Amherst architect Geoffrey Cornish. As Duxbury's commitment to golf expanded, so did its influence in the larger world of the game. Three of its members rose to become president of the MGA: Laddie Butler, John Arnold and Paul Evans. Only The Country Club in Brookline has supplied more MGA chiefs over the years.

Meanwhile, the Sprague-Parker barn dating from the 1780s, acquired in 1926, was remodeled in 1936

to serve as the main clubhouse for the golfers and tennis players. (The Ellison Waterfront Clubhouse on Duxbury Bay serves the sailing interests.) This beautiful but sparsely furnished farm building reflects the club's long-standing belief in simple, unpretentious facilities. "The club does not try to do more than it can, but what it does it always tries to do first-rate," wrote club historian David Mittell in 1995. "It is always trying to improve its properties and its programs. This is perhaps a natural corollary to the care, thoughtfulness and staunchness of the sailor."

Hard times being the great test of fiscal policy, it is interesting to observe how Duxbury Yacht Club's flinty conservatism managed to keep the club afloat during the Great Depression and again during World War II.

After President Roosevelt closed the banks in March of 1933, the yacht club's officers went to work. They reduced dues; they formed a membership committee to seek new members; they admitted two-week members; they created the status of absentee members. Non-members were allowed to play in tournaments with the payment of a fee. These and other penny-pinching measures kept the club from a fate that many less fortunate clubs suffered: going into receivership.

The Japanese attack on Pearl Harbor in 1941 produced another set of challenging circumstances for private clubs. Gas rationing was instituted in the fall of 1942 after German submarines along the coast began threatening tankers and other Allied shipping.

Use of cars for pleasure including golf, tennis or sailing was soon forbidden. All drivers east of a line running approximately through Worcester had to paint the top third of their headlights black. Near the shore, motorists had to drive at night on

dim lights at about 10 miles per hour. But once again, Duxbury's tight-fisted finance committee managed to hold things together, inevitably with the sacrifice of certain creature comforts.

For many years the locker rooms were inadequate and members were content to change into their golf shoes in the parking lot. To this day there is no bar, the serving of liquor being limited to certain senior events, and then only with special permission. Mittell, who has been a Duxbury member for more than half a century, believed this restriction enhanced the family aspects of the club, helping to make it, as someone once remarked, "the best day camp anywhere in the world." As Mittell once observed, "The predominance of athletic activities—sports, competition—over social activities is a reality truly practiced," and he quoted from a 1927 club booklet: "The true sportsman plays the game to the utmost with keenness and courage, but above all with fairness to all."

Opposite, clockwise from top left: Duxbury's 4th hole, a 475-yard double dogleg par-5; inside the clubhouse, a renovated farm building dating from the 18th century; the 11th hole, a 363-yard par-4, viewed from the right-hand side; a clubhouse detail acknowledging two major concerns of golfers—time and luck. *Above at right:* Lowering the flag at the end of a day of sporting activities at Duxbury Yacht Club.

NEW ENGLAND'S
"HOME FOR PRO GOLF"

~

For more than four decades, golf fans in the tens of thousands
flocked to Pleasant Valley in Sutton, in the words of one golf writer,
"as if it were free tomato plant day at Spag's."

I T WAS PLANNED as a modest nine-hole golf course for the employees of a central Massachusetts construction firm called Bayer & Mingolla Industries. In the late 1950s, Cosmo "Cuz" Mingolla personally walked the hilly terrain of an apple or-chard chosen as the site of Pleasant Valley Country Club, along with the club's first golf professional, Don Hoenig, delineating fairways, greens and bunkers. So golf-friendly was the land that Mingolla could not resist expanding his pet project to 18 holes.

When the course finally opened for play in 1961, Mingolla realized he had something of a tiger by the tail—a golf course worthy of hosting not just garden-variety golfers but players of the highest caliber. Never mind that Sutton was a town of 8,200 with one traffic light, one motel and three gas stations. In 1962, barely before the paint on the clubhouse was dry, Pleasant Valley was host-ing its first women's professional event, the Lady Carling Women's Open. It marked the start of a 13-year run with the LPGA.

Plaques honoring former Pleasant Valley winners Tom Shaw (1969) and George Archer (1984) await re-hanging following a clubhouse renovation. *Opposite:* The 365-yard 13th hole was stretched to 386 yards for the pros; the second shot is uphill.

Good-sized galleries turned out to watch the likes of Kathy Whitworth and Mickey Wright compete in the LPGA events, but when the male touring pros came to town, there were throngs. In 1997, the year before the PGA Tour finally pulled the plug on Pleasant Valley, more than 40,000 people were on hand for Sunday's final round, when Loren Roberts shot 64 to beat Bill Glasson by a stroke. A tour official had once complained that Pleasant Valley was "in the middle of nowhere," but, situ-ated 55 miles from Boston and 35 from Providence, it always received staunch support from area golf fans. The Worcester County Convention Bureau once estimated that the tour stop was worth "something in the $10 million range" to the Worcester/Providence economy.

Throughout the clubhouse and locker rooms are mementoes of the famous and not-so-famous golfers who have competed at "P.V."

Men's professional golf started in 1965 with the Carling World Open. The event offered the biggest jackpot the tour had ever seen — $200,000, put up

Clockwise from top: Kids and parents alike enjoy an after-school clinic, here unfolding on the 2nd hole; cartoon preview of the 1969 Avco Open at Pleasant Valley, including tribute to founder Cuz Mingolla; the 415-yard 17th hole, calling for two carries over water; lush seasonal plantings, as on No. 15, are a familiar sight on the course.

by Carling Brewery, located just up the street in Natick. A drop in the beer bucket by today's standards, but more than enough back then to entice an unusually strong field, including Ben Hogan, Sam Snead, Arnold Palmer, Gary Player, Jack Nicklaus, Billy Casper, Julius Boros, Ray Floyd, Gene Littler and Tony Lema. Champagne Tony, who would die in a plane crash the following year, won the inaugural event. Snead hurt his chances on the last day when he broke his putter in disgust after three-putting the 10th green and was forced to putt with his driver and 1-iron for the final eight holes.

After Carling Brewery folded, the scramble for a new sponsor began, a pattern that would endure. In all, 32 tour events were played at Pleasant Valley under 12 different names. In years when no sponsor could be found, Pleasant Valley underwrote the event and called it the Pleasant Valley Classic or the New England Classic or the Jimmy Fund Classic. But even in lean years and when fields were poor, as when the event was scheduled the week before or after the British Open, galleries turned out in force. Week-long attendance seldom dropped below 130,000.

When Cuz Mingolla died of cancer in 1979 at age 64, his son, Ted, ran the event. Eventually Ted's son, Stephen, took over from his father as tournament director. A 1984 Boston College graduate, Stephen worked at the TPC at Sawgrass in Florida for a year to learn the business. All three generations of the family established close relationships with the touring pros.

From the landing area for the tee shot on the 359-yard par-4 15th, golfers face a steep approach to an elevated green guarded by two bunkers.

"My favorite champion without question was Paul Azinger," recalled Ted Mingolla. "The first time he came here he stayed with his wife in a motor home in our parking lot. They didn't have much money. We set them up with electricity. It developed into a friendship." Azinger won the tournament in 1993, but not without difficulty. Before the third round, his right shoulder hurt so much he took 12 Advil

On No. 11, a par-5, the 60-yard-deep green with its range of bunkers on both sides requires thoughtful club selection. *Inset:* Pleasant Valley's floral monogram between two holes can be seen from the golf shop.

before teeing off. He shot 64 on Saturday, 68 on Sunday to win, but later underwent surgery for a lymphoma found in the ailing shoulder. While recovering, he missed most of the 1994 season.

Pleasant Valley exposed untold numbers of New Englanders to the rigors and rituals of professional golf. It was the first tournament Rhode Island's Billy Andrade saw as a kid, long before turning pro himself. "It was where I first dreamed of playing on tour," he said. When Andrade himself competed at Pleasant Valley, he witnessed a bizarre performance in the pro-am, playing with an amateur golfer, another victim of cancer who in fact died several months later. "The man made five putts over

50 feet," Andrade recalled. "It was like God said, 'This is your last hurrah and it's going to be a good one for you.' It was unbelievable, and we all felt the emotion of it."

Another Rhode Islander, Brad Faxon, became the first and only player from New England to win the tournament, shooting a final-round 68 to edge out rookie Phil Mickelson in 1992. In 1977, among many other dramatic finishes at Pleasant Valley, Ray Floyd overcame a double-bogey on the 71st hole to beat Jack Nicklaus by a stroke. In 1983, Mark Lye came back from nine shots down on the final day to shoot 64 and win by a shot, birdieing the last two holes for his first tour victory. In 1988, Mark Calcavecchia rolled in a 30-foot birdie putt on the final hole to win. In 1991, Bruce Fleisher, who had

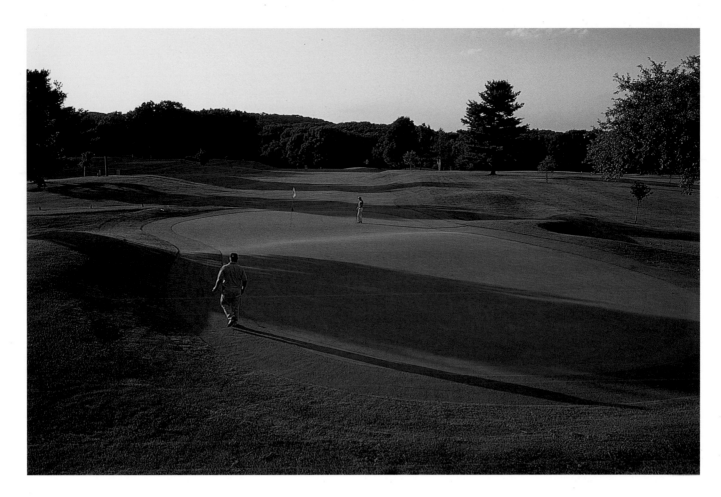

Playing at 455 yards for the pros, the tough par-4 10th hole is a dogleg-right calling for an uphill carry to a two-tiered green. *Below:* For the 1998 pro finale at Pleasant Valley, *Boston Globe* cartoonist Paul Szep depicted a golf cart labeled "Finchem PGA Tour" running over Ted Mingolla.

gotten into the tournament at the last minute as an alternate, shot a final-round 64 to reach a playoff with Ian Baker-Finch that went seven holes. Fleisher won with a 50-foot birdie putt. In that same year, a rookie named John Daly electrified galleries by consistently driving the green on No. 15 (359 yards) and on one occasion driving the green on the dogleg-right 12th (420 yards).

The year 1998 marked the last year a PGA tournament would be played in Sutton. Appropriately, it was won by Steve Pate, a loyalist. "I've played here 13 years and the people have always treated us first class," he said afterwards. "I think I can speak for many of the players—it's not our choice to leave."

In fact the tour had gone global and corporate and there was no longer room on the schedule for small-town venues like Pleasant Valley. With hindsight, one could trace the likelihood of this happening all the way back to 1968, the year the touring pros went to war with the club pros for control of the schedule. That year Arnold Palmer arrived at Worcester Airport in his private jet to compete at Pleasant Valley. Stepping from the plane, he announced to the press that he was siding with the touring pros in the dispute. It was an agonizing decision for Palmer because his father had been a loyal PGA member for years and he was closely associated with it himself. But it was momentous for golf, shifting power over professional golf from the PGA of America to a new entity to be called the PGA Tour.

The week wasn't all agony for Arnie, however: he won the tournament.

AT WORLD'S END,
BEAUTY OR THE BEAST

~

*The Kittansett Club offers golf as unpredictable as the winds
that blow in from Buzzards Bay.*

ONE GRAY, overcast day in September, Ray Dennehy, long-time golf professional at The Kittansett Club in Marion, set out from the first tee for a round of golf with two members, Charlie Peirson and John MacDonald. Kittansett, a links-style layout exposed on three sides to the winds of Buzzards Bay, is noted for its unpredictable weather, so the golfers weren't surprised to see the wind brought to bear on some of their golf shots.

On the signature par-3 third hole, all carry over a tidal shore, for example, MacDonald left his tee shot in a large bunker left of the green. Hitting directly into the wind, he blasted out successfully, then watched as his ball struck the green, stopped, then rolled backward across the putting surface, over the edge and down the bank to his feet.

When they came to the par-5 seventh hole, the wind was at their back. Peirson hit a prodigious drive that placed him within striking distance of the

Above and opposite: The 165-yard par-3 3rd hole at Kittansett can be reached with anything from a 3-iron to a 9-iron, depending on the wind. "There is no such thing as a bad day at Kittansett," one member quipped, "only bad scores."

green. He had never reached home with a middle iron on this hole, but today he reached for his 5-iron. When his shot carried straight and true toward the flag, he couldn't help but smile. But his smile faded as he watched the ball continue its flight toward the flagstick, pass over it well above treetop height, and disappear far into the woods beyond.

At this point the threesome decided that conditions warranted they play an abbreviated round. They cut over to the 11th tee, but when their drives into the wind all finished less than 100 yards from the tee, they picked up and struggled homeward in what were now gale force winds.

They stopped for a drink in the Beverly Yacht Club clubhouse. At the time, the building, facing the water at the end of Butler Point, was shared by golfing and boating members. From the club they could see the ocean waves lapping across the parking lot. Peirson put down his drink and headed for his car, anxious to check on his waterfront home not far away. Dennehy

The 13th hole, a dogleg par-4, requires an approach shot often directly into the wind or into a strong right-to-left wind, to a green guarded by bunkers.

and MacDonald lingered long enough to see MacDonald's car, parked nearest the water, disappear into the sea. At the same time the causeway linking the point to the mainland also vanished.

With all haste, Dennehy and MacDonald gathered up a handful of stranded caddies, tumbled into Dennehy's car and headed for the high ground near the 18th green. There, atop the only part of Butler Point that remained above the storm-driven waves, they rode out the Great Hurricane of 1938.

Kittansett had only come into existence in the previous decade. First play was in 1924, the layout's design largely the handiwork of one man, Frederic C. Hood, a founding member who was inspired by his experience of seaside courses in Scotland and England. Apart from having been lengthened somewhat, to 6,631 yards, this design has remained essentially unchanged to this day, a testament to its

golf-friendly site and to Hood's vision. Four Massachusetts Amateur championships have been staged here, including a windblown affair in 1990. "I can remember standing on the first tee and seeing a guy hit three balls into the hazard on the right," recalled Ray Wright, the champion that year. "Literally, you had to aim it dead left to keep it straight." A U.S. Amateur qualifying round held here a few years ago revealed how challenging the layout can be even without wind. "The course was played at moderate length with the pins set near the middle of the greens," recalled head professional Steve Demmer. "The

Opposite, clockwise from top left: The bronze golfer on the 1st tee, modeled after a sundial at Pinehurst, is dedicated to the memory of Ray Dennehy, Kittansett's golf professional from 1927 to 1973; a bench in front of the golf shop is named for another longtime club fixture, caddiemaster William "Spike" Barros; a caddie of today, insouciant in spite of posted admonition; the lunch room adjoining "Hurricane Hall" in the main clubhouse.

The Kittansett Club

The
KITTANSETT CLUB
AUGUST ORGY

Year	Winners	
1952	Miss Daisy O'Donnell	— W.G. Lyle, Jr.
1953	Mrs. A.H.B. Peabody	— W. Howard
1954	Mrs. F.G. Crocker	— J.W. Goodrich
1955	Mr. & Mrs. A. Lawrence Peirson, Jr.	
1956	Miss Elizabeth Hood	— C.H.B. Davison
1957	Mr. & Mrs. Walter A. Friend, Jr.	
1958	Mr. & Edwin H.B. Pratt	
1959	Mrs. Theodore G. Bremer	— C.L. Peirson
1960	Mr. & Mrs. Hewitt Morgan	
1961	Dr. & Mrs. Howard C. Davis, Jr.	
1962	Dr. & Mrs. Howard C. Davis, Jr.	
1963	Robert & Jeanne Watson	
1964	Miss Mary Nicholson	— D.E. May
1965	Mr. & Mrs. Frantz Warner	
1966	Mr. & Mrs. A.W. Rice	
1967	Mr. & Mrs. A.W. Rice	
1968	Mrs. A.O. Wellman, Jr.	— Robert I. Bryden

ATTENTION ALL CADDIES

I EXPECT THE CADDIE YARD TO BE CLEANED AT THE END OF EVERY DAY.

IT IS A TOTAL MESS... I AM SURE THAT EVERYONE WILL PITCH IN AND HELP.

THANK YOU IN ADVANCE FOR YOUR COOPERATION!

THANKS...GLENN.

Above: Irishman Joe Carr blasts out of a bunker during the 1953 Walker Cup matches played at Kittansett, won by the U.S. side, 9 to 3. *Left:* The talented American team, back row from left to right, Ken Venturi, Jim Jackson, Don Cherry, captain Charles Yates, Charlie Coe, Bill Campbell and Jack Westland; front row, Sam Urzetta, Gene Littler, Harvie Ward and Dick Chapman. Chapman lived in Connecticut but summered on Cape Cod and was well known in Massachusetts golf circles; a three-time Walker Cupper, he also won the amateur championships of Massachusetts, Connecticut, New England, France, Italy, Britain, Canada and the United States.

Clockwise from above: Sails are familiar sights on the horizon at Kittansett during golf season; the club's shell symbol, re-created with antique golf clubs, in the dining room; assistant professional Karen Nicoletti fits a set of clubs with new grips; the view from the 1st green looking back to the clubhouse compound.

Fairway bunkers narrow the approach to the 400-yard par-4 16th hole. *Below left:* A plaque on the course marks some of the problematical high points in Kittansett history.

lowest score was even par and some scores rose up to over 100. Considering how talented the field was, I'd say Kittansett won again!"

If fault is to be found with Kittansett, it is its vulnerability to the ocean; indeed its very name derives from two Indian words meaning "near the sea." The 1938 storm reduced the yacht club, golf shop and various cottages and other buildings to driftwood. Hurricane Carol so thoroughly devastated the site on August 31, 1954, that some fairway areas did not fully recover for 10 years. The recovery from Hurricane Bob, which roared through Kittansett on August 19, 1991, cost the club nearly a half million dollars.

When the Walker Cup was played here in 1953, the British side looked forward to competing in the kind of windy conditions they were used to at

home. Instead, it was calm, hot and humid and the U.S. side, clearly superior in depth in any case, prevailed, 9 to 3. The event was notable for an unusual display of sportsmanship. Playing in the third foursome on the first day, Americans Gene Littler and Jim Jackson were one down on the second hole when Jackson discovered he had 16 clubs in his bag, two more than permitted under the rules. The obvious remedy was disqualification, but the Brits insisted that play continue, allowing only that the other side be penalized the loss of two holes. The U.S. pair in fact came back from three down to win the match. The English columnist Henry Longhurst termed the incident "Britannia waives the rules."

The Shot Heard
'Round the Factory

*When MIT grad Phil Young lost a match in 1932 because of a lopsided golf ball,
the stage was set for the creation of Titleist.*

The GOLF COURSE MURDER MYSTERY!

SOLVED!

He was an earnest golfer. Every so often he broke 95—but every member of the club knew he was a golf ball murderer. Big and powerful, he loved to "smack 'em out!" But when he was a bit off his game "death" rode his irons to the green. His golf ball split from pole to pole, putted like a flat wheel and piled up strokes to 6's and 7's.

This went on month after month. Then one day his Pro, who had been racking his brains for a solution said, "I've got it!—from now on you play the Acushnet Bedford."

Our friend, the golf ball murderer, took this advice and—hung up an 88! The first one of his life!

The wonderful Bedford has been solving golf mysteries like this all summer. Thousands of them. It's the ball that "can take it"—*without sacrificing distance!* The Bedford has the sweetest "click" off the club you ever heard. An entirely new method of construction is the secret—the secret of a ball that although topped and hacked, comes up white, bright and fresh, hole after hole. Try a Bedford yourself. Your pro has it. *And get ready to pick up the bets.* Acushnet Process Sales Co., New Bedford, Mass.

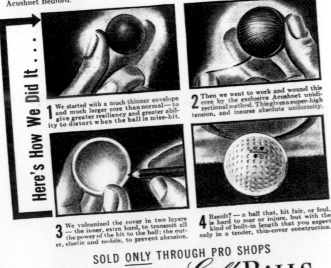

Here's How We Did It . . . .

1 We started with a much thinner envelope and much larger core than normal—to give greater resiliency and greater ability to distort when the ball is miss-hit.

2 Then we went to work and wound this core by the exclusive Acushnet unidirectional method. This gives a super-high tension, and insures absolute uniformity.

3 We vulcanized the cover in two layers—the inner, extra hard, to transmit all the power of the hit to the ball; the outer, elastic and mobile, to prevent abrasion.

4 Result?—a ball that, hit fair, or foul, is hard to mar or injure, but with the kind of built-in length that you expect only in a tender, thin-cover construction.

SOLD <u>ONLY</u> THROUGH PRO SHOPS

ACUSHNET *Golf* BALLS

BEDFORD 75c
The ball that "can take it"

TITLEIST 75c
"For experts only"

GREEN RAY 50c
PINNACLE 35c

WITH ITS HEADQUARTERS now in Fairhaven, Acushnet Company has grown into a giant corporate presence in the world of golf, with more than 4,000 employees in 14 countries. It produces not just golf balls but clubs, putters, shoes, gloves, bags and a myriad of accessories. Yet it started in 1910 as an enterprise with a much different product in mind—an improved version of the natural rubber then being used to make tires for the infant automobile industry.

The founder of the company, Philip E. Young, was born in Dorchester, the son of a Unitarian minister, and grew up in Dedham. After graduating from the Massachusetts Institute of Technology with a degree in mechanical engineering, Young went to work for Goodyear Tire and Rubber Company in Akron, Ohio. There he discovered that the raw material coming in from Brazil's Amazon Valley, where natives tapped rubber trees and sold the sap for $3 a pound, was very poor in quality. Young and a Goodyear chemist named Frank Peabody found a way to extract a sap from a shrub that grew in abundance in Mexico, called guayule, which, after the resin was removed, provided a superior and more consistent rubber product.

When Goodyear balked at the heavy investment the new process would require, Young and Peabody decided to start their own company. For financing, Young turned to Allen Weeks, a fraternity brother from MIT who happened to be from a wealthy family living in Marion. Weeks agreed to join in the business on condition that the company be located somewhere in the Buzzards Bay area. Weeks had a 36-foot boat that he loved to sail. (So did Young, whose nickname was "Skipper.")

That location proved to be an abandoned two-story building in Acushnet. This is how the firm name became Acushnet Process Company—named for the town and the process of deresinating the guayule.

In the years that followed, the core business evolved with the vagaries of the marketplace. It was a casual golf match that Young played, and lost, one Sunday in 1932 that would seal the company's future. In his regular foursome at the Country Club of New Bedford, where he was a member, Young this day could not keep the ball in the fairway, slicing some shots, hooking others. Normally a fairly good golfer, he decided the fault lay with the ball. Over drinks in the club afterwards, he convinced his partner in the match, who happened to be head of the X-ray department at St. Luke's Hospital in New Bedford, to put the suspect ball under the X-ray machine. Arriving at the hospital, they not only submitted Young's ball to scrutiny, they examined a couple of dozen of every make of golf ball that they had taken from the pro shop for that purpose.

The result: even though the outside of each ball was fairly round, X-rays showed that all the cores were cockeyed—off center. "So that afternoon," Young's son, Richard, recalled, "with no Sunday dinner and about six rounds of drinks under his belt, Skipper decided that if he could make a round ball, he could sell a few."

It would take a couple of years to develop machines that would wind rubber thread uniformly on the center of the golf ball, a couple of more years to produce the first balls known as Titleist, and some years after that to gain broad acceptance for the product. In the watershed year of 1949, the U.S. Open was played at Medinah Country Club in Chicago, and for the first time more contestants played with Titleist golf balls than any other brand.

Opposite page: A golf ball ad from 1939 combined humor and technical information. *Right:* The ad appearing in the January 2, 1945, edition of the *Saturday Evening Post* was couched in the military parlance of World War II. *Above:* Titleist's distinctive script was designed as the result of a contest among employees.

Ceiling Zero, mission incomplete! — golf hasn't changed.

There's a lot of fun and a lot of good golf in a ball reprocessed by us here at Acushnet. Lucky thing, too! — because that's the *only* kind of Acushnet ball you can get until the Army and Navy give us "cease firing" on the vital war items we're molding for them of rubber and synthetics. But even we can't reprocess balls we haven't got, so keep the old ones coming in to us — send them to us through your Pro, of course. Acushnet Process Company, New Bedford, Mass.

ARE YOU SHOOTING
PAR ON THIS NINE?
1. Buy War Bonds.
2. Give blood.
3. Conserve paper.
4. Save gas.
5. Save tires.
6. Save fuel.
7. Share your car.
8. Don't travel.
9. Buy *more* War Bonds.

ACUSHNET
GOLF BALLS

SOLD AND REPROCESSED THROUGH YOUR PRO SHOP ONLY

VENERABLE VESPER

~

The club that hosted the first Massachusetts Open championship
in 1905 has since survived floods, fire, tornadoes—and an infamous liquor raid.

"**V**ESPER COUNTRY CLUB is one of the most fascinating courses in the country," declared the *Spalding Official Golf Guide* of 1907. "Members are the nicest and most jovial set of golfers ... keep out of the woods and your medal play will be OK."

The early years of Vesper, a charter member of the Massachusetts Golf Association, were indeed fascinating. Located on Tyng's Island at the confluence of the Merrimack River and the Pawtucket Canal, it actually began life as a boating club, in 1875. (For many years the oars to a pair of rowing sculls hung over the dining room entrance in the clubhouse.) Despite resistance from some members opposed to any further development of the island, the club hired Scotsman Alex Findlay to lay out six golf holes in 1895, and three more were added by the end of that year.

In October of 1900, Vesper's par-40 layout was judged good enough to host an exhibition match featuring the famous British professional Harry Vardon, who was fresh from victory in the U.S. Open at the Chicago Golf Club. After spending the night in a tent set up for him on the banks of the Merrimack, Vardon went out and set a course record

Vesper's 14th hole, 163 yards from the ladies' tees, crosses the Merrimack River, which inundated the entire course in the Flood of 1936. *Opposite:* No. 17, a 211-yard par-3.

of 78 at Vesper. Vardon was 30 and would go on to win a record six British Opens. He had been touring the country in behalf of A.G. Spalding & Bros. of Chicopee, drawing crowds wherever he appeared and gaining fresh converts to the game. In a stop at Jordan Marsh in Boston he smashed balls into a net while store customers gathered around and applauded wildly; the store sold out its stock of golf clubs in a matter of hours.

Vesper hosted the MGA's first statewide open championship in 1905. Donald Ross, at the time head pro at Oakley, shot an even-par 320 for 72 holes to defeat amateur Arthur Lockwood by a stroke and collect the $100 first prize. Galleries were modest. Before the Age of the Automobile, Vesper members and guests reached the club by means of a ferry from North Chelmsford. In 1908 a wood suspension footbridge was completed at a cost of $8,000. To finance the construction, a turnstile was installed on the North Chelmsford side, requiring visitors to deposit a toll of a nickel to cross onto the island. The bridge was destroyed by a tornado in 1914.

The relative inaccessibility of Vesper did little to affect the aforementioned joviality of its membership.

"Back in those days, many members were expelled

The 8th hole at Vesper is a 392-yard par-4, viewed here from the wrong side of a fairway bunker designed to catch errant drives.

from the club for misconduct," reported club historian George B. Leahey, "and many others were suspended for various periods of time for minor infractions such as being too boisterous at a social gathering or failing to register a guest."

Such antics apparently came to the attention of teetotaler and reformer the Reverend Charles E. Merrill. In 1910 he staged a liquor raid on the club that made headlines in the *Boston Post*.

"There was enough liquor to stock a city barroom," Rev. Merrill declared, adding, "And let me tell you it was high class stuff. I have pulled off many raids, but never in my experience have I scooped up so much classy liquor."

Speaking of class acts, Vesper member Henry H. Wilder was the medalist in the 1908 U.S. Amateur. He lost in the second round to Walter J. Travis. Earlier that same year, Wilder, playing out of Yale,

won the National Intercollegiate Golf Championship. Active in New England golf circles for many years, Wilder was elected president of the MGA in 1917.

That was the year Donald Ross returned to Vesper, not as a competitor but as an architect. The club had purchased a large tract of farmland across the creek from the island and retained Ross to design nine new holes. While he was at it, he re-designed several of the existing holes. When the new nine opened for play in 1921, the result was a par-72 layout of 6,341 yards.

The Massachusetts Open returned to Vesper three times. Jesse Guilford won in 1929, Charles Volpone in 1971, and Fran Quinn, Jr., in 1990.

Opposite, clockwise from top left: Vesper's clubhouse, built in 1924 after the original clubhouse burnt to the ground, seen from across the putting green; a solitary golfer on the par-5 7th hole; flag marking launch date of the original boating club in 1875; bunker maintenance on No. 6; footprints in the dew on the green of No. 12; high-fiving on the green on No. 13, a 373-yard par-4.

BIRTH OF
THE RYDER CUP

~

*One of the greatest international rivalries in all of sport began
at historic Worcester Country Club in 1927.* BY GEORGE KIMBALL

NEVER LET IT BE SAID that we
New Englanders don't recognize a Big Deal when we see
one. An entire nation was still
basking in the afterglow of
Charles Lindbergh's transatlantic flight two weeks
earlier, and here in Massachusetts,
a committee of concerned citizens met with Governor Alvan T.
Fuller, urging him to reconsider
the impending executions of
Nicola Sacco and Bartolomeo
Vanzetti.

On the day the British Ryder
Cup team arrived, Babe Ruth
hit the 15th and 16th home runs
of what would be a 60-homer
season, while across the Atlantic
in Paris, Big Bill Tilden beat
Henri Cochet in straight sets at
the French Open.

In the newspapers of Boston
and Worcester, the above stories were rivaled by the
international golfing competition that was about
to take place at the Worcester Country Club.
Contested barely 50 miles from The Country Club,
the first Ryder Cup Matches might have been
considered an obscure competition by most of the

**Above and opposite: Program for the
inaugural Ryder Cup banquet depicts
a finishing-hole scene that has not
changed substantially over the years.**

sporting world, but in these parts it was a major story
from the outset.

Although these were the first Ryder Cup
Matches, it was hardly the first international clash
between teams of professional golfers. In fact, had
things gone a bit differently, an earlier rivalry between
professionals from the United
States and France might have
taken root.

Informal international matches
were sometimes arranged by
small groups of professionals in
those early days, and in 1913 an
American squad consisting of
Johnny McDermott, Mike Brady,
Tom McNamara and Alex Smith
took on a distinguished French
team at Versailles. The French, a
powerful force in golf in that
early era, were led by Arnaud
Massy, the 1907 British Open
champion, along with teammates
Louis Tellier, Jean Gassiat and Pierre Lafitte.

Only the outbreak of World War I prevented the
establishment of this rivalry, and in 1921 when the
possibility of another international competition was
suggested, it was the British who took up the challenge. Just prior to the 2,000 Guineas at Gleneagles

tournament, held that summer at Gleneagles Hotel in Scotland, a team of Scottish and English professionals beat a squad of American-based professionals by a 10½ to 4½ score.

Five years later, when the R&A ordered regional qualifying for the 1926 British Open at Lytham & St. Annes, another competition was arranged, following the qualifying round at Wentworth, with the assistance of a wealthy seed merchant from St. Albans in Hertfordshire named Samuel Ryder. With Abe Mitchell leading the way, the home professionals administered a fair trouncing, taking 13½ of a possible 16 points. After, Ryder donated a trophy for regular competition (at a cost of £250) with the condition that the figure atop the lid resemble Mitchell, his friend.

It is important to note that Ryder, a self-made millionaire, was probably exempt from certain attitudes prevalent in the upper-class circles in which he traveled. Joe Carr, the most accomplished amateur golfer in Irish history and who would go on to become captain of the R&A, once recalled an episode from his own boyhood which aptly illustrates the station of the professional golfer in the late 1920s.

Carr grew up in the clubhouse at Portmarnock, where his father, a retired British Army warrant officer, was the club steward. He recalls the day Henry Cotton arrived to play an exhibition on the fabled links north of Dublin, and even more vividly remembers that once the match was completed, the membership repaired inside, leaving Cotton to be served refreshments by his white-gloved butler beside his Bentley out in the car park. Professional golfers were not allowed to set foot in the clubhouse.

Ryder harbored no such prejudices. In fact, he positively idolized the professionals, and delighted in their company. He had come to the game fairly late in life and was over 50 when he played his first round, but

went on to earn a very respectable six handicap.

As early as 1923, Ryder had sponsored a professional tournament, the Heath and Heather. It was there that he met Mitchell, who may have been the best golfer of his era never to win a British Open. Mitchell, a sometime gardener, hit it off with the seed merchant, resulting in Ryder engaging Mitchell as his personal instructor at the then princely sum of £1,000 per annum.

The next Matches were scheduled for the following June 3–4, 1927, at Worcester Country Club, where in 1925 Willie Macfarlane defeated Bobby Jones in a playoff for the U.S. Open title. The dates were chosen for their proximity to the U.S. Open, which would be played at Oakmont the following week. The 1927 Matches would be regarded as the first "official" Ryder Cup competition because it was the first using an all American-born U. S. team.

The British magazine *Golf Illustrated* initiated an appeal to raise the £3,000 it would cost to send the British team. Although £400 rolled in the first week of the drive, donations subsequently lagged, and at the deadline the team was still £500 short of its goal. The shortfall was ultimately made up by Ryder himself, and although the team was a man short, it set sail in May from Southampton on the *Aquitania*.

Mitchell, who had been appointed team captain, was suffering from stomach pains that were later diagnosed as appendicitis, and withdrew. He was replaced on the team by Herbert Jolly, who sailed aboard the *Majestic* four days later and joined the others in New York, while Ted Ray, already on the team, was named captain.

There were, of course, no tabulations of "Ryder Cup points" in those early days. The makeup of the visiting team was determined by Harry Vardon, James Braid and J. H. Taylor, who had been appointed as selectors by the British PGA. The selection process

Mementoes of the 1927 Ryder Cup hanging in the clubhouse at Worcester include an artist's rendering of an exhibition match between American and British professionals held the year before at Wentworth, England. *Opposite:* Club members take a whirl around the course with a canine friend.

in this country was even more informal. The swashbuckling Walter Hagen would captain the American side for the first six meetings, and, recalled Gene Sarazen, "Hagen just picked the team from among his golfing buddies."

Sarazen, who was the last surviving member from those inaugural teams before his death in 1999, had won the U.S. Open in 1922 and the PGA Championship in 1922 and 1923, and said, "I suppose I'd have been automatically qualified."

The foreign-born players who had represented the United States in 1921 and 1926 scrimmages were now ineligible. In fact, 5 of the 10 players on the 1926 U.S. team were born overseas. Only Hagen, Bill Mehlhorn and Al Watrous remained from the team that had played at Wentworth the year before. Along with Sarazen, the other "rookies" were Leo Diegel, Johnny Farrell, Johnny Golden and Joe Turnesa. (Al Espinosa was also named to the American team, but did not play in a match.)

Bon vivant that he was, Hagen "rolled right up to the clubhouse in a Rolls-Royce, driven by a chauffeur, with his own traveling caddie," recalled Fred Hill, a Worcester resident who served as Sarazen's caddie that week.

"Sarazen was staying at the Bancroft Hotel downtown with a Hollywood couple, an actor and actress who were making a movie that had some golf scenes. Sarazen gave them lessons out at the Worcester Country Club, and they followed him around that week.

"He and Hagen were both former caddies themselves," remembers Hill, who would himself go on to win the New England Public Links Championship four times. "They were such rivals for the spotlight they'd sometimes push each other off the

The par-5 5th hole at Worcester, viewed here from the extreme left of the hazard, requires a carry over water on the second shot for long hitters.

tees if there was a camera around."

The Worcester Country Club had been established in 1900, but the course wasn't built until 14 years later. Designed by the estimable Donald Ross, it had officially opened in September of 1914, in a dedication ceremony presided over by a former president (and future chief justice) of the United States, William Howard Taft, who frequently visited a favorite aunt in nearby Milbury and held an honorary club membership. It was recalled by old-timers that when the 332-pound Taft struck the first ball opening the course, he topped it.

All aspects of the 1927 Matches were first class. "Everywhere we went, we were submerged by hospitality and kindness," British team member Arthur Havers would recall later. "Suddenly we were in a world of luxury and plenty, so different from home. It was something we had never expected.

Even the clubhouses were luxurious, with deep-pile carpets, not like the run-down and shabby clubhouses at home."

On the eve of the Matches, it became clear that this Era of Good Feeling might end somewhere between the door exiting the locker room and the first tee. The Americans wanted to be good hosts, but they had no intention of becoming the first country to lose the Ryder Cup.

To that end, a delegation from the American PGA met with Ray and British team manager George Philpot with four proposals to amend the rules of competition. The original understanding of the rules, as formulated by Ryder, had called for the matches to precisely follow the format of the Walker Cup, which had begun some five years earlier. The Americans, however, wanted to substitute four-ball matches for foursomes, the latter being a form of competition rarely played in this country even then.

Although essentially a parkland course, Worcester has stands of trees that lend a distinct New England character to the layout.

The hosts also proposed that any match finishing all square continue to a sudden-death result, that two points instead of one be awarded for victories in two-man team events, and that both teams should be allowed to substitute a player in singles on the second day.

The British conceded only on the last point, for both captains had reason to anticipate that some line-up juggling might be in order. George Gadd had become so violently seasick on the crossing that he had not fully recovered his form. He had played so poorly in practice rounds that at his own suggestion he was held out of the competition. The Americans feared that Watrous, who was nursing what the local newspaper described as "a split finger," might be similarly indisposed.

"It is doubtful that Watrous will be able to play tomorrow," predicted the June 2 *Worcester Gazette.* As it turned out, Al was a trouper: He not only played but won in both foursomes and singles.

"With good weather a big crowd is expected to watch the play which will continue through Friday and today's perfect offering of the weather man was accepted as a hopeful augury of the brand that may prevail tomorrow. The forecaster had nothing worse than 'cloudy' to predict," noted the Worcester paper on the eve of the big match.

On Friday, a photo in the evening *Gazette* of Hagen shaking hands with Ray identified the nascent competition as "the Ryder Cup Matches for the professional championship of the world." The afternoon paper also contained an overview of the morning portion of the 36-hole foursomes matches: "At the start of the afternoon rounds the teams seemed to be playing a better brand of golf, especially those who finished on the wrong side of the ledger at the end of the morning session."

Frank Hickey, who caddied for the English captain, remembers Ray as "a big man, a huge man. Believe me, the ground shook when he swung the club! Ray was 50 then, considerably older than anyone else in the field, but he was longer off the tee than any of them by a good 40 yards!"

That first day's play saw Watrous team with Sarazen to win their 36-hole foursomes match against Havers and Jolly, 3 and 2, while a closer match involving both captains saw Golden and Hagen defeat Fred Robson and Ray, 2 and 1, as the Americans rallied from 3-down to 1-up by winning the 12th, 13th, 14th and 15th.

Farrell and Turnesa put what the visitors described as a "dog license" on George Duncan and Archie Compston ("8 and 6" being the standard price of a dog license in England), while the invaders' lone consolation came from Aubrey Boomer and Charles Whitcombe, who between them scored level fours for the 31 holes necessary to finish off Diegel and Mehlhorn, 7 and 5.

"One of the chief reasons for our failure was the superior putting of the American team," Ray told the *Worcester Telegram* after the first day. "They holed out much better than we did." His caddie, now 87, recalls that as an understatement.

"The British players were almost all better strikers of the ball than the Americans were," said Hickey. "Their short game just wasn't there. Not only did they putt badly, they had a lot of trouble around the greens, too."

But Ray was also impressed by the Americans' superior long-iron play.

"If the same number of holes had required brassie shots to reach the green, I would certainly look more favorably on our chances," he told reporters, while maintaining that the early results had "not killed our team spirit."

Ray's hopes for a comeback in singles were dashed almost from the outset. After Mehlhorn edged Compston, 1-up, the next three matches were U.S. runaways: Farrell defeated Boomer 5 and 4, Golden walloped Jolly 8 and 7 and Diegel crushed the British captain by a 7 and 5 score.

Only Duncan, who beat Turnesa, 1-up, and Whitcombe, who halved the day's last match with Sarazen, salvaged points for the visitors. And the latter should probably be marked with an asterisk: Down five with nine to play, Sarazen had charged from behind to draw level on the penultimate hole. Aware that the competition had already become a rout, he sportingly (and intentionally, insists caddie Hill) three-putted the last to produce the all-square result.

The other two matches saw Hagen post a 2 and 1 win over Havers, and Watrous beat Robson 3 and 2 for what proved to be a 9½ to 2½ triumph for the U.S. in the inaugural Ryder Cup Matches. The hometown press was somewhat smug in victory. In the following morning's paper, cartoonist Al Banx depicted Hagen as a "Big Game Hunter," dangling the pelt of the British lion from his mashie, above the gloating caption "Britannia rules the world, but what about the fairways?"

"When it comes to getting the little round ball into the little round hole," conceded Captain Ray, "there's no talking. You Americans have us whacked!"

And thus the Americans were first to take possession of the Ryder Cup, even though its benefactor never saw those Matches. In the end, Ryder, who died in 1936, only twice witnessed the contest he'd helped found, in 1929 at Moortown Golf Club, and in 1933 at Southport & Ainsdale Golf Club.

"It was a few years later that I finally met Samuel Ryder himself," recalled Sarazen. "He was a great gentleman and a great lover of golf."

And a man who would doubtless be both shocked and proud to see what the product of his imagination had become these many decades later.

George Kimball is an award-winning columnist for the Boston Herald *and a member at South Shore Country Club in Hingham. His article originally appeared in* The 1999 Ryder Cup Journal.

Scenes from the Massachusetts Amateur Championship

WORCESTER COUNTRY CLUB, AUGUST 14, 2000

Counterclockwise from above: R. D. Haskell, Jr.; teeing off on the par-5 5th hole; suggested line of play from a dad serving as caddie; medal-round scores; a busy practice range.

Memoirs of a Massachusetts Golfer

～ BY JOHN UPDIKE ～

I THINK OF MYSELF as a Pennsylvania native and a New York writer, but 100% a Massachusetts golfer. I never touched a club until, at the age of twenty-five, I became resident in the Bay State; an aunt of my wife's put a driver into my hands on her side lawn in Wellesley, and complimented me on my swing at a phantom ball, and thus sent me haring, for over forty years now, after my unfulfilled golf potential.

It was in Wellesley, the bards of golf history tell us, that golf took root in the Commonwealth. A Miss Florence Boit (who can be seen in the Museum of Fine Arts, in the celebrated John Singer Sargent portrait of the four Boit sisters) had played the game in Pau, France, and in 1892 she brought some clubs and balls back to her uncle's home in Wellesley, Arthur B. Hunnewell. To demonstrate the purpose of these curious implements the athletic lass proceeded to lay out a seven-hole course on her uncle's land and that of some neighbors. Among the astonished audience of her exhibition play was one Laurence Curtis, of Boston, who, ere the year was out, persuaded

REGARDED as America's foremost man of letters, John Updike was born in 1932, in Shillington, Pennsylvania. He graduated from Harvard in 1954, and spent a year in England, at the Ruskin School of Drawing and Fine Art in Oxford. From 1955 to 1957 he was a member of the staff of *The New Yorker,* to which he has contributed poems, short stories, essays and book reviews. Since 1957 he has lived in Massachusetts, where he took up golf. His novels have won the Pulitzer Prize, the National Book Award, the American Book Award, the National Book Critics Circle Award and the Howells Medal. While his witty musings on golf were previously collected in the book *Golf Dreams*, the following essay was composed expressly for *A Commonwealth of Golfers*.

The Country Club in Brookline to devote some of its turf to golf. So, without young Florence Boit and her good times at Pau, there might have been no course at The Country Club, and hence no venue wherein Ouimet would beat Vardon and Ray in a 1913 playoff for the U.S. Open, and Julius Boros would vanquish Arnold Palmer and Jacky Cupit in a 1963 Open playoff, and Curtis Strange would hold off Nick Faldo in yet another playoff at the U.S. Open, in 1988 — and thus Massachusetts golf would have missed out on three of its epic moments. Likewise, if that aunt-in-law hadn't played golf, I would have spent a lot more summer afternoons working in the yard or answering my mail.

I had moved, as it happened, to the North Shore, where the virus imported by Miss Boit was festering within a year or two, causing primitive layouts to spring up on the Essex County Club land in Manchester, the Appleton farm in Ipswich, the Moraine farm on Wenham Lake, and at Prides Crossing. The Myopia Hunt Club in Hamilton, against the better judgment of the red-coated fox chasers, had nine holes by 1894; the club

hosted the first of its four U.S. Opens in 1898 and the last one in 1908.

My own obscure golfing career, however, developed, in the 1950s and '60s, far from these storied private venues, on a number of public courses in the area. Each had its distinctions. Candlewood Golf Course, on Essex Road in Ipswich, was a converted farm, and the farmer's widow, gracious Mrs. Whipple, took your fees (less than a dollar, can it be?) in a roadside cottage distinguished, if my faltering memory serves, by a soft-drink cooler as murmurous as a mountain stream and a large photograph of Dr. Cary Middlecoff's swing as captured by stroboscopic camera. The Candlewood layout was on the flattish, shortish side, but a sufficient challenge to my novice skills; my majestic beginner's slice posed a considerable threat to the motorists on the roads passing to the right of the first and ninth fairways. There were two long holes, and then two short ones, and a fifth which asked that you walk back to a tee framed by apple trees and hit a blind drive which, if errant, could threaten players on the sixth

tee and fairway. At the center of the course, a number of fairways came together on a knoll of desolate bareness, all its grass and mayflowers worn to dust by the intersection of many wheels and dragging cleats. From this lunar knoll, the highest point on the layout, there was a 360-degree battle panorama of loping pre-adolescents, white-haired retirees, and off-duty clammers as they struggled to move the ball along the circuits of the hard-used little course. My older son, at the age of ten, would play Candlewood all of a summer day, working in as many as fifty-four holes.

A mile farther down Essex Road, in the hamlet of Essex, where clipper-ship building had, within a century, given way to the fried-seafood business, the Cape Ann links offered nine holes of greater length and less harrowing contiguity than Candlewood, with some exhilarating views of marsh and sea. The seventh hole, a longish par-three, asked that you hit across a stretch of mudflat; more than once, at icy high tide, we took off our shoes and socks to reach the hole and, on a parallel causeway to the eighth fairway, waded back. Beside the green of the ninth hole one was rewarded with a handshake from the owner, who proprietorially basked in one of the few golf carts available. It was a Depression-vintage course of minimal amenity and maximum intimacy; the owner's son drove the gang mowers, the daughter-in-law sold the Cokes and second-hand balls, and the aging holder of the course record (64, I think) often acted as starter. Weekends saw long waits on the first tee. Greenheads, an insatiable fly bred in marshes, were a seasonal torment. You teed off on broken tees pried into the interstices of rubber mats. There were soggy patches and parched stretches on the fairways at the same time of year. But the sea air and short-sleeved bonhomie were hard to beat. It was on this modest par-70 that I had my best round ever: a 38 on the first nine was topped by a par 35 on the second (the same nine), making a marvellous 73. My opponents refused to pay their debts, I had played so far above my head.

> "Amid the laconic courtesies of an afternoon foursome one is not permitted to forget that golf is, as well as a competitive ordeal, a form of socialization."

And other courses beckoned, a bit inland: Ould Newbury, with its aggravatingly elevated greens and pleasantly elevated screened clubhouse veranda; the Rowley Country Club, constructed as a lark by a retired Peabody contractor, its fairways newly seeded and its third hole an imposing watery dogleg; New Meadows, where the buzz of traffic along Route 1 mixed with that of the mosquitoes. Some public courses boasted eighteen holes: Wenham, whose linkslike back nine throbbed to the periodic passage of Boston and Maine commuter trains; Lynnfield's Colonial, where Canada geese and their offal were superabundant and Red Sox players could occasionally be spotted, treading lightly; Boxford's Far Corner, its precipitous fairways on one witnessed

occasion the scene of a spectacular roller-coaster ride, the rubber-tired golf cart doing slow wheelies on the wet grass all the way down to the eleventh green, while its duo of passengers yelped.

It was a happy and varied world, public golf, but an increasingly crowded one, as televised tournaments gave the sport glamour, and the population of eastern Massachusetts grew, and a prospering economy freed ever more wage slaves to the joys of recreation. My old companions in driving miles to make a hard-won publinx tee time slowly faded away, and my sputtering battery was recharged by membership in a private club. Thus was I admitted to the privileged, curried terrains of Myopia and Essex, of Peabody's Salem and Salem's Kernwood, of Brookline's Country Club and Newton's Brae Burn and Wellesley's Wellesley. Gradually I acquired a country-club manner, an ease with chits and caddie tips, and an expectation of lush green spaces populated by discreetly scattered golfers, of three- or even four-level tees and carts equipped with grass-seed ladles that make replacing divots a faux pas, of clubhouses whose walls shone like those of Byzantine churches with gold-lettered walnut plaques proclaiming tournament results from bygone ages and with silvered clubs and balls of intense historic interest, and of pro shops stocked as densely as a flower shop with fanned bouquets of high-tech multi-metal clubs, and of locker rooms scaled like the Baths of Caracalla, and of dining facilities that make upstairs at the Ritz look like a pizza parlor. However hard I endeavor to blend in, in costume and manner, my golf, I fear, has betrayed me, remaining ragged and unmannerly—public-course golf, formed in the school of hard knocks. Never mind; onward I go, spring, summer, and fall, in pursuit of that vision glimpsed in Wellesley nearly half a century ago.

Now what, in all this motley experience, is distinctly of a Massachusetts character? The Puritan founders of this Commonwealth have contributed, it may be, a certain Spartan tang to the sport, a tang less to be tasted in the plush precincts of Connecticut, so much of it suburban to New York City and its grotesque megabucks, or even in the precious courses carved from Rhode Island's meagre, inlet-nibbled acreage. Massachusetts clubhouses, by and large, rarely are cast in the mock-Tudor, half-timbered style favored in Greenwich, Stamford, and the Hudson Valley, nor are the waiting lists for membership as elaborately staged or as cruelly prolonged as there. Easier and quicker to help crew a spaceship to Uranus and back than run the hurdles at, say, Darien's Wee Burn. On the other hand, Massachusetts golf is not as rugged, nor as truncated in the length of its season, as that in the three states of northern New England. Cape Cod can entertain play in any month of the year, and even north of Boston a good season stretches from a muddy start in April to a balmy last round in November. As opposed to Florida golf, that of Massachusetts offers an entertainingly unflat terrain, rich in sidehill lies and blind shots over this or that immediate horizon. Hilly, but, unlike that of Vermont, not showily dependent on mountain views and prodigious feats of bulldozing to achieve a teeing area.

And, in distinction from Florida or Arizona or Alabama golfers, those of Massachusetts can venture out under the noon sun of most any summer day without suffering heat prostration. The summer is slow to come, with many a Maytime feint, but when it does it is a temperate sweetheart that rarely lacks a cooling breeze and a bearable humidity. No dawn risings to avoid the cruel scorch of midday; no late-afternoon rounds dragging past dinnertime. In Massachusetts one strides or rides cheerfully into the heart of the day, as through the warm months the scenery rings its changes from blossom-time to leaf season, each with its own glories, its height and texture and tint of rough, its qualities of turf underfoot and of cloud overhead. Golf becomes an exhilarating reason to get outdoors and take a long soak in Nature. Insects, except for spring blackflies and August greenheads in some locales, are no problem; nor does an alligator threaten to slither ravenously up from a water hazard, or a rattlesnake to uncoil from behind a red rock, or a scorpion to skitter hissing out of a burrow in a sand trap. Nature has been tamed, but for the wilderness within that produces wild and woolly golf shots.

> "As opposed to Florida golf, that of Massachusetts offers an entertainingly unflat terrain, rich in sidehill lies and blind shots over this or that immediate horizon."

The character of one's companion Massachusetts golfers deserves to be particularized. They are not the high rollers of Palm Springs and Winged Foot; a dollar a side, or a quarter a skin, is enough to whet a thrifty Yankee's competitive edge and to bring the excitement of financial concern to a four-foot putt. In keeping with the Commonwealth's Puritan heritage, we (if I may) know that life is a vale of tears, all is vanity, and earthly comfort is not the main issue. Cold days, damp days, nasty days are nevertheless days for golf.

Having been weaned on the essays of Ralph Waldo Emerson, Massachusetts golfers know that "a foolish consistency is the hobgoblin of little minds"; the inconsistencies of their game do not trouble them so much as philosophically amuse them. Aware, too, that "if the single man plant himself indomitably on his instincts, and there abide, the huge world will come around to him," they are loyal to their instinctive, untutored swings, and do not hurry off to seek instant relief in the faddish lessons of the golf pro, who comes from California and winters in Sarasota. The Massachusetts golfer wears his golf as he wears his turtleneck and creaseless corduroys and ten-year-old golf shoes; they may sag and hurt a bit, but they are his own, and "in self-trust all the virtues are comprehended." Yet the self-trust is tempered by, as Emerson's disciple Thoreau put it, knowledge that "the mass of men lead lives of quiet desperation" and each man is "a parcel of vain strivings." Vainly striving together on the golf course, Massachusetts golfers evince a puckish stoicism and, usually, an unforced good humor. "Manners," to quote Emerson once more, "are the happy ways of doing things," and amid the laconic courtesies of an afternoon foursome one is not permitted to forget that golf is, as well as a competitive ordeal, a form of socialization.

One might wonder if the common philosophical wealth that Massachusetts inherits hasn't sapped our lust for victory. A relatively few native golfers have excelled at the national level. There was Ouimet and his epic feat in 1913, but in modern annals the non-sportswriter is hard pressed to come up with names beyond those of Paul Harney, Bob Toski and Pat Bradley. Toski rapidly won six tournaments in 1953–54, and then slumped into a distinguished career as a golf instructor. Little Rhode Island and Connecticut have done slightly better, producing Julius Boros, Brad Faxon and Ken Green. The climate can be blamed, but is it much worse than that of western Pennsylvania, which produced Arnold Palmer, or of Rochester, New York, whence came Walter Hagen? It is certainly better for golf than that of Sweden, but look at Jesper Parnevik and Annika Sorenstam. Compared with, say, bleak and windy Texas, with its parade of greats from Byron Nelson and Ben Hogan to Lee Trevino and Ben Crenshaw and beyond, Massachusetts has kept its golf to itself, a green secret tucked here and there among its spired towns and bravely surviving farms. I like it that way. I never feel closer to my adopted state than when perambulating those green spaces, searching for the philosopher's stone behind a sweet, repeatable swing while casting a sideways glance at the early-budding willows and late-budding oaks, the swampy groves with their mossy stumps and springtime skunk cabbage, the wooden-bridged rivulets, the shimmering high rough of summer, and autumn's blazing fringe of hickories and maples all along the fairway.

Western Massachusetts lends
a bucolic charm and serenity to
golf not commonly experienced
elsewhere in the state. The
Berkshires and the Pioneer
Valley, lying astride the
Connecticut River, have long
attracted summer visitors seek-
ing relief from the heat, noise
and congestion of the cities. It
didn't hurt that art, dance and
music of the highest order came
to be part of the summer reper-
tory in these locales. Some well-
to-do families built their own
"cottages" in the Newport,
Rhode Island, tradition, while
others stayed at elegant hostel-
ries like the old Berkshire Inn in
Great Barrington. Golf inevitably
followed, first as a diversion for
the "tourists." In this way,
makeshift nine-hole courses were
built to serve the summer hotels
that sprang up in hill towns like
Ashfield and Northfield. The
hotels are long gone, but the
courses survived. Country clubs
in Springfield, Longmeadow,
Pittsfield and Stockbridge were
formed to serve both permanent
and summer residents, and
these have not only survived
but prospered.

IV. INTO THE WEST

Wyantenuck Country Club, Great Barrington, Massachusetts

A PIONEER IN
THE BERKSHIRES

~

*After building one of the country's earliest golf courses
in 1895, Stockbridge Golf Club invented the invitational, today
the heart and soul of American club golf competition.*

"THE CHARMING COURSE lies in the flat of the sunken meadows which the Housatonic, in the few thousand years which are necessary for the proper preparation of a golf course, has obligingly eaten out of the high accompanying bluffs."

Thus is Stockbridge Golf Club described by Owen Johnson in "Even Threes," a short story first published in *The Century Magazine* in 1912. The classic tale tells what happens when two members of average skills inexplicably play the rounds of their lives, only to find that no one else in the club will believe them. As a member at Stockbridge for more than 30 years, the author well understood the foibles of the golfers at his club and the impact of the ubiquitous Housatonic, which bears on play to some degree on 13 of 18 holes, on them.

"The river, which goes wriggling on its way as though convulsed with merriment," Johnson continued, "is garnished with luxurious elms and willows, which occasionally deflect to the difficult

For its centennial year in 1995, Stockbridge Golf Club produced a poster bearing its distinctive crest. *Opposite:* **The par-5 15th hole, 485 yards long, finishes near the 1st tee and golf shop.**

putting greens the random slices of certain notorious amateurs."

Even when the Housatonic inundates the course, as has happened on numerous occasions, sometimes more than once in a single golf season, Stockbridge members seem to have the capacity to find "merriment" in the disaster. In one early flood, club member Walter Tuckerman recalled canoeing happily "over practically every part of the course," and coming upon an even happier angler "who caught 15 or 20 pounds of carp near the great willow tree."

Tuckerman, a semi-finalist in the 1910 U.S. Amateur at The Country Club, was one of several multiple winners of the Stockbridge Golf Club Men's Invitational, first held in 1897 and arguably the oldest invitational in the country. At its inception and until 1941, the Invitational was an individual match-play tourney. Jesse Guilford, a U.S. and Massachusetts Amateur champion, was another early winner at Stockbridge. After 1941, the tournament became the four-ball team event it is today.

No. 7 at Stockbridge, a 504-yard dogleg par-5, requires an approach shot over the Housatonic River to a green backed by a rock outcropping and maple tree.

Once described as "one of the great, great granddaddy tourneys with an uninterrupted history," the Stockbridge Invitational was the model for inter-club competitions throughout the Northeast and beyond, as visiting golfers took back to their home clubs word of the format's many desirable features, including its capacity for fomenting friendship and affability as well as intense rivalry. In the post–World War II years, the Invitational developed mostly into a contest pitting Berkshire County against invaders from the Springfield-Holyoke area.

While a number of male golfers have made their mark at Stockbridge over the years, a single woman stands out in the club's entire history, and that is Rosamond 'Ros' Sherwood. In 1920, at age 20, the Stockbridge member was chosen for a team of four women sent to England by the USGA to represent the U.S. against the best women golfers of Great Britain—the precursor to the Curtis Cup. On the same trip she played in the British Ladies' Golf Championship at Newcastle, County Down, Ireland. After running a stake through her foot vaulting a fence, however, Sherwood was forced to play on crutches, and lost her match. Undaunted, she went on to compete in France, then, on a flight to Scotland for more golf at St. Andrews, barely escaped with her life when the airplane she was in developed engine trouble and fell into the English Channel, fortunately not far from land.

Back home, Ros settled into a much less precarious existence and assumed a near total lock on the Stockbridge ladies' club championship. She won the Stockbridge Women's Invitational

Opposite, clockwise from top left: A schematic of No. 12, showing the river "wriggling on its way as though convulsed with merriment"; No. 12 in real life, from the 90-yard mark; young parents and son having sport on the 4th green; view from the championship tee box for No. 16; graveyard behind the green on No. 2.

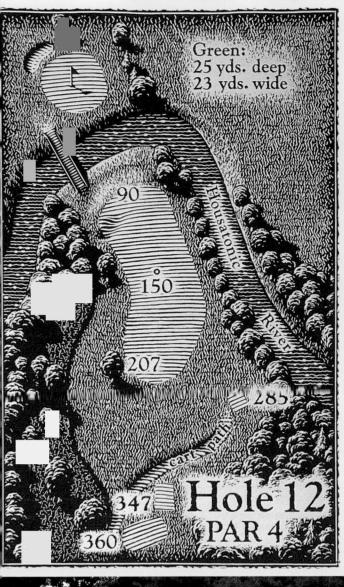

Green:
25 yds. deep
23 yds. wide

90

150

207

285

Housatonic River

cart path

347

360

Hole 12
PAR 4

The par-3 5th hole is short, at 121 yards, but all carry over the Housatonic. Stockbridge's flat terrain makes it a popular walking course.

Tournament three times and the Women's Amateur Championship of Berkshire County once. She and fellow Stockbridge member Don Ingram also won the Allied Mixed Foursomes Tournament several times. In 1930, when the event was hosted by Stockbridge, she and Ingram played the 13th, 14th and 15th holes in seven shots—five under par— including a double eagle on the 15th.

The most dominant player coming out of Stockbridge since the era of Ros Sherwood has been Jim Salinetti, who turned professional in the fall of 2000 after another outstanding year in amateur competition. Successfully defending his title, he won the Massachusetts Amateur in an exciting 36-hole final staged at Worcester Country Club. Trailing Larry Nuger by as many as 3-down after 13 holes, the 22-year-old Salinetti took his first and only lead after 29 holes. The pair halved the next six holes with Nuger conceding the 36th. His victory made him the first player to win back-to-back titles since Kevin Johnson in 1987–88. He's the seventh player to win the crown three or more times—he also won in 1997.

Stockbridge's club history closes with a verbal snapshot of the diverse membership attracted to this pioneering golf (and tennis) club in the Berkshires:

"Seasoned competitors with vivid memories and teenage golfers with bright futures play alongside each other. A violinist and a film director make a foursome with a bank president and a paving contractor. An artist and an engineer battle an interior designer and a theologian in mixed doubles."

Rosamond 'Ros' Sherwood, whose picture hangs in the clubhouse at Stockbridge, was "the shining light of women's golf in the Berkshires" from the 1920s to the 1960s, according to the club's history, winning the Stockbridge Women's Invitational three times, numerous club championships and various regional titles. She was the sister of playwright Robert Sherwood.

LAYOUTS OF
HIGHER LEARNING

~

*Williams College's Taconic and Mount Holyoke's
The Orchards get straight A's from discriminating golfers.*

ON THE WALL next to the bar at the Taconic Golf Club in Williamstown, photographs of Williams College golf teams span nearly a century, a fashion parade that reveals young men in plus fours and argyles in the 1920s, white bucks and crewcuts in the 1950s, long hair and jeans in the 1970s, spikeless shoes and Ralph Lauren Polo in the 1990s. In contrast, the clubhouse at The Orchards Golf Club in South Hadley has framed photos of Mount Holyoke girls of the 1930s and 1940s (and they were invariably called "girls," or "coeds," in that era), taking putting lessons in long skirts or teeing off wearing circle pins and penny loafers.

Both clubs bear lightly but unmistakably their close association with the schools that own the land on which today's members play golf in their own inimitable fashions. They also have in common several other things. The natural beauty of the countryside surrounds and shapes them.

An admonition dating from Taconic's earliest days is posted on the golf shop door. ***Opposite:*** **As seen from the 12th fairway, the tower of Thompson Memorial Chapel, on the Williams College campus, provides an elegant counterpoint to the smokestack.**

Taconic is hillier, but both layouts are fraught with the uneven lies that come with mountainous terrain. Both have their roots in Scottish golfing traditions in the persons of their first golf professionals. Taconic hired Dick Baxter, a Scot who came down from Canada, in 1924, initially to help build the course and plant it with trees, ultimately to serve both as club pro and greenkeeper for four decades. His legacy is found most evidently in a sign he prepared and which still hangs outside the pro shop, its Scots-laconic message:

"No preferred lies. We play golf here!"

Donald Ross is credited with the design of The Orchards but according to Mount Holyoke archives, James D. Young, a blacksmith's son from a village not far from St. Andrews, Scotland, was hired by Holyoke silk mill mogul Joseph Skinner to lend a hand in building the first nine holes at The Orchards in 1921. Himself an avid golfer, Skinner had the course built primarily for his daughter, Elisabeth, a crack amateur who would

go on to win the Endicott Cup, among many other prizes. Young was made pro and greenkeeper the following year and stayed on for nearly four decades, working as an accountant at Skinner Silk Mills in the off-season, eventually retiring in 1959. When he began teaching golf to students in the 1930s, Mount Holyoke, the oldest college for women in the United States, became the only college in New England with that sport in its physical education program.

The two courses are also on common ground as tests of golf. Taconic has hosted numerous national and state championships, including a U.S. Women's a U.S. Senior, a U.S. Junior and three Massachusetts Amateur championships. When the NCAA National Championship was held here in 1958, the field included numerous players who went on to successful careers as tour pros, among them Phil Rodgers, who won the event, Tommy Aaron, Al Geiberger, Don Massengale and Deane Beman. Sixteen-year-old Jack Nicklaus was in the field when Taconic hosted the U. S. Junior Amateur in 1956. Although he lost in the semi-final, he made his presence felt that year by holing an 8-iron from 175 yards on the par-3 14th hole. It took place on the second day of practice rounds.

The Orchards, which Ben Crenshaw once declared "the best kept secret in the Northeast," was the annual site of one of the

Clockwise from top left: From behind the green of the 390-yard uphill par-4 2nd hole at Taconic, a panoramic view of the mountains surrounding Williamstown; fall foliage adds its distinctive beauty to the course in October; a trio of students on the 385-yard par-4 3rd hole, the No. 2 handicap hole, which narrows as it descends to a bunkered green.

biggest amateur events of its time in the 1940s, the Eastern Area Air Force Golf Championship, which attracted teams from 18 bases. Since then it too has hosted a number of national and state championships, including the 2001 Massachusetts Amateur. The USGA has announced that The Orchards will host the U. S. Women's Open in 2004.

In 1973, the equivalent of today's NCAA championship for women was held at The Orchards. Westford native and LPGA Hall of Fame member Pat Bradley broke Elisabeth Skinner's long-standing course record of 72 in the opening round, but soared out of contention with an 85 on the next day. The U. S. Girls Junior Championship played here in 1987 was dedicated to Elisabeth, who was then in her 90s, living a reclusive existence in South Hadley. According to Bob Bontempo, the head professional at The Orchards from 1970 to 1996,

Arnold Palmer gives it body English as he urges a putt toward the hole at the 1981 U.S. Senior Open. The tournament took place at the Oakland Hills Country Club, designed by legendary golf architect Donald Ross. Palmer won the tournament in a playoff with Billy Casper and Bob Stone.
Photo courtesy of USGA.

Elisabeth rose to the occasion by speaking for 10 minutes at the preliminary banquet held for the 150 junior girls in the field that year. "And on the day of the final match," added Bontempo, "she had her chauffeur drive her up to the first tee, where she rolled down the window and shook hands with both of the finalists." A few weeks after Michelle McGann beat Lynne Mikulas in that final, Elisabeth died.

Finally, Taconic and The Orchards both bear the imprint of notable golf course designers. Taconic came into existence as a three-hole course laid out on athletic fields adjacent to the present 18th fairway, with tomato cans for cups, but it did not truly come into its own until Wayne Stiles of Stiles & Van Kleek, a Boston firm, was commissioned to design and construct an 18-hole course in 1927. Stiles was noted for large teeing areas, dramatic bunkering and greenside mounding, which tended to narrow the target for approach shots. In the same year, Joseph Skinner hired Donald Ross to build nine new holes at The Orchards as, in the words of the architect's associate, Walter B. Hatch of North Amherst, "an excellent addition to your present course...of better golfing value than those which you now play." Hatch's estimated cost for building what are presently holes 4 through 8, 12 through 15, and a portion of 16, was $34,349.

Upon his death in 1941, Skinner, who had presided over Mount Holyoke's board of trustees from 1912 to 1931, deeded The Orchards to the col-

Opposite: A triumphant moment for Arnold Palmer, whose management company runs The Orchards Golf Club in South Hadley, is captured in a photograph inside the refurbished clubhouse. *Above:* Just beyond the practice putting green, the clubhouse looks down on the 1st and 18th holes.

The 14th hole, descending from the highest point on the course at The Orchards, is a 405-yard par-4 with a right-to-left-sloping fairway and a green canted from back to front. Legend has it that the green mirrors the contours of the Mount Holyoke range in the background. *Opposite:* On the practice range, a convenient aiming point is the steeple of a former church, now housing the museum dedicated to silk mill mogul Joseph Skinner.

lege for the token sum of $25,000. (It would cost at least $15 million to build the course today, according to one recent guesstimate.) Operated as a private membership club for many years, owned by but independent of the college, The Orchards was turned over to the Arnold Palmer Management Company in 1999 on a 25-year lease agreement. In return, the firm established a $500,000 endowment fund for the school's golf team, named in memory of Arnold Palmer's recently deceased wife, Winnie. The new operator invested heavily in returning the layout to Donald Ross' original design, recapturing the actual sizes of many of the greens. Even the new scorecard at The Orchards capitalizes on the Ross mystique.

"Nestled in a rich maple and birch tree forest, this gem from 1922 is truly a shotmaker's delight," the card reads. "Decision making begins with the tee shot, the first piece in a puzzle that evolves from hole to hole."

Bontempo organized Mount Holyoke's first golf team when he arrived in 1970 and still teaches golf to undergraduates here. He considers his biggest achievement the role he played in nurturing the game of Anne Marie Tobin, Class of 1978. "When she first arrived she was shooting in the 90s," he recalled, "but by her senior year she won the Massachusetts State Intercollegiate, the New England Women's Intercollegiate and the Penn State Invitational. She was and is my pride and joy."

Incidentally, Donald Ross's daughter, Lillian Grace Ross, was a 1932 graduate of Mount Holyoke College, but her yearbook entry makes no mention of her famous golf connection, reporting only that she majored in French and played goalie on the field hockey team.

Open champion Harry Vardon came to America to play in a series of exhibition matches for Spalding and to promote the Vardon Flyer, a new gutta-percha ball with a bramble-patterned cover. Vardon won the U.S. Open during his visit, but the Vardon Flyer failed to take off: the Haskell rubber-core ball had come on the scene to displace the gutta-percha.

Spalding introduced its own rubber ball, the Spalding Wizard, in 1903. Soon thereafter, it developed a cover made of balata, a natural rubber that adhered securely to the rubber windings inside the ball and that was easier to control. Discovering that a dimpled cover made the golf ball fly farther and truer, Spalding brought this innovation into the market in 1909 in the form of the Spalding Domino Dimple.

Meanwhile, the company had moved from Chicago to a new facility on Front Street in Chicopee, Massachusetts, in 1904, where it established its executive offices and chief manufacturing operation. (In 1948 it moved to its current location on Meadow Street.) A. G. Spalding, who had retired from active participation in the early 1900s, died in 1915 in Point Loma, California, but his company's pioneering role in the sporting goods business, and increasingly in golf, would continue throughout the 20th century.

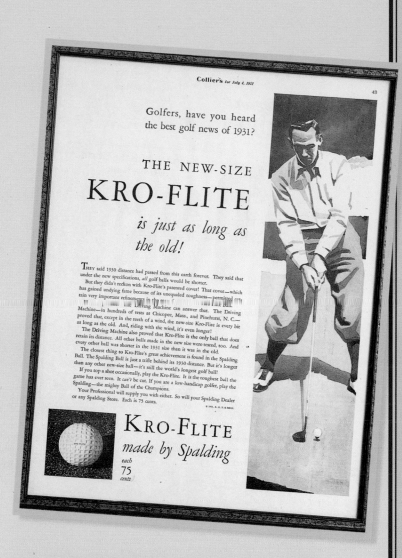

Spalding's Jones-designed flanged irons from the 1930s were an improvement on such straight-backed irons as the Chicopee firm's J. Victor East line. *Top:* **A print ad for a best-selling ball from the same era.**

A "set" of early golf balls from Spalding display the variety of dimpled surfaces designed, then as now, to help golfers in their quest for distance with accuracy. The firm's archive contains materials dating back more than 100 years.

A WILY CRUMPIN-FOX
COMES OF AGE

~

*It got off to a rocky start, and then things took a turn for the worse,
but after many years, this remote hill-town layout matured to become the first public
golf course to host the Massachusetts Open.*

LIKE ANCIENT CELTIC CAIRNS, the piles of rocks stand alongside fairways at the Crumpin-Fox Club in the rugged hills north of Northfield near the Vermont border. The unusual 150-yard markers date from the earliest days of the golf course, when it was a struggling nine-holer.

"There were two old farmers who used to come over to play the course in their overalls," recalled course architect Roger Rulewich, who now runs his design business from an office behind the 17th green. The course was built on the stony soil typical of the region, and the two golfers, with the instincts of New England farmers, cleared the land even as they played. "They were hillbilly-type characters and for some reason they started making piles out of the rocks they would come upon as they played their match. Eventually it dawned on us to put the piles to good use."

David Berelson, a young novelist who hired Rulewich in 1969 to design Crumpin-Fox as his personal "field of dreams," envisioned a walking course limited to middle-handicap golfers

or better, that would one day rival the legendary Pine Valley in New Jersey for its capacity to make grown men weep. Berelson was long on vision but short of funds. "We started clearing the land in 1972 but what with all our construction delays, the course wasn't ready for play until 1978," Rulewich recalled, "and it took almost another 12 years for the second nine to be completed."

From the beginning, Rulewich recognized the potential in the site, with its dramatic terrain and beautiful views, for creating a challenging golf course. It's just that he wasn't sure Berelson could get anyone to come play it. "It's hard for me to explain how it took off," he said. "There was no great population base to draw upon. It was hard to find—you wouldn't just come across it, you had to purposely set out to get to it, compass in hand. And yet even when it had only nine holes, Crumpin-Fox developed a kind of cult following. Golfers did not mind traveling to the place. It was remote, rustic, informal and cast a certain charm." Perhaps the curious name of the club alone attracted some golfers. It had noth-

Owner Bill Sandri flaunts his club's dapper mascot on his golf bag. *Opposite: At end of day, magical light floods the 175-yard par-3 15th hole at 'Crump.'*

ing to do with golf, having been derived from the Bernardston-based Crump Soda Company that was sold in 1853 to Eli Fox, thus becoming the Crump & Fox Soda Company.

After Berelson finally went broke on the project, he sold Crumpin-Fox to a local plastics manufacturer and enthusiastic golfer, Andy St. Hilaire, who held on to it until 1987, building a clubhouse in the meantime. In that year he sold the property to a friend, local heating-fuel magnate William A. Sandri of Bernardston, who bankrolled completion of the second nine. The 18-hole course opened to belated fanfare in the spring of 1990 and almost immediately proved its mettle as a worthy host of the 1990 Massachusetts Senior Amateur, won by Ed Myers. *Golf Digest, Golf Magazine* and *GolfWeek*

all sang its praises, and since then it has hosted U.S. Open qualifying three times, as well as the 1997 Massachusetts Open, won by Geoffrey Sisk.

Rulewich's affection for Crumpin-Fox stems in part from its humble origins, so much in contrast to the many major-league golf designs he executed during the 34 years he worked with Robert Trent Jones, most of them as chief design associate.

"Of all the projects I've been involved with," he declared, "Crumpin-Fox is my favorite."

Rulewich's former employer went even further after visiting Bernardston. "Crumpin-Fox," Jones predicted, "will someday be mentioned in the same breath as Pinehurst and Pine Valley."

So maybe the bankrupt visionary David Berelson (in whose memory the Berelson Challenge, an annual team match between Crumpin-Fox members and Robert Rulewich Group staffers, is played) had it right all along.

WHY THE GRASS
IS GREENER

~

Beginning in the 1920s, a Mass Aggie prof named Lawrence Dickinson
led the golf world in defining and developing the profession of golf course superintendent.

BY GEOFFREY S. CORNISH

GOLFERS of the Commonwealth, the nation and indeed the world are indebted to the University of Massachusetts in Amherst, formerly the Massachusetts Agricultural College, for the perfection of their greenswards.

In 1927, Amherst native Lawrence S. Dickinson (1888–1965) established the first course ever at college level on the subject of turfgrass management and science. It was designed specifically for course superintendents, then known as greenkeepers, and was devoted to the development and maintenance of fine turfgrasses on golf courses and other large lawn areas. The Dickinson program survived and expanded despite depression and war and constant flux resulting from unsteady financing. It also became the forerunner of many similar schools in the United States and abroad, while still remaining a leader.

By 1927, studies on turfgrass and related research in the United States and elsewhere were being pub-

Opposite: **Early American golf clubs like Essex used herds of sheep to keep their fairways in trim.** ***Above:*** **Amherst-based Lawrence Dickinson was the first educator to create a curriculum to help greenkeepers take care of turf professionally.**

lished in relative abundance. Yet the greenkeeper found it difficult if not impossible to apply this information to those endless practical problems that arise on a golf course. One of Dickinson's major objectives was to make it easier for the professional guardians of turfgrass to apply the lessons of scientific research to the successful design, construction and maintenance of their greens, tees and fairways. Yet like other successful educators, he felt strongly that his students should understand the principles on which the practical solutions to turfgrass problems depended.

Lawrence Dickinson was a visionary to say the least. Those of us who knew him continue to be astonished by the relevance of his observations made 60 or more years ago. Only recently this writer learned that evolutionary biologists now posit that the habitat of savannahs, where the human species experienced its early evolutionary development, relate to the contemporary golfer's yearning to be in open areas with a low greensward, scattered

trees—and with a club in hand! Dickinson speculated on the connection between man and his environment before World War II. In fact, he routinely talked about what is now known as environmental awareness.

The Dickinson Winter School for greenkeepers and course managers was of 10 weeks' duration with attendees arriving in Amherst direct from the field. Two-year students in the Ornamental Horticultural Department of the Stockbridge School of Massachusetts "Aggie" could also attend under certain conditions until 1946, when a formal two-year course in turfgrass science was established. By 1950, a large proportion of the nation's greenkeepers had attended one of the Massachusetts programs. The Winter School and the two-year program continue to flourish, and a four-year program and graduate program have been added.

Dickinson also recognized the relationship between golf course architecture and greenkeeping. To this end, his first part-time assistant was Walter Hatch, an associate of the esteemed Donald Ross. Hatch was based in North Amherst at what was then the Ross northern office. The tradition of a course architect assisting part-time was continued by Dickinson's successors with this writer assisting him and his successors until the mid-1980s when course architect Brian Silva took over. Other UMass faculty members ably supported the program, with Professor John Zak of the Department of Agronomy assisting Dickinson and all his successors until 1995.

Another noteworthy Dickinson assistant from beyond the campus was Carl Treat, a prominent Boston attorney who had become greenkeeper before World War II at Woodland Golf Club in Auburndale, when his eyesight failed as a result of long hours of reading. Treat's work at Woodland soon attracted wide attention and he was lured to

Maintains and Enhances It." Both points of view have since become virtually axiomatic among design and maintenance professionals.

Professor Dickinson retired in 1958. Dr. Eliot Roberts, a young and distinguished scientist, took over but left within a few years to take a similar position in Iowa. Dr. Joseph Troll, who had assisted Dr. Roberts, then became head of the program. He expanded both it and the annual turfgrass conference, another Dickinson pioneering effort. It is now held annually under the auspices of the six New England states and is attended by thousands of golf course superintendents and green committee members. Dr. Richard Cooper followed Dr. Troll and remained for a decade. During that time he too introduced notable improvements in the curriculum.

It is not possible to catalog all the accomplishments of those who have attended UMass's turfgrass programs and have gone on to "maintain and enhance" the golf courses of this nation and other countries. Their contributions to the excellence of the greenswards of golf are impressive. Without them and those who have graduated from programs at other universities, the playing fields of the game would never have reached their present state of excellence, providing "the turf the golfer wants." This includes the nearly 400 courses that take up more real estate in Massachusetts than all fruit and vegetable crops combined.

Greenkeeping would not be what it is today had it not been for the visionary turfgrass educator Lawrence S. Dickinson.

A native of Manitoba, Canada, golf course architect Geoffrey S. Cornish has lived and worked in Massachusetts for more than 50 years. In addition to his original designs, he has contributed to the restoration of such historic courses in the Bay State as Brae Burn, Myopia, Worcester and Longmeadow.

Montclair Golf Club in New Jersey, from where he visited Amherst regularly to assist Dickinson. This remarkable person was also a visionary. He introduced management and finance skills to the Dickinson program while emphasizing the impact of a golf course on its community, both socially and environmentally. Dickinson was also adept at enticing well-known visitors to the campus. Two of the many who came more than once were Francis Ouimet, whose chosen subject was "Turf the Golfer Wants," and a dynamic but then little-known course architect, Robert Trent Jones, whose favorite subject was "The Architect Provides the Cornerstone of the Game While the Greenkeeper

Above, from left: At Essex, state-of-the-art equipment in a vintage maintenance barn, tokens of tournaments past, and a 10th tee view from the office of the golf course superintendent. Inset: Worcester Country Club professional Willie Ogg praised Lawrence Dickinson's turfgrass course in the February, 1929, issue of *Golfdom*.

"UNDER SMILING SKIES"

~

*The club motto of the Country Club of Pittsfield captures
the countrified ambience there and at Longmeadow, two western Massachusetts clubs
where the presence of the great Bobby Jones still can be felt.*

Most golf fans are aware that Robert Tyre Jones, Jr., studied English literature at Harvard, but his deepest connections in the state of Massachusetts actually lay well west of Cambridge. When Jones retired from competitive golf at the age of 28, having completed his 1930 Grand Slam, he became affiliated with A. G. Spalding & Bros. of Chicopee, with the goal of developing a matched set of steel-shafted clubs to be marketed under the Jones name. Thus began an association that would last nearly 30 years and bring the great man to western Massachusetts summer after summer, an immense treat for all of those who came into contact with him during that time, for, as the golf writer Charles Price once observed, "He had flashing good looks, a personality that could charm the blossoms off a peach tree, and the thoughtful grace of a man twice his age."

The Massachusetts connection widened when his son, Robert Tyre Jones III, went into business as the distributor of Coca-Cola in the Pittsfield area and became a member of the Country Club of Pittsfield,

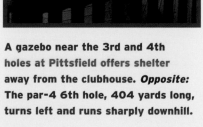

A gazebo near the 3rd and 4th holes at Pittsfield offers shelter away from the clubhouse. *Opposite:* The par-4 6th hole, 404 yards long, turns left and runs sharply downhill.

serving as its president in 1969 (and winning its club championship 10 times). The club's coat of arms carries the motto Benigno Numine, meaning "By the favor of Providence," or, in terms of play, "Under Smiling Skies," and that precisely describes the privilege of playing the course on a fair summer day.

The Pittsfield club was founded in 1897 by nine golf enthusiasts led by Dr. Henry Colt, a prominent physician and surgeon. Determined to "establish and maintain a house and grounds…for social meetings and to encourage athletic exercise," the group purchased 230 acres of land and a large, square mansion dating from 1781. This edifice, a portion of which is incorporated into the clubhouse as it exists today, positively reeks with history. The original owner, Henry VanSchaack, a member of the first board of trustees of Williams College, was a politician and scholar. A history of the club published in 1990 portrays VanSchaack as a busy host. Lawyers "after every adjournment of the court at Lenox flocked to his hospitable mansion," as well as Williams College trustees en route to commencement exercises, and the "magnates of the Federal Party," including Alexander Hamilton, "with whom

A successful escape from
a greenside bunker on the
562-yard par-5 8th hole at
Country Club of Pittsfield.

it was his greatest pleasure to share his rich wines and sparkling cider."

In the early 19th century the clubhouse building, which came to be known as "Broadhall," was owned by Elkanah Watson, the founder of the Berkshire Agricultural Society, the first such society in America. He sold the place to Major Thomas Melville of Boston, uncle of Herman Melville, whose son became the owner in 1837 and turned it into a boardinghouse. Prominent guests who stayed here included Henry Wadsworth Longfellow, Nathaniel Hawthorne and President John Tyler after he left the White House. In 1848, Longfellow used the house as his summer residence. For a time the house was used as a link in the "underground railway" which concealed escaped slaves on their way to freedom in Canada.

The property changed hands two more times before becoming the possession of golfers in 1900. Willie Anderson, the Scotsman who won four early U.S. Opens, was the club pro from 1901 to 1905.

But to return to 1931, Longmeadow Country Club, not very far from Spalding's headquarters in Chicopee, happened to be the home club of Milton B. Reach, vice president and general manager of Spalding. It was "M.B." who had persuaded Jones to sign one of the sporting-goods industry's first equipment royalty contracts, and then focused the company's design and production capabilities on the club project. (The smashing success of the Jones line of clubs is in fact credited with helping Spalding survive the Great Depression.) At Reach's suggestion Jones also became a member at Longmeadow, and the two of them, along with the club's head professional, J. Victor East, a renowned teacher and club designer in his own right, spent the better part of that first summer playing the course while they tested prototypes of the new clubs.

"To keep their experiment under wraps, they would play the first hole with their regular wood-shafted clubs," recalled Reach's son, Milton Reach, Jr. "Then they would switch to the prototypes. After

A familiar trio at Longmeadow Country Club in the summer of 1931 comprised, from left to right, Milton Reach, Sr., vice president and general manager of A. G. Spalding & Bros. in Chicopee; Bobby Jones, Spalding consultant; and J. Victor East, head professional at Longmeadow at the time. Jones, having retired from competitive golf after his Grand Slam year of 1930, was working with Reach and East to develop the golf industry's first matched set of steel-shafted irons. In the background on the right is Reach's son, Milton Reach, Jr. *Below:* Milton Reach, Sr., tees off on No. 10 at Longmeadow while Jones and others look on.

Longmeadow's No. 7 hole is a 184-yard downhill par-3, its green bunkered left and right. A portion of the 3rd fairway is seen beyond the creek to the right.

THE PRIZE FOR MAKING THIS HOLE IN ONE STROKE WILL BE THE VALUE OF ACCUMULATED INTEREST ON A THOUSAND DOLLAR ENDOWMENT

A plaque behind the tee box of the 4th hole, a 134-yard par-3, offers a bonus to anyone acing the hole, but the endowment, created by industrialist and Longmeadow member Alfred H. Chapin, was apparently lost, along with Chapin's own fortune, in the stock market crash of 1929.

playing with them and comparing notes on their performance, they would switch back to the old clubs coming up the 18th." Prudently stowed, the precious cargo would then return to the factory for modifications and more field tests.

The first sets of Jones irons, as tested at Longmeadow and refined at the factory in Chicopee, reached the market in 1932 and were an instant hit. "Prior to that time there were no satisfactory iron clubs made in this country," Jones wrote in his book, *Golf Is My Game.* "The American-made irons were too long from heel to toe and had a 'tinny' appearance and feel. Striking the ball off center produced a most unpleasant shock in the hands of the player.... By making the blades more compact, with a thicker top line, and providing a flange sole on the back of the head, we succeeded in bringing the center of gravity of the head more nearly behind the center of the striking surface, or 'sweet spot.'"

Although only a teenager at the time, Milton Jr. vividly remembers Jones' mastery of the difficult, par-70 Longmeadow course designed by Donald Ross. "For example, take the first three times he played our 10th hole, a par-5. All three drives were within 10 yards of each other on the flat in the left center of the fairway. The pin was tucked left the first day, so he drew a 4-wood 15 feet from the pin.

Clockwise from top left: Longmeadow member Cary Jubinville, a past MGA president, powers out of rough along No. 5, a short but treacherous par-4; the 5th hole seen from behind the well-bunkered green; a view of the Tudor-style clubhouse from the 1st fairway. *Opposite:* Near a summer day's end on the front nine at Longmeadow.

The second day it was in the middle, calling for a 3-wood that found the center of the green 12 feet below the hole. On the third day he faded a 2-wood to the right rear pin position, four feet from the cup. Birdie, birdie, eagle." In fact, during that third round, Jones established a new course record of 66, followed later by a 65. As of 2001, the 65 had been equaled only once from the back tees, by Joe Henley in 1999.

With the Jones and Reach families becoming friends and traveling together, Milton the younger had many chances to observe Jones the golfer, including his competitiveness. Playing as a two-some at The Highlands in North Carolina, Milton recalled, "I was playing pretty well that day and when we came to the 15th tee, I said, being a brash youth, 'Let's play in for a Coke.' The final four holes played to pars of 4, 3, 5 and 3. I shot 4, 3, 4, 3. Jones shot 3, 2, 3, 2. It didn't matter what you did, he could raise the level of his game to beat you."

The younger Reach recalls his father as "a tire-less promoter of the game, always trying to create new golfers. The promotion of golf through exhi-bitions actually began in 1900 when Dad brought Harry Vardon and Ted Ray from England to tour the States, including a match at Springfield Country Club. He organized countrywide exhibition matches with Lawson Little, Horton Smith, Lighthorse Harry Cooper and Jimmy Thomson, who could hit the ball a mile—I once saw him hit a drive 340 yards on the 18th at Longmeadow after missing a short putt on 17 in the Massachusetts Open!"

Since Spalding was just down the road from Longmeadow, other visitors to the club had names like Armour, Nelson, Runyon and Diegel. But it is Jones who has left the deepest impression. And thanks to Longmeadow's most famous member, four tickets to the Masters Tournament are reserved in the club's name every spring at Augusta National.

Besides appearing in numerous exhibition matches in the Bay State, Walter Hagen made his mark here by winning the 1915 Massachusetts Open at The Country Club in Brookline and the 1919 U.S. Open at Brae Burn Country Club in West Newton. In 1927 he captained the U.S. team to victory in the inaugural Ryder Cup Matches, staged at Worcester Country Club.

Golf Notes of a Native Son

~ BY HERBERT WARREN WIND ~

Walter Hagen at Thorny Lea

SHORTLY AFTER his return from Europe that year (1929), Hagen embarked on an exhibition tour with Horton Smith, a tall, handsome young man from Missouri, who had won the French Open that spring. One of the clubs they played was Thorny Lea, in Brockton, Massachusetts, where my family lived and where I was in school. I had been playing golf for a few years by then, and I made sure to watch Hagen. As I recall, school let out at one-fifteen, and Hagen and Smith were playing the sixth when I picked them up. Two of the club's best players rounded out the foursome. I arrived just in time to see Hagen play a shot that remains as clear in my mind as if he had played it yesterday.

The sixth is by far the best hole on the course. In those days, it was a 445-yard par-4 from the back tee, and the fairway crested about two hundred and sixty yards from that tee. It ran down to two small ponds, and then slowly rose to a two-level green, bunkered on both sides. Woods extended all along the left side of the fairway, and there were clumps of tall trees in the heavy rough bordering the fairway on the right. That day, the pin was set on the upper level, at the back of the green. A gallery of about a thousand people was trailing behind the players. It was easy to pick out Hagen as the players walked up the fairway to their balls. His black hair shone in the sun, his face was tanned a mahogany brown, his nose was tilted up a bit, his eyes were fixed on the distant green, and he carried himself like a grandee. He stopped and waited while the two local players and Smith hit their seconds, and then he walked about three yards into the woods on the left, where his drive had finished. The contours of the sixth fairway funnelled a drive hit down the left side farther to the left. Hagen had a good lie and a small opening back to the fairway, but he had no opening in the direction of the green. Not for one moment did he modify his composed expression as he walked from his ball to the fairway, returned to his ball to study the situation, and repeated these movements several times. All this was so much in

AMERICA'S preeminent golf writer of the 20th century, Herbert Warren Wind was born in Brockton, Massachusetts, and was educated at Yale and Cambridge. His career as a staff writer for *The New Yorker* began in 1947 and spanned more than four decades, during which time he wrote not just on golf but tennis, baseball, football, basketball and hockey, as well as many other topics. His meticulously wrought accounts of the major golf championships, as much history as journalism, appeared with virtually unbroken regularity under "The Sporting Scene" rubric in the magazine from 1963 to 1989. The following excerpts from that column provide a small sampling of the author's range, virtuosity and humor.

character that it was like watching someone playing Walter Hagen. Finally, he selected a club from his bag. It looked like a mashie. The pin was about a hundred and seventy yards away, but he seemed to be aiming his shot to come out of the woods well to the right of the green. He took a full swing and hit the ball hard. It rose rather quickly and broke sharply to the left. It cleared the bunker on the right side of the green, hopped up onto the upper terrace of the green, and stopped some twenty feet from the pin. He had played an intentional hook, drawing the ball at least fifteen yards to the left. I had never seen anything like it. He made a good bid for his birdie, and then tapped the ball in for his par.

Hagen was out in 35 after holing from about ten feet to birdie the short ninth. His impact on the members of the gallery was much different from Smith's. They regarded Smith as a well-mannered young man with a splendid golf swing. Hagen came across as visiting royalty and a master golfer. The greens at Thorny Lea were not easy to read, but he read them perfectly. He gauged the distance of his shots surprisingly well on a course he had never played before, making only one mistake. On the fourteenth, a long dogleg par-4 that bends to the left, he drove through the fairway and into the wooded rough on the right. After having his caddie remove several rocks, he played a stunning recovery shot through a narrow gap between two trees. The ball bounced onto the green and stopped about fifteen feet from the pin. His iron play was magnificent. I don't believe I have ever seen another golfer who got as much of the ball on the face of his irons as Hagen; he finished with a 70, two under par. Smith had a 73. Hagen was the first great golfer I had ever seen, and

both his ability and his presence surpassed anything I had expected. Not until Arnold Palmer came along, in the late nineteen-fifties, did another golfer establish a relationship with his galleries that was as strong and dramatic as Hagen's.

—*May 18, 1987*

~

The Arnold Palmer Years

WHAT LAY BEHIND Palmer's enormous popularity? First, his galleries were attracted by the attacking style with which he played the game. He was not afraid to gamble, and three times out of four he pulled the shot off. He got into trouble quite often, because he was an arms-and-hands hitter who came through the ball with such velocity that he had to block out his shots a bit with his left arm to prevent his right hand from taking over and hooking the ball. Besides being an extremely strong and long hitter, he was a superlative putter. He holed many long, sinuous putts because he had complete confidence that if he missed them he would make the three-footer or four-footer coming back. Palmer brought Walter Hagen to mind in the way he could recover from seemingly impossible positions and, all in all, make a round of golf seem like an adventure. Like Hagen, he had the kind of personality that dramatized everything he did on the course. In other respects, though, he was the exact opposite of Hagen, the suave, pomaded, impeccably dressed internationalist. Palmer was a handsome, clean-cut, rugged, All-American type that people could easily identify with. He had a natural manner and an unusually mobile face, which expressed his thoughts and emo-

> "Palmer brought Walter Hagen to mind in the way he could recover from seemingly impossible positions and, all in all, make a round of golf seem like an adventure."

tions vividly, and these traits enhanced the closeness the members of his army felt for him. People were charmed by his politeness and his patience. He was never too busy to autograph a book or a program. His coolness under pressure was the real thing. During a tournament round, he would walk over to a friend he had spotted in the gallery and begin a conversation. The friend would be as tight as a drum, fearful that he might be disturbing Palmer's concentration, but that was never the case. Palmer was the right man to be the dominant personality in golf at a time when it was enjoying a gigantic boom for several reasons—among them General Eisenhower's well-known fondness for the game, and the advent of color television and better coverage.

—May 28, 1984

~

Bing Crosby, Golfer

ONE REASON Crosby was so fond of golf was that he had discovered it at the age of twelve, when he started to caddie at the old Riverside Golf Club in Spokane, where he grew up. From then on, he was fascinated by the game. He played it periodically during his years at Gonzaga University, in that city, and much more often when he became a band vocalist, ending up with Paul Whiteman's orchestra as the lead singer of the Rhythm Boys—a marvelous group, which was as far ahead of its time as the band's cornettist Bix Beiderbecke. After the Whiteman band completed the motion picture "The King of Jazz," in 1930, Crosby decided to go out on his

Bing Crosby inaugurated his Pro-Am in 1937 in part for the great pleasure he derived from the company of crack professionals.

own, and settled in Los Angeles. In no time, he had his own coast-to-coast radio program and was making two or three movies a year. During this period, he developed his fine golf game. He joined the Lakeside Golf Club, to which many people in the film industry belonged, and, despite the rigors of his schedule, managed to play nine or eighteen holes several times a week. A well-coordinated man with a natural sense of timing, he got his handicap down to 2 and carried off the club championship five times. In 1940, he won a spot in the sectional qualifying round for the United States Amateur Championship, but failed to make the match-play rounds in the subsequent thirty-six-hole qualifying test held at Winged Foot, in Westchester, the scene

of the championship. During the war, he played many exhibitions—as did his friend Bob Hope, himself a more than creditable golfer—to promote the sale of war bonds.

Golf is a game that demands constant application, and during this stretch of his career hardly a day went by when Crosby didn't have a club in his hands. For example, he used to keep a shag bag of balls at the Paramount lot and, between scenes, practice chipping with a 7-iron on a small strip of lawn. I first saw him in action near the end of the war, when he was playing with some friends at Cypress Point, one of the courses on the Monterey Peninsula. Two things about that afternoon remain clear in my mind. First, I had long wondered whether Crosby was really as good a golfer as he was cracked up to be, and discovered that he was; he had a very legato, nicely grooved swing, and, while he wasn't particularly long, he hit crisp, straight shots down the fairway or toward the flag with the assurance of a man who knew exactly what he was doing. Second, I recall the astonishing way his voice travelled. You would be walking down an adjacent fairway, anywhere from a hundred to two hundred yards from his foursome, and, while you couldn't hear the three other players in his group talking at all, or you caught what they said merely as an unintelligible mumble, Crosby's voice had such timbre that every word he spoke in an ordinary conversational tone carried like the peal of a bell, and he invariably sounded as if he were no more than forty feet away.

—*May 8, 1978*

~

Eternal St. Andrews

THE TOWN OF St. Andrews (present population: just over eleven thousand) edges into the North Sea at the tip of the Fife Peninsula, between the Firth of Forth, to the south, and the Firth of Tay, to the north. The town itself sits on top of a rocky plateau that falls gently downhill to the Old Course, which occupies a sweep of linksland running north along the shallow curve of St. Andrews Bay to the mouth of the Eden River. As the crow flies, St. Andrews is only thirty miles from Edinburgh. Since 1964, when a bridge for motor traffic across the Firth of Forth was completed, the touring golfer on a tight schedule has been able to breakfast in Edinburgh, drive to St. Andrews for a round on the Old Course, get in a pleasant stroll around the town, and return to Edinburgh in plenty of time for dinner and some entertainment in the capital city. Close by the motorway bridge stands the Michelangelesque railroad bridge that spans the firth. A mile long, its tracks a hundred and fifty-seven feet above the inlet, it was considered a marvel of engineering when it was finished, in 1890, seven years after work on it began. Whenever an old-movie buff takes in this gigantic, muscular structure, his thoughts invariably go back to "The 39 Steps," Alfred Hitchcock's first great success, and to the theatrics aboard the train on which Robert Donat and Madeleine Carroll were crossing the firth. For the golf enthusiast who is making his first visit to the Old Course and has a malleable schedule, perhaps the best time to arrive in St. Andrews is around six o'clock on a summer's evening, when the sun is streaming across the links and turning everything to gold. At this hour, there are many golfers still out on the course, and there will be until darkness falls. On such a long, lingering evening, the weather-beaten sandstone clubhouse of the Royal and Ancient Golf Club of St. Andrews looms sturdier and more regal than it does on any official R. & A. Christmas card. Beyond the clubhouse, nearer the bay, the vast eighteen-hole municipal putting green on the Bruce Embankment is filled to capacity with residents of the town, ranging from tots scarcely as tall as a putter to perky octogenarians. Everybody is totally absorbed in his match. The fee for a round is thirty British pence—about forty cents. A little north of the embankment is the three-acre green of the Ladies' Putting Club, a private club, established in 1867, which is now composed of a hundred and forty members and approximately thirty gentleman associate members. They all pay annual dues of five pounds. Because of its fanciful undulations, the green is referred to by the members as the Himalayas. In good weather, they are out in force, full of merriment.

—August 27, 1984

~

The Essence of Amateur Golf

ON THE SIXTH OF JANUARY, the day when the hundred-and-twenty-five-thousand-dollar Los Angeles Open, the first event on the 1972 American professional golf tour, got under way, a tournament of considerably less surface glitter was beginning at the Rye Golf Club, a few miles to the east of that ancient Cinque Ports town on the English Channel. This was the President's Putter, a four-day, match-play affair that the Oxford and Cambridge Golfing Society annually holds early in January. It would be hard to imagine a more amateur occasion. As a rule, the galleries are very small, rarely exceeding three or four hundred spectators—and an equal number of dogs—even on the day of the final. And whereas first place in the Los Angeles Open is worth twenty-five thousand dollars nowadays, all that the winner of the President's Putter gets to take home is a silver medal with the inscription "Primus inter pares." Literally translated, this means "First

> "While Bernard Darwin the writer was the soul of serenity and balance, Darwin the golfer had one of the shortest fuses in history."

among equals," but most of the members prefer the freer translation proposed decades ago by Arthur Croome, a famous secretary of the Society: "He was lucky to win."

It is precisely this low-key amateur ambience that makes the President's Putter special and significant. . . . However, what really sets the President's Putter apart is that it is played under the worst conditions of any golf tournament in the world. . . . Gale-force winds and cold, sluicing rains from off the Channel frequently rip over the links. As often as not, the fairways and greens are frozen bone-hard. Every now and then, for good measure, there is snow to contend with. In 1960, for instance, with the links coated white on the final day, the players were provided with red golf balls and forecaddies were stationed along the fairways, and the tournament was able to finish on schedule. Two years after that, when the President's Putter was beset by perishingly cold weather, David Phiri, a black Zambian who was on the Oxford team, appeared for his first match wearing three pairs of socks, underwear, pajamas, a pair of rain trousers over his regular trousers, a heavy shirt, six sweaters, two scarves, two pairs of gloves, a woolen hat, and the kind of face-protecting hood called a balaclava. Somehow or other, he won that match.

Why, you might ask, have the members of the Society not chosen to come in from the cold, like sensible men, and shift their tournament to a more reasonable time of the year? Because they are English, by and large, and, ipso facto, born eccentrics. . . .

I found the President's Putter a world of its own, an entirely different world from anything I had ever before encountered in golf. During my four

Regarded as Great Britain's finest golf writer, Bernard Darwin, a grandson of Charles Darwin, was a fine golfer in his own right, good enough to play in the 1922 Walker Cup.

long. On Thursday night, for example, a number of us who were staying at the Hope Anchor Hotel settled in the bar after dinner, where, supplemented by visiting friends, we talked golf solidly for the next four hours. The star turn was provided by Tony Duncan, one of the Society's old lions (he was the winner of the Putter in 1948 and 1958), who told a series of Bernard Darwin stories. While Darwin the writer was the soul of serenity and balance, Darwin the golfer had one of the shortest fuses in history, and this is what Duncan's stories were about. One incident he related had taken place at the Putter. Darwin, it seems, was playing a man named Speakman, a rather ordinary golfer, but as they came to the twelfth it was still anybody's match. On that hole, Darwin hit a magnificent approach shot that barely missed the pin, but, unluckily, it was a shade too strong and just slid over the green, where it caught a downslope that plunged it into deep rough. Speakman followed with a terrible half-topped approach that hopped through a bunker and onto the green, where it finished close to the pin. The injustice of all this was too much for Darwin. Hurling his club to the ground, he roared, "God damn this blasted course! God damn this blasted hole! And you, Speakman, God

days at Rye, I lost all track of what was going on anywhere else. The daylight hours were spent at the golf club in the company of the stalwarts of the O. &. C. G. S., and at night, since the residents turned in early and there were no other visitors, they were the only people you encountered as you made your way around the cobbled streets. Rarely did a subject other than golf command a conversation for

damn you!" Another Darwin story that Duncan told had as its setting the annual Medal Day at Woking— a competition that Darwin took very seriously. On the first green, after a fine approach, he missed a five-foot putt. On the second, he missed an eight-footer. After another perfect iron to the third, he missed from six feet. Now he was seething. On the fourth hole at Woking, a tight par-4, the place to be on your drive is between the principal fairway bunker and a railroad track on the right. Darwin threaded the needle with his tee shot, nursed a delicate pitch-and-run three feet from the pin but then blew the putt, whereupon he sank down on his hands and knees, bit a huge piece of turf from the green, and, lifting his hands toward the heavens, said in a voice that trembled with emotion, "O God, are you satisfied now?"

—April 1, 1972

~

Jack Nicklaus' "Ideal Temperament for Golf"

GOLF MAY BE THE MOST DIFFICULT of all games to play well. For one thing, it is the only major outdoor game in which the player must generate his own power as he strikes a stationary ball from a stationary position. To do this and at the same time hit the ball accurately toward a target requires mastery of a very sophisticated technique. For another thing, since the game is played on natural terrain the player must continually adjust his hitting action to the lie of the ball, not to mention the wind and weather. All the great champions have necessarily been extremely sound shotmakers, but what really separates them from the talented golfers on the level just below them is their deep, unshakable belief in themselves. This engenders the determination and the self-possession that enable them, in this game where the slightest faulty movement can lead to a costly error, and even to disaster, to rise to the occasion and produce their finest golf at the most important moments. For all the gracefulness of his swing, Jones was a high-strung young man who felt the stress of tournament play so acutely that during one championship he lost eighteen pounds. He had the ability, however, to gather his concentration as he prepared to play each shot. Hogan, from the begin-

ning to the end of a round, could insulate himself from the world and go about his golf with white-hot intensity. He was oblivious of everything else. Nicklaus's mind works unceasingly during tournament rounds, but at the same time he appears to be cooler and calmer than any other golfer of the modern era. He seems to actually thrive on pressure. Out on the fairway, surrounded by thousands of exuberant fans, he wears the tournament golfer's invariable frown of concentration, but he seems completely relaxed—as much at home as if he were taking a solitary walk in the country over a pleasant stretch of land he has known all his life. In a word, Nicklaus has the ideal temperament for a golfer, and, combined with his physical stamina and phenomenal will to win, it helps to explain the miracles he has performed at many critical moments.

—May 30, 1983

~

Goats and Shamrocks

GOLF STARTED IN LAHINCH the way it did at practically all the older Irish homes of golf. A Scottish regiment—in this instance, the Black Watch, stationed in Limerick—was looking for a suitable place to pursue its national passion. Until 1891, the Black Watch golfers had made do with a rude layout in the middle of the Limerick race-course, but that spring one of their number made a trip into Clare and returned to report that there was some honest-to-goodness golf country along the coast there. From that time on, the regiment made Lahinch its golfing headquarters. At first, the players stuck feathers in the untended ground to demarcate the teeing areas, the direction of the holes, and the greens. Two years later, a rough course was created, and the Lahinch Golf Club was formally founded, on Good Friday, 1893, with members of the local gentry installed as the officers. Shortly afterward, the club hired Old Tom Morris to design a proper course. Dissatisfied with the character of the existing layout, which mainly occupied dull inland ground, he reconnoitred the sand hills along the edge of the sea and rerouted many of the holes over their profusion of ridges and grassy hollows. He adjudged the revised layout to be one of the five best courses in the British Isles—a statement that he made not in a spirit of self-congratulation but, rather, out of a wish to point up that the terrain constituted "as fine a natural course as it has ever been my good fortune to play over." In 1927, the Scottish architect Dr. Alister MacKenzie, who is best known in this country as the designer of Cypress Point and as the co-designer, with Bob Jones, of the Augusta National, was engaged to modernize the course. He did this by building some splendid new holes in a distant stretch of sand hills that had been left untouched, by remodeling most of the holes he kept, and by extending the total length of the composite eighteen to 6,544 yards. Like Old Tom before him, he fell in love with the links, and declared that Lahinch might come to be regarded as "the finest and most popular course that I or, I believe, anyone else ever constructed." Most objective golfers would probably consider MacKenzie's assessment to be a shade exuberant. While Lahinch is an excellent course, with a high percentage of vivid and provocative holes, few connoisseurs, I think, would put it in a class with, for example, Portmarnock, or, for that matter, with County Down or Portrush, in Northern Ireland. However, because of the way the course is interwoven with the life of the village, the Lahinch Golf Club has a truly extraordinary vitality. A few years ago, in order to thin out the heavy traffic on the course, the club built a new nine-hole course, designed by John Harris, an able English architect. Counting both regular and affiliated members, over six hundred and fifty golfers at present belong to the club. The annual dues for all mem-

bers are around thirty dollars. (The green fee for visitors is also shockingly low—a little under two dollars on weekdays. and a little over on weekends—and since Lahinch is only thirty miles north of Shannon Airport, it is hardly surprising that the club does the briskest transient business of any in Ireland except for Portmarnock.) The old clubhouse was also enlarged not long ago, by the addition of a spectacularly modern wing, all glass and highly polished wood. When a visitor is taking his ease in the new wing, it is hard for him to realize that he is in Ireland until he notices that the barometer on the wall in the bar is broken and that taped to it is a note that reads, "See Goats." He learns, on inquiry, that three ancient goats who are allowed the freedom of the links head for the clubhouse the moment they sense that rain is coming, and huddle against the building until it is over. They have proved to be such reliable weather prophets that the club officers long ago concluded that repairing the barometer would be economically redundant. Instead, they voted to change the club emblem, adding to the original motif, which was a shamrock and a thistle, a goat rampant.

—April 1, 1971

~

Ben Crenshaw and The Country Club

OF THE MANY PEOPLE who helped Ben Crenshaw to attain the unique breadth of his knowledge of golf, two men stand out. One was Harvey Penick, who quickly understood that the young Crenshaw boy preferred to learn golf by playing it rather than spending sedulous hours on the practice tee....

The other man who helped Crenshaw to comprehend and enjoy the full scope of golf was his father, Charles Edward Crenshaw IV. When Ben was thirteen, the elder Crenshaw gave him Charles

Price's wide-ranging "The World of Golf" to read, having just finished reading it himself. Ben had no idea until he got into the book that golf was as old as it was.... He was entranced by its gradual development in Scotland and its progress from the feather ball to the gutta-percha ball and then to the modern rubber-core ball. He and his father took turns reading the book to each other, and this really laid the basis for Crenshaw's exceptional interest in golf throughout the world and in all its phases.

In 1968, Mr. Crenshaw, noting that the United States Golf Association would be holding the national junior championship in midsummer at The Country Club, in Brookline, Massachusetts, decided that it would be an excellent idea for Ben to play in it. Through reading and re-reading "The World of Golf," they were well aware that in the game's long history few rounds could compare in drama and importance with those which had been played at The Country Club in the 1913 U.S. Open, when Francis Ouimet, a twenty-year-old ex-caddie, first tied the famous English professionals Harry Vardon and Ted Ray and then, on the following day, went out in the rain and defeated them soundly in the playoff. The senior Crenshaw thought that it would be both educational and enjoyable for him and Ben to see that renowned home of golf, and Ben duly sent in his entry form to the USGA.

"I had been to St. Louis as a boy, but this was my first trip up East," Crenshaw told some friends not long ago. "The Country Club made a tremendous impression on me. That yellow wooden clubhouse on the oval driveway was so handsomely spread out under those big old trees. There was a fine atmosphere about the club. The people dressed properly.

Ben Crenshaw, shown here playing in the 1968 U.S. Junior Amateur at The Country Club, later called it "one wondrous week [in which] golf history, architecture, and big-time competition hit me over the head."

There was nothing fancy about the food, but it tasted unusually good. And that wonderful course—it far surpassed my expectations. I'd never played on bent-grass fairways before or putted on real bent greens. The greens were faster than the ones I was used to and much smoother. There was no excuse for failing to putt them well. Those bent fairways were so beautiful I was scared to take a divot. I was struck by the variety of holes.... I had never seen comparable natural relief in a course—such rolling fairways, such deep bunkers, such shallow greens, like the one on the seventeenth hole, which Francis Ouimet birdied on the last regular round and again in the playoff. Francis's winning the Open was such a romantic story that walking over the course where he had played his memorable rounds was a little like visiting the Alamo for the first time if you were in the least historically inclined. Thank goodness, I played pretty good golf and got to stay around a few days. There were two qualifying rounds, and then the match play began. I won my first two matches but lost in the quarter-finals. I got beaten on the last green by Larry Griffin, the New Orleans junior champion. I think I was a shot or two over par. I loved everything about the trip East. The climate was so different—when you got up in the morning, you had to wear a sweater. It was a perfect place to play your first national championship. While we were there my father and I saw a Red Sox game at Fenway Park, and we took two historical tours—the Freedom Trail tour and the Liberty Trail tour. We made the most of our trip."

—*June 10, 1985*

~

The Last Days of Bobby Jones

ALMOST INVARIABLY when the subject of Bob Jones's sportsmanship comes up in a discussion, someone will mention how he twice called penalty strokes on himself in our Open—once in the second round of the 1925 championship, at the Worcester Country Club, in Massachusetts, when, after he had addressed the ball, it moved slightly in high grass as he was preparing to play a recovery from the rough on the eleventh hole, and once in the second round the next year, at Scioto, in Columbus, Ohio, when his ball moved the tiniest fraction as he was addressing it with his putter on the fifteenth green. Both times, no one else saw his ball move. In 1926, as it happened, Jones went on to win the Open, but in 1925 he finished in a tie for first with Willie MacFarlane, to whom he subsequently lost in an extended playoff, so it is often argued that the penalty stroke Jones called on himself cost him the championship.

> "We were lucky we had Jones so long, for he had a rare gift for passing ideas and ideals on to other people."

Maybe yes and maybe no. One can't alter one fact and presume that all the others would have remained unchanged. In any event I think there is a certain danger of missing the point about Jones's sportsmanship if one places the primary emphasis on those two instances. They are better viewed, I believe, as dramatic examples of Jones's tenet that there is only one way to play golf, and that is by the rules. . . .

In the nineteen-sixties, when Jones was confined to a wheelchair, the word went round each winter that his condition had become worse, and everyone in golf speculated on whether he would be able to attend that year's Masters. He had suffered from heart trouble since 1952, and now that, too, became increasingly debilitating. Somehow he got to Augusta each April, though by then his body had so wasted away that he weighed scarcely ninety pounds. His arms were no bigger around than a broomstick, and he could no longer open his fingers to shake hands or grasp a pen. Yet this indomitable man kept going. For many years on the day before the start of the Masters, I called in on him in company with Ed Miles, of the *Atlanta Journal*, and Al Laney, of the *New York Herald Tribune*, who was one of his oldest and closest friends. We would walk over to Jones's cottage, near the tenth tee, torn by mixed feelings—the prospect of pleasure and the prospect of sorrow. Mrs. Jones or their son Bob or his wife, Frances, would be there to greet us. There would be a few cordially jumbled minutes during which personal news was exchanged and it was computed how many people wanted Coca-Cola and whether they wanted it in a glass or a bottle. By this time, Jones would have appeared and would be contriving a seating arrangement that enabled him to see everyone. He never looked as bad as you dreaded he might. While his body had withered to nothing, his handsome head and features had remained relatively untouched, and his mind was as good as ever. We would ask him all sorts of questions we had stored up about new golfers and old tournaments, and he would answer them with amusement and flair. You could listen to him all day. He had the same feeling for words as Adlai Stevenson, and the same wonderful self-deprecatory sense of humor. Inevitably, as the session continued you became aware that you and your friends were doing all the talking—telling Jones what you had been up to and what you thought about this and that. Jones did not bring this about by any conscious technique; he simply was extremely interested in what his friends were doing, and you felt this interest. Leaving was always hard. When he put his twisted, folded-up hand in yours as you said goodbye, you never knew whether you would be seeing him again. Each year when Miles and Laney and I left the cottage, we would walk seventy-five yards

Riding in an early golf cart, brand name "Autoette," Bobby Jones watched the Walker Cup matches unfold at The Kittansett Club in 1953, with W. Myron Owen of New Bedford.

or so—nearly to the practice green—before we exchanged a word. My God, we felt good at that moment! We were so proud of Bob Jones! There was no need to feel sorry for a man like that. If he could rise above his misfortune, you could jolly well rise above his misfortune. I think that everyone who called on him responded this way....

While I gather from medical authorities that it would be wrong to credit Jones with living on for years after the average person would have picked up his ball and torn up his scorecard—how long anyone lives is not necessarily dictated by his will to live, they say—Jones deserves incalculable credit for how he lived out his life. Where he got the courage and energy to do all that he did there is no knowing. However, I think that Hogan put his finger on at least a part of the answer when he said, shortly after Jones's death, "The man was sick so long, and fought it so successfully, that I think we have finally discovered the secret of Jones's success. It was the strength of his mind." About three days before Jones's death, when he knew he was dying, he said to the members of his family, "If this is all there is to it, it sure is peaceful." That is good to know. We were lucky we had Jones so long, for he had a rare gift for passing ideas and ideals on to other people. I think he probably enriched more lives than anyone else I have known. He enriched mine beyond measure.

—*April 29, 1972*

V. BY THE SEA

With its rolling terrain, sandy soils and relatively benign climate, the archipelago of Cape Cod, along with its offshore neighbors, Nantucket and Martha's Vineyard, would constitute, by most measures, a golf course architect's dream. However, it was not until the last decades of the 20th century that the area truly came into its own as a golfing destination of national renown. Early implantations of the game, such as Cummaquid Golf Club and Highland Golf Links in North Truro, have survived, and some of the Cape's acknowledged masterpieces, like Hyannisport Club, Eastward Ho! and Oyster Harbors, date from the early days as well, but new golf course construction ground to a halt during the period from World War II to the 1960s. Growth in both the transient and permanent population in the area triggered a golf boom, and today the more than 50 golf courses on the Cape and Islands—the largest concentration of golf facilities north of the Mason-Dixon line—host two million rounds a year. Some say that the boom is only beginning.

Highland Golf Links, North Truro, Massachusetts

STYLE AND SUBSTANCE

~

Historic Oyster Harbors captures the sophistication
and wistful beauty of golf on Cape Cod.

IT WAS ONE of the first golf-centered planned communities in the country, the vision of a Boston real estate developer with the oddly rhyming name of Forris W. Norris. In 1925 Norris, with the help of a few backers, paid $500,000 for a 600-acre wilderness island on Nantucket Sound, between Hyannis and Falmouth on Cape Cod. In fewer than three years, he transformed it into a resort complete with roads, utilities, stylish Cape Cod Colonial houses and cottages and a golf course designed by Donald Ross.

Called Oyster Harbors, the complex was described in Norris' first sales brochure as "the wonder colony of Cape Cod—not a real estate development, but a private residential park, sharing its manifold advantages with all who lived within its confines." In keeping with the park theme, Norris had hired the Olmsted brothers—the redoubtable landscape architects who designed Central Park in New York and the Back Bay Fens in Boston—to plan roads and home sites for Oyster Harbors and to approve all plans for new houses to be built there. The Cape Cod vernacular was ascendant: no flat roofs, no more than three stories, no oversized outbuildings.

Donald Ross, operating out of his summer home office in Newton Centre, had by this time quietly established a reputation as a golf architect of the first rank, and Norris gave him carte blanche to build a course for Oyster Harbors. Actually there was one caveat. Because the golf course was to be the centerpiece of the selling effort, it had to be built swiftly. The construction project was described in some detail in a history of Oyster Harbors published in 1993, thanks to the input of John R. Blackinton, who became Ross's stepson in 1926 and actually worked on the course. Blackinton's testimony cast light on the arduous nature of golf course construction in the early part of the 20th century:

"The heavily wooded site was cleared in the fall of 1925. An estimated 800,000 trees were removed from the 140 acres set aside for the course. Crews cut trees, pulled stumps and then wielded grub hoes for clean-up. Large stumps were dynamited. A horse-drawn disc harrow was used to level the ground, and then the greens and traps were located. That Oyster Harbors might have the finest fairways and greens, a farm in West Barnstable, nine miles away, was purchased and 37,000 yards of loam were transported to the site by truck. Cow manure was shipped in from Maine

Opposite: The 6th hole at Oyster Harbors, a 400-yard dogleg left, is the No. 1 handicap hole on the course, and reputedly a favorite of the course designer, Donald Ross. Inset: A china pattern from the early 20th century bears the club's familiar emblem.

View from behind the green of the finishing hole at Oyster Harbors, a 420-yard par-4. *Opposite, clockwise from top:* Teeing off on the par-3 5th hole, 198 yards long, against a backdrop of June-flowering rhododendron; windmill belonging to a private home, overlooking tee box on No. 9; the club's distinctive hole identification; the Oyster Harbors practice range with its infinite supply of ammunition.

WATER DOG

6

390 YDS

PAR 4

HDCP 1

Oyster Harbors' elegant clubhouse was designed by Boston architect Royal Barry Wills, a renowned practitioner of the Cape Cod architectural style. *Inset:* Notable Oyster Harbors trophies include the Governor's Cup for the club four-ball championship and the Mrs. William H. Danforth Trophy, won 16 times by Patricia A. Lynch beginning in 1976.

to West Barnstable in 30 or 40 freight gondolas. It was then loaded by hand from gondolas to trucks and taken to the golf course where eight manure spreaders took two weeks to spread it. At the height of activity, 348 men were engaged, assisted by 96 horses, six tractors, two steam shovels, 42 trucks, two tree pullers and a steamroller."

Many years after this Herculean effort, with most building lots surrounding the golf course sold, Oyster Harbors became what it is today, an exclusive private community inaccessible to the general public, but in its first decades, it was ever in the public eye. A great deal of promotional effort was expended to attract visitors—potential buyers of land—to the island, and the golf course was used as the main draw. Players like Walter Hagen, Horton Smith, Gene

Sarazen, Babe Didrickson and trick-shot artist Joe Kirkwood came to Oyster Harbors in response to invitations or as part of commercialized promotions.

Oyster Harbors also welcomed the publicity that came with hosting the Massachusetts Open seven

times from 1932 to 1942. In those years, the state open championship was on a par with most of the stops on the nation's fledgling pro tour and it attracted strong fields, which in turn brought in large galleries. As it happened, a lifelong amateur, Francis Ouimet, won the first of those state titles staged in Osterville.

Golf tournaments for duffers were also held to attract visitors who came and stayed at the Oyster Harbors Club. The original clubhouse, functioning as a summer resort hotel, could accommodate more than 100 guests. Special package trips with group discounts were offered through upscale realtors in the region. Owners often rented their homes for part or all of the season with the help of Forris Norris' real estate manager—which introduced the "colony" to more potential buyers.

William H. Danforth, Sr., one of the early investors, attracted a coterie of players to the club, including Francis Ouimet, Johnny Fischer, "Trailer Bill" Holt and *Boston Transcript* golf writer A. Linde Fowler.

Aspiring tour player Ken Venturi also received encouragement from Danforth and returned the favor by playing at Oyster Harbors. On a visit here on August 23, 1959, Venturi went so far as to set a course record of 65, handing in a scorecard that consisted of eleven 4's and seven 3's.

The Oyster Harbors project was a brilliant real estate marketing scheme and it succeeded, in spite of bumps in the road like the Great Depression of the 1930s, the devastating hurricanes of 1938 and 1944, and the threat of a commercial takeover of the island by the likes of Howard Johnson's and the Ramada Inn in the 1960s. In the last-named crisis, when the club had fallen on shaky times economically, homeowner Paul Mellon came to the rescue by buying up stock in the Oyster Harbors corporation, then leasing and eventually selling the club, course and a few house lots to a newly constituted entity, a move which ensured that Oyster Harbors would survive as a private golf club indefinitely.

The green of the 355-yard par-4 9th hole is in plain view from the club's dining room.

CIVIC VENTURES

INTO GOLF

~

*The success of The Captains, a full-service
36-hole complex in Brewster, and Cranberry Valley, in Harwich, signaled
an encouraging new direction in public golf in Massachusetts.*

IN HIS ESTIMABLE *Complete Guide to Golf on Cape Cod, Boston Globe* golf writer Paul Harber tells the story of the hairdresser who changed the course of public golf in the mid-Cape town of Brewster. One day back in the early 1980s, while cutting hair at her beauty salon, Leona Leary heard about a proposed development of 150 house lots on a tract of scrubby woodland in town. An avid golfer, Leona only the day before had been frustrated in her efforts to get a tee time at Brewster's only public course, a crowded nine-holer unable to keep up with the population's fast-growing appetite for golf. She decided to collect signatures for a petition urging the town to build a full-length golf course on the parcel of land, rather than to burden Brewster with "another 150 toilets flushing," as she put it, "another

150 youngsters in our overpacked schools."

After some initial resistance, Brewster passed a $2 million bond issue, then hired Brian Silva of the Uxbridge-based design firm of Cornish, Silva and Mungeam to create an 18-hole course on 167 acres just off Route 6. The Captains was the first solo effort for Silva, a Massachusetts native and a graduate of the University of Massachusetts turf-grass program at Amherst, who has since acquired a national reputation as a golf architect of the first rank. The first public course on the Cape to be planted with bentgrass tees, greens and fairways opened to widespread praise in 1985, *Golf Digest* naming it the Best New Public Course in the country, and golfers flocked to it.

"It was a great way for the town to maintain open space, and it made for good public relations," said Silva. "Plus, it made money for the town the first year it was open." In fact, the new course was so successful the town acquired an adjoining parcel of rolling, windswept dunesland marked by dramatic elevation changes and commissioned Silva to build an additional 18 holes. "The new acreage was more

Opposite: The finishing hole at Cranberry Valley is a rugged double-dogleg par-5 playing to 584 yards from the gold tees. **Above:** A visiting Japanese golfer takes time to record a golf vista for the photo album; about 35 percent of daily-fee golfers at Cranberry Valley are out-of-towners.

Cranberry Valley Golf Association strong man Tidal B. Henry, Jr., right, confers with starter/ranger Bill Burke as a club tournament gets under way.

'active' in that it had more up-and-down topography, so we decided to blend some of that into the first layout," Silva recalled. "It happened that four holes began and finished near the clubhouse on that layout, so re-routing really wasn't a problem."

The new and revised courses opened in 1998 as The Port, with 10 of the new holes, and The Starboard, with eight of the new holes, complete with a $1 million clubhouse and golf shop. Holes were named in honor of the sea captains who had made Brewster their home port two centuries ago.

Other municipalities had built golf courses on the Cape long before Brewster got into the business. The Town of Dennis opened Dennis Pines in 1965. Twenty years later, the town built a second public course, Dennis Highlands, using revenue from Dennis Pines to carry most of the debt service for the new construction. Other towns, including Yarmouth, Chatham and Barnstable, have also gotten into the act. Instead of building a course, the Town of Chatham purchased an existing layout, the course belonging to the Chatham Bars Inn, and made it a public course named The Seaside Links of Chatham.

The result of all this growth is that only Myrtle Beach, South Carolina, and Wilmington, North Carolina, can boast more public golf courses per capita than Cape Cod. (When the more than 50 golf courses on the Cape are taken into account,

No. 11 at Cranberry Valley is a 351-yard par-4, a dogleg right to a green protected by bunkers in front and on the right.

Playing No. 17 on Port at The Captains, a father and son are joined by a canine version of a slow-play marshal.

profit-making aspect of the golf course in order to get the votes of the non golfers in town. They succeeded and the course was built for the relatively modest sum of $780,000.

A Geoffrey Cornish/William Robinson design, Cranberry Valley opened in 1974 and was soon ranked among the Top 75 Public Golf Courses in America by *Golf Digest.* "It's a very challenging course, but enjoyable to play because it does not totally brutalize you and there are no repeat holes," observed director of golf Dennis Hoye. With larger-than-normal tees and greens, the course wanders through woods, marshes and the cranberry bogs for which it is named. There are seven dogleg holes, including the double-dogleg 18th, at 584 yards from the gold tees a very testing finishing hole. "Actually, the gold tees are removed for normal play," noted Hoye.

The course is kept in remarkably good condition considering it supports 55,000–60,000 rounds a year. "To handle that much traffic, we had to increase the number of top dressing and aeration programs," said Hoye. "We'll aerate as many as seven times during the season, but most of the members understand it is for the good of the course."

With more than 1,600 members paying annual dues of $420, and non-members, who represent about half the total number of golfers, paying $55 in green fees, the course has paid for itself every year and has handed over as much as $600,000 in profits. With everyone— golfer and non-golfer— now happy among the local citizenry, Cranberry Valley was poised in 2002 to finally build what it had so long been denied—an honest-to-goodness clubhouse.

the area's per capita golf count rivals the entire state of Florida.)

As for The Captains, it set a new standard for public golf with its esthetically pleasing design, impeccable playing conditions and pre- and post-round amenities. It was as good as if not better than many a private club.

And "business" was the operative word for the venture. In most years since the 36-hole complex opened, after all expenses have been deducted, The Captains facility has poured more than $500,000 into the town's coffers. Cranberry Valley, an 18-hole course in neighboring Harwich, is just as lucrative for its township. But it was many years before Cranberry Valley got off the ground.

"In the late 1960s when the golf course project was first presented to the townspeople, it failed to pass several times," recalled Tidal B. Henry, Jr., a past president of the Cranberry Valley Golf Association. "The biggest problem seemed to center around the idea of a 'clubhouse' and the feeling in town that the taxpayer was building and would have to maintain a 'country club' for the small number of the town's golfing citizens."

It was not until 1973 that the project gained approval. At that time advocates studiously avoided using the word, "clubhouse," speaking of a "pro shop" instead, and they also stressed heavily the

Opposite, clockwise from top left: **Headgear for the home team; nautically inspired tee markers, with each hole at The Captains named for a sea captain from Brewster's storied maritime past; two par-5s on the Port course, including one with water challenging the approach shot; the 2nd hole on Starboard, a spectacular 162-yard par-3.**

LINKS TO THE PAST

~

*One of the Cape's oldest and most venerated courses, Hyannisport Club,
has been blowing golfers' minds, and scores, since it was laid out — by a man
who never played golf in his life.*

"IT WAS A FRIDAY IN EARLY APRIL and I was lying on a beach in Nassau, sipping a Bahama Mama and soaking in the sun. The following morning, at exactly 7 a.m., I was standing on the first tee at Hyannisport, not having touched a club since the previous October, and I was getting snowed on. And my question to myself was, 'What am I doing here?'"

Robert "Sandy" Dowling III, a former club champion at Hyannisport, was recalling the last time he participated in the Seagulls Four-Ball, an annual spring fixture since 1951, one almost always accompanied by "godawful weather," in the words of head professional Rick Johnson.

"We get the conditions that tend to come through here toward the end of winter," Johnson added. "A few years ago it was so cold and snowy, we just had to cancel the championship final." In the event, two-man teams play an 18-hole qualifier on the first day, then compete at match play through seven flights of 16 over the following week, using their gross better-ball scores. Despite the often brutal weather, the Seagulls is oversubscribed by 20 to 40 teams every year, a fact which speaks to the hardiness of the Cape Cod golfer in general and the Hyannisport variety in particular.

The Seagulls was started by club member G. Winthrop Moore, in whose memory the tournament scoreboard is named. Moore was a local auto dealer with so much enthusiasm for the game that he would sponsor area professionals on what was known as the winter tour in the 1940s and 1950s. Bill Ezinicki, the hockey star turned golf pro, was one of his protégés. His daughter, Connie, married Jay Tracy, another longtime member at Hyannisport. Tracy, Dowling and Dowling's father, Robert Dowling, Jr., all served on the executive committee of the Massachusetts Golf Association. Sandy Dowling was MGA president in 1990–1991.

"Hyannisport is similar to Kittansett in that it blows like the devil most of the time, and when the wind shifts, the nines play quite differently," said Dowling. The prevailing winds off Nantucket Sound are from the southwest, but at times the wind comes from the north. Westerly winds make the course uniformly harder because they create crosswinds on

Opposite, at top: Hyannisport's 15th hole is a downhill par-3 stretching to 177 yards. *Bottom:* During a practice round, a local high school team comes onto the 141-yard par-3 17th green, reachable, depending on the wind, with anything from a wedge to a 2-iron. *Inset:* Live rabbit squares off with a quail tee marker.

every hole. "Another unique thing, you can see water from every hole on the course, and from the elevation of the clubhouse, you can see a portion of every hole—so if someone is looking for you, there's no place to hide."

Hyannisport was first laid out as a nine-hole course in 1908 by Alex Findlay. In 1936, the club hired Donald Ross to re-design the existing layout and add a second nine. Ross drew up a preliminary routing plan but withdrew from the project when the club decided it could not afford his services. Frank Paine, a founding member and for 25 years the club president, took on the job himself, using some of the routing proposed by Ross. Self-trained as an architect, Paine was one of New England's most esteemed designers of colonial buildings. Although it begs disbelief, Paine was not even a golfer, yet he had the ability to grade land to any contour and to

interpret any specification. Effectively, he read Ross into the Hyannisport site.

If the Seagulls ushers in the season on the Cape, the Cape Cod Amateur, also played at Hyannisport since 1951, ushers it out. Staged at the end of October, it too is "a hardcore event," according to Johnson, with unpredictable winds and weather the norm, but the field is much smaller than the spring event, with 32 players qualifying for the championship, and 16 for the senior title. Jim Hallett, who grew up a mile away from Bass River Golf Course and played at Dennis Pines as a youngster, won the Cape Cod Amateur four times. (Hallett's father, Ollie, won the Seagulls with various

Clockwise from bottom left:
The 10th hole at Hyannisport, with marshes in background; No. 5, a 176-yard uphill par-3; an uninvited foursome on one of the greens bordering marshes. **Inset:** A sign along the 9th hole in behalf of wildlife more welcome on the course than Canada geese.

partners four times over four decades.)

Speaking of champions at Hyannisport, Bob Toski won the 1958 Massachusetts Open here in dramatic fashion. Trailing seven other players by as much as six strokes with 18 holes to play, he turned loose a 32-34— 66 to edge Bob Crowley of Pine Brook Country Club in Weston by one shot.

More than four decades later, the native of Haydenville vividly recalled the victory. "I had to make a sweeping, fast-breaking putt of about 15 feet on the 18th green to avoid a playoff," Toski said. "Lining up the putt, I remember seeing Bob Crowley standing at the back of the green. He had already finished and he had an expression on his face that said, 'Well,

In the early 1960s, Hyannisport was the home club of President John F. Kennedy, but he rarely played, and even more rarely allowed photographers to take his picture. "It's true that my predecessor did not object as I do to pictures of one's golfing skills in action," he once wrote. "But neither, on the other hand, did he ever bean a Secret Service man." *Opposite page:* The 3rd hole is a 354-yard dogleg left requiring an accurate approach shot to avoid the marshes on all sides. Most of the greens at Hyannisport are quite small, firm and fast.

Tosk, chances are we're going to be in a playoff or, who knows, you might even three-putt.' In fact, three-putting was a distinct possibility, so all I was trying to do was lag the putt, hoping it would wind up no more than three or four feet below the hole, giving me a chance to make par. I would say the odds were 50-1 against making the birdie, but I did, and I immediately looked over to where Crowley had been standing. He was gone. When I saw him later in the locker room, he looked shell-shocked.

"I don't ever remember making a putt of quite that magnitude," Toski added. "I'd played in the state open a number of times but had not succeeded, so it meant a great deal to me to win, and to have my name on a trophy with so many great champions."

Toski's three older brothers, Jack, Ben and Tom, were all golf professionals. Starting when he was 10 years old, Bob worked as a caddie for them at Leeds Country Club, a nine-hole course outside of Northampton. After finishing military service in 1945, Toski himself turned professional. He became one of the top players on the pro tour in the early 1950s and was the leading money winner in 1954, when he won George S. May's World Championship and a record first-place purse of $50,000. He went on to even greater fame as one of the pre-eminent teachers in the game, helping to develop *Golf Digest*'s instruction schools and authoring numerous instruction books. In spite of his commitment to teaching, Toski never lost his taste for competition, winning five titles on the senior tour in the late 1980s and early 1990s. In 1997, at age 70, he became the oldest qualifier ever in the U.S. Senior Open.

It was about the time of Toski's triumph at Hyannisport that the "Kennedy Compound" came into being just a few blocks from the club, when both John F. Kennedy and Robert Kennedy bought cottages near the family's summer home on Marchant Avenue, which Joseph P. and Rose Kennedy had purchased in 1927. The nine Kennedy children and their various cousins had spent summers in Hyannisport, learning to sail, swim and play golf and tennis. Ambassador Kennedy reportedly had been blackballed by the "Yankee membership" at a country club on the South Shore, but the businessmen who belonged to Hyannisport, some of whom had been helped by the elder Kennedy through hard economic times, made him and his family welcome.

"I remember seeing Rose Kennedy out on the course on several occasions," recalled Sandy Dowling. "She'd carry an old canvas bag with five or six clubs in it and would keep three or four balls in play. If a group came up behind her, she'd quickly gather up her balls, hurry off the fairway and let them play through."

BY THE LIGHT
OF SANKATY HEAD

~

Founded by a man for whom capitalism came naturally,
Sankaty Head Golf Club on Nantucket has more recently spawned a summer camp
program that teaches boys sound values for business and pleasure.

GOLF FIRST CAME to Nantucket in 1897 when nine holes were laid out near present-day Wannacomet on the western side of the island. Less than a year later, another nine holes graced the rolling landscape north of the village of Siasconset (pronounced Sconset) on the more sparsely settled eastern side of the island. Called the Sankaty Golf Club of the Siasconset Moors, this course faded from active use in the first decade of the new century.

Sankaty Golf Club was resurrected by David Gray of Detroit, Michigan, in 1921, a man with the means to do such a thing. David's father, John Gray, a native of Edinburgh, Scotland, had come to America with his family in 1849, at the age of eight. By the end of the century, he had become an investor in a number of small Detroit-area manufacturing businesses. According to Sankaty Head historian Paul R. Rudy, John Gray was known to possess "a rare combination of push and conservatism" and he "knew the merit of economy as an adjunct to the spirit of enterprise."

In 1903, John Gray's nephew Alex Malcolmson had become deeply overextended as a result of financing an eccentric inventor. Despite obvious risk, John Gray invested $10,500 in the nephew's enterprise, and was elected president. On his death three years later, the value of Gray's investment in the Ford Motor Company had already reached a startling multiple of cost. When John Gray died, David became a director of Ford. By 1919, when Ford redeemed the company's shares held by John Gray's estate, the original investment of $10,500 had generated, through various avenues, in excess of $35 million.

In 1921, David Gray could well afford to indulge in his expansive vision for bringing Sankaty Head Golf Club back to life, and in fact personally donated 280 acres and a clubhouse for the fledgling club.

He approached three-time U.S. Amateur champion Walter J. Travis to lay out the course, but deemed his $3,000 design fee too high and turned

Inset: Teeing off under the vigilant eye of Nantucket's Sankaty Head Lighthouse, a beacon visible from many locations on the golf course. **Opposite:** The 15th hole is a 396-yard dogleg-right par-4, called 'Light Ahoy' on the scorecard.

to H. Emerson Armstrong, an island dweller familiar with the proposed site and a fine amateur golfer in his own right. Supervising construction, Armstrong had the first nine holes ready for play in September of 1922. The second nine was completed the following year. Among a number of pioneering innovations, many of the greens were watered from wells equipped with electrically driven pumps.

"This is a simple course, and I hope that future grounds committees will leave it so," Gray stated in a newspaper interview in 1923, after Sankaty was already in play. "We want this whole club to be in keeping with 'Sconset: simple.' Why, down here you go along and come to a little piano-box of a cottage and see a man out front dressed in an old golf suit, and perhaps he is the president of the Southern Pacific; but you'd never know it to look at him."

Although the Great Depression eroded the wealth of many of the barons of industry on the island—Armstrong himself lost his cottage to fore-closure—Nantucket re-gentrified itself yet again in the years following World War II. By the end of the 20th century, Sankaty Head claimed members who were among America's most influential business leaders, such as Jack Welch and John Akers, the former longtime CEOs, respectively, of General Electric and IBM.

The same individuals have been among the most ardent supporters of Camp Sankaty Head which operates out of a compound of cabins and berthing huts on golf club property. The camp began in the 1930s to provide jobs for young men cast out of work by the Depression, but it has since evolved into a non-profit summer camp offering boys aged 14 to 18 a chance to participate in a unique resident camping experience, one designed in part to bring out the budding capitalist in every youth.

"We teach the campers money management by having them open bank accounts, which are supervised," explained camp director Doug Ellsworth, who brings 39 years of teaching experience in the public schools of West Orange, New Jersey, to the task of running the camp. "Fees and tips earned by caddieing are credited to the camp account of the individual camper. Many of them save a good amount, perhaps several thousand dollars, by the end of the 10-week program." In addition to money management, Ellsworth noted, campers are encouraged to develop the virtues of responsibility, honesty, integrity and industry.

Some of the campers develop friendships with the members they caddie for over the summer and these contacts sometimes extend well beyond camp days. "Some members have tremendous business experience as well as a natural capacity for mentoring," said Ellsworth. "Kids have been helped into graduate school and landed jobs through these channels."

Besides caddieing, campers participate in a wide variety of group and individual athletic programs. A popular banquet at summer's end honors achievement in both sports and academics. By emphasizing a sense of responsibility to the club membership, as well as devotion to team and camp internal unity, the camp nurtures group and individual loyalties.

A total of 70 campers, including older boys who serve in staff positions, lived and worked at Sankaty Head in the summer of 2001. Over the years about half the campers have come from Massachusetts and the other half from just about every other state as well as foreign countries. A percentage of the campers are given scholarships based on need. In addition, campers are eligible for scholarship money for high school and college expenses. In 2001, the non-profit foundation which oversees the camp handed out $92,000 in financial aid to the campers who qualified through a process of essay-writing, grade reviews and interviews.

With almost two-thirds of the campers returning each season, there are never many open spots. "Believe me, we don't have to advertise," said Ellsworth. "The program is so successful, word of mouth is all we need."

Opposite, clockwise from top left: Redtail hawk coming in for a landing on No. 17; view of the long 5th hole from the 6th tee at Sankaty Head; playing through fog, a not uncommon phenomenon on Nantucket; inside the clubhouse, a distinctive record of winners in a popular team event. *Following pages:* The par-4 16th, a dog-leg-right stretching to 392 yards, named 'Round the Horn.'

Camp Sankaty Head

A unique summer experience for young men 14 to 18 years of age has emerged on Nantucket as a 21st-century version of the Bay State's caddie programs of old, with a capitalist twist.

Opposite page, clockwise from top left: Campers in relaxation mode, waiting for a loop; tribute to Charles M. Goetz, a prominent Washington, D.C., attorney and longtime club member, who created the legal basis for the caddie camp foundation; sequence of forecaddies at work, with happy result; a camper/caddie on the job on the 16th at Sankaty Head; another camper packing double, a more lucrative task and the special province of the more senior camp members — all campers are required to develop financial management skills through control of earned money.

This page, clockwise from top left: The camp compound, situated between two fairways at Sankaty Head, including three bunkhouse-style buildings erected in 1995, where 60 of the 70 campers reside; the quasi-military routine of morning roll call, featuring campers in varying states of alertness; polishing the ship's bell, which sounds at 8:10 a.m. sharp every day; senior camper making inspection rounds along with the day's work assignments for each youth.

TILL LAND DO US PART

~

The site of this Cape Cod course, "an awesome spit of land buffeted by swirling winds on the shores of Pleasant Bay," is what puts the exclamation point in Eastward Ho!

COMBINING the rolling terrain and ocean setting of a links with the tree-lined fairways and raised greens of a heathlands course, Eastward Ho! poses a singular challenge to any golfer. In an exhibition match marking the formal opening of the course in 1922, the legendary Francis Ouimet could do no better than shoot 87, prompting him to declare it "the most difficult course I have ever played."

Located on a peninsula called Nickerson's Neck in Chatham, Eastward Ho! is wedged between the Atlantic Ocean on one side and the popular sailing venue of Pleasant Bay on the other. Winds are near constant and ever-changing and the convolutions of terrain present an extraordinary variety of sidehill, downhill and uphill lies. As *Boston Globe* columnist Paul Harber has observed, "This is one course where the elements beat you all the time."

Development of the site got off to something of a false start in 1890 when a group of investors from Boston, including Eben Marsh of Jordan Marsh, built a luxury hotel on the highest point of land, approx-

Not far from the No. 7 tee at Eastward Ho!, "casting from the top" takes on a whole new meaning. *Opposite:* With Pleasant Bay in the background, No. 6, a 405-yard par-4, drops sharply before rising to the green.

imately where the fourth green is located today. It was the last word in summer resorts, with 76 rooms, steam heat, a bathroom on every floor, bowling alleys and billiards rooms, tennis courts and, along the beach, a long line of bathhouses. But within three years the resort had folded for lack of public interest in the idea of vacationing on Cape Cod.

Subsequently, the property caught the eye of G. Herbert Windeler, the Boston insurance broker who had been instrumental in organizing the Massachusetts Golf Association, serving as its first president in 1903. Windeler and Charles Hardy, a Boston architect with family roots in Chatham dating back to the Revolution, formed a group to evaluate the possibilities of the site. They hired the Scottish champion Willie Park, Jr., to visit Chatham. When he reported that a course could be built "equal to, if not better than, any course this side or the other [of the Atlantic]," the Great Point Golf Club (named for the highest promontory, where the since demolished resort hotel had stood) was formed.

The English-born Windeler was a sportsman of renown whose pursuits included cricket, golf, riding, tennis and curling. W. Herbert Fowler, the Englishman he and the Great Point Golf Club hired to lay out their Chatham course, was of comparable stature in the sporting world. Born into an affluent family, Fowler was an outstanding cricket player in his youth, his 6'4" frame making him an intimidating opponent. He took up golf at the age of 35 and was soon playing at scratch. A barrister and banker by profession, he discovered an affinity for golf course architecture and soon had a reputation to equal Donald Ross, two of his most famous designs being Walton Heath in England and Westward Ho! in England. Eastward Ho! would be one of only four courses he designed from scratch in America.

Fowler had his first look at the Chatham site in 1920. According to Virginia Doherty's early history of the club, "the huge, dignified visitor" made a somewhat quixotic sight perched upon a polo pony (sent down from Myopia Hunt Club) as he somberly rode about the land, but Fowler was a firm believer in making an exhaustive study of any site to be transformed into a golf course. Placement of greens was of paramount importance to him.

"Layers-out of courses should, I think, strive more to get suitable places for the various greens than to get the holes any particular length," he wrote in an essay entitled "Links Architecture," published in 1907.

Opposite, at top: A golfer on the par-5, 467-yard 5th hole, after moonrise. *Below:* The par-3 4th hole, 167 yards long, may require a long iron off the tee if the wind is blowing in from Pleasant Bay.

"Much can be done by judicious placing of the tees to get the desired length, but if the greens are badly placed the result will be that the holes will never command the respect of the good golfer."

Fowler disliked blind shots, an irony not lost on Eastward Ho! golfers who, owing to the hilly terrain of Nickerson's Neck, face blind shots at almost every turn. Fowler also regarded cross hazards within 50 yards of a green as unfair. But he was a strong advocate of what he called side hazards in fairways and near greens. "As time goes on I believe golfers will as a body prefer courses which are well guarded," he wrote, "to those where the game is principally a question of holing out on the green."

It was Charles Hardy who turned Fowler's vision into reality. Hardy spent a number of months consulting with Fowler over the plans at Westward Ho! in England, and when work began on the Chatham links in 1921, Hardy took charge of the construction. When the course opened for play in 1922, the *Boston Herald* ran a full-page feature under the headline "Cape Cod's Wonder Links Opened Up for Play," and reported that some of the holes were "nothing short of majestic." In fact, the course was not considered close to completion at that time and work continued on it for years.

"Wonder links," though it was, Chatham Country Club, as it was called at the time, soon ran into financial difficulty. By 1927 there were only 75 members, one of whom, Roy E.

The Eastward Ho! clubhouse, which opened on July 5, 1930, is a clever amalgam of old structures moved to the site, including one local homestead formerly belonging to the Nickerson family, and a 1700s cottage brought intact from Acushnet.

Tomlinson, stepped forward to save the day. A Chicago native with family roots in New England dating from the mid-1600s, Tomlinson was president of National Biscuit Company. Summering in Chatham, he had grown so attached to the club and course that he bought the property for $75,000, thus keeping it out of bankruptcy, and a year later sold it back to the former members for what he had paid for it. Tomlinson served as first president of the newly constituted club, re-named Eastward Ho! Country Club, and remained influential in its affairs. He donated two oil paintings now hanging in the grill room to the club in 1958. *Captain Hunter,* a portrait of a Cape seaman in his oilskins, and *Obed Bassett,* a portrait of a hunter in the marshes, were executed by

Harold Brett, a noted artist and illustrator who himself served as club president from 1941 to 1945.

Symbolizing the club's resurgence, a pro-am exhibition match on August 9, 1929, featuring Jess Sweetser, Francis Ouimet, Johnny Farrell and Tom Kerrigan, drew nearly 400 spectators at $1 a head and produced a spectacular round of golf by Sweetser. Winner of both the U.S. and British Amateurs, Sweetser scored a 68, a record for the course that would not be beaten for the next 30 years. That record is commemorated by Harold Brett's painting of Sweetser on the 15th hole, also hanging in the grill room.

U.S. and British Amateur champion Jess Sweetser set a course record of 68 at Eastward Ho! when he played in a pro-am exhibition match as a benefit for Cape Cod Hospital on August 9, 1929. The painting now hanging in the club's grill room commemorates his feat; it was executed by Harold Brett, a former president of the club, and shows Sweetser teeing off on the 142-yard par-3 15th hole. *Inset:* The club's elegant monogram oversees the bar in the grill room.

Inside the clubhouse, a pair of oil portraits by Harold Brett pay tribute to figures distinctly of the region surrounding Eastward Ho!: *Obed Bassett*, a hunter in the marshes, shotgun at the ready, and *Captain Hunter*, a Cape seaman in his oilskins.

W. H. Fowler on Learning Golf

The English designer of Eastward Ho! had strong opinions on everything related to golf.

After playing golf for some years I came to the conclusion that golf is like billiards: if you want to get beyond a certain stage you must practice, and not be continually playing matches. . . . I am certain that no one can come to their best unless they go through a long period of practicing, or rather I should say learning, with all the different clubs, including the niblick [*equivalent of the 9-iron or wedge– Ed.*]. How often one sees quite a good player who has no idea of how to play the proper bunker shot, and how important it is, and yet you hardly ever see a man in a bunker learning how to get out. There is a great deal that the individual must find out for himself; but I am convinced of one thing, and that is that the player who cultivates a slow swing when beginning will never regret it. He will play quite as well when he is young, and he will retain his game for a far longer period than if he had begun as a quick swinger.

–From "Links Architecture"
   by W. Herbert Fowler, an essay published in
   Great Golfers in the Making, 1907

While much of Eastward Ho! plays in the open in traditional links style, a portion of the course inland from the sea is thick with the trees and other vegetation native to the interior sections of Cape Cod.

WALK ON THE WILD SIDE

~

Nantucket Golf Club offers a classic test of golf on windswept grassland and sand dunes, at the same time preserving open space and natural habitat on an island where the environment comes first.

GOLFERS and environmentalists have often been depicted as at odds with each other. "Many who practice the sport see environmentalists as tree-hugging fanatics unwilling to base their opinions on true science," observed one contributor to the Audubon Society's magazine in 1998. "Golfers in turn are stereotyped as uncaring elitists fixated on manicured fairways and oblivious to the effects of such artificial conditions on local birds and other wildlife."

While this dichotomy exists even in Massachusetts, one of the more environmentally sensitive states in the country, it has also been proven false on occasion. A case in point is Nantucket Golf Club on the southeast corner of Nantucket Island, adjacent to the town of Siasconset (pronounced Sconset). The course opened in 1998 to rave reviews both from golfers and environmentalists.

Designed by Rees Jones, it was cited as the best new private course of the year by *Golf Digest*. "Rather than isolate each hole with high mounds," Ron Whitten, the magazine's architectural editor, noted, "Jones let the natural humps and dips of the

Young caddies at Nantucket Golf Club learn the ropes by being paired with more experienced practitioners. *Opposite:* Sunset lends its glow to island landscapes, such as the green of the 6th hole, a 572-yard par-5.

land dictate the routing, so there are long-range views across adjoining fairways toward the coast to the south and a neighboring wildlife refuge to the north." *MassGolfer* magazine reported that the club "adds a world-class facility to the Bay State's already distinguished roster of golf gems." *Links* magazine pronounced the Nantucket course "golf's latest great walk, sweeping so gracefully from one hole to the next that you're liable to lose track of what hole you're playing." In fact, the 7,081-yard layout was designed to be walked, with tees close to previous greens, and no paved cart paths anywhere. To ride the course in one of the club's small fleet of golf carts, one must present medical evidence that walking isn't possible.

In order to build its masterpiece, the Nantucket club agreed to several conservation conditions, which in turn pleased environmentalists on an island where more than 40 percent of the land is already under protective covenants. Faced with the possibility of a real estate development on the site, the idea of a naturalistic golf course was attractive even to staunch open-space advocates.

"It really does a fabulous job of fitting into the

Apart from the clubhouse and adjacent guest cottages at Nantucket Golf Club, there are no buildings to distract from the natural beauty of a course laid out among island dunes, knolls and grasses. *Opposite:* **The 475-yard 15th hole, here seen from across waste bunkers along the 12th hole, features a range of cross bunkers that extend back from the green for 350 yards.**

landscape," said James Lentowski, executive secretary of the Nantucket Conservation Foundation. "On a continuum of choices, this certainly is a choice closer to the most desirable rather than the least desirable."

The club entered into an unusual arrangement with the Massachusetts Department of Fisheries and Wildlife to manage an 1,100-acre habitat for the endangered northern harrier hawk, also known as the marsh hawk, in partnership with the Nantucket Conservation Foundation and Massachusetts Audubon, both of which control portions of the land surrounding the golf course. The club will contribute $800,000 to this program alone over the next 50 years.

"The partnership between the club and state and local officials has been highly successful, and has become a model that is being used with other proposed golf course projects in Massachusetts," said golf course manager Mark Lucas. "We have been pleased by the research to date, which has shown that the harrier hawks are using the course to forage. And this is only the beginning, with more research and land management to come."

Nantucket's sand plain grassland has been slowly disappearing, overrun by scrub oak, a low-growing tangle of woody branches that's friendly to no one. The harrier hawk depends on the grassland habitat for food and nesting grounds. By removing the scrub

A view from behind the green at No. 11, a 416-yard par-4, on a moderately breezy day; the club logo at Nantucket is a flagstick, bowed by what seems like gale-force wind. Days when such conditions prevail are called "logo days" by members.

oak from areas and planting them with fescues and other grasses, the club and its partners have begun to resurrect an ecological niche for voles and moles, the food source for the hawks, and nesting pairs of the birds have already been identified not far from the course.

The club has also built a nursery to nurture and propagate several species of endangered plants, such as the St. Andrews cross and the bushy rock rose, and various grasses indigenous to the sand plain grassland. Lucas, calling the program "cutting edge for a golf facility," will re-introduce the plants into the grassland areas that are being restored. The deal between the state and the club calls for a total of 70 acres of grassland to be restored. Most of the grassland remaining in Massachusetts is found on Nantucket.

Rees Jones first gained national attention as a restorer of classic courses in connection with his work preparing the composite course at The Country Club in Brookline for the U.S. Open in 1988, but he is just as well known for his original designs. After graduating from Yale in 1963 with a B.A., and doing graduate work in landscape architecture at the Harvard School of Design, he joined the firm of his father, Robert Trent Jones, Sr., in his hometown of Montclair, New Jersey. He designed and built 25 courses before setting forth on his own in 1974.

In recent years he has designed a number of courses in coastal areas, including Ocean Forest in Sea Island, Georgia, and Atlantic Golf Club in Bridgehampton, New York. Those projects well prepared him for the task at Nantucket, where coastal breezes add a significant dimension to play. Most of the bunkers on the new course were built as old-fashioned flat-bottomed pits, with steep faces of grass, to keep the sand itself out of the wind. Most greens are simply extensions of the fairways, so running shots kept beneath the wind can hit and hold. Jones designed the course's longest two par-4s, the 471-yard 7th and the 475-yard 15th, to run in opposite directions so at least one would actually play like a par-4. The prevailing wind on the island comes from the southwest, but seldom stays that way for the length of a round, yet when the wind switches and comes from the north, the holes simply exchange their degree of difficulty.

"Rees and I talked about the responsibility we felt to the land out here," said course developer Fred Green, whose other projects have been the centerpieces of real estate developments. "We knew it had the potential to be one of the great golf clubs ever built in America, and it was a personal challenge to me to build a golf course like they did 80 or 90 years ago." Hummocks, knobs and other natural contours were accentuated by the relocation of some 350,000 cubic yards of earth.

"Nantucket is a throwback course," Rees Jones told *Golf Digest*. "It's an old-time, hands-on job, done with my own shaping crew. We used the site in its natural state, and I think we optimized it. I made probably 25 trips to the site. That's what it takes to get all the subtle details right.

"It's not designed to play the same every time," Jones added, "because of the wind. It provokes thought on every hole."

"The term 'links' is overused or misused when describing some courses," stated head golf professional Kevin Walker. "But there's no other description for this course. The holes look like they belong, and when you factor in the conditions and the elements, it's pure links. This course is just an absolute joy to play."

Nantucket's extensive practice facility includes a range, bunkers, target green and plenty of balls. *Below:* Downwind, the 387-yard par-4 17th hole might be negotiated by a better player with a 3-wood and 8-iron, but the approach still must carry the large, cloverleaf bunker.

Trouble in the Locker Room

~ BY JOHN P. MARQUAND ~

ETTER to Mr. Albert Magill, President Emeritus, from Mr. Roger Horlick, Board of Governors of the Happy Knoll Country Club.

DEAR ALBERT:

I have never known a golf season at the Happy Knoll Country Club when there have not been a number of complaints lodged before the Board of Governors regarding conditions in the men's locker room, and added to this, there are now complaints from the ladies' room as well. But the conditions in the men's locker room, I would say, are more social than physical. Unfortunately, the usual groups and juntas seem to be more at daggers drawn than usual and consequently it may be necessary to issue and enforce some new regulations.

There are, as always, the drinking and the non-drinking groups, or if you wish to put it in another way, the shower-and-change and the simple shoe-changing cliques. You would think that the shoe-changers, who pay as much for their lockers and who simply sit in front of them and take their spiked shoes off as rapidly as possible and then retire to the men's bar, where they can discuss their golfing difficulties in comparative comfort, would not be a source of trouble. Old Tim—who, I must say, is getting forgetful and seems even worse this year than last—has only to take the shoe-changers' shoes, clean them and place them beneath their lockers. Then his work is done. If the shoes are mixed up—for instance, as occasionally happens, one of Mr. Bentley's crepe shoes is found beside Mr. Robinson's spike shoe in Mr. Lockforth's locker, and both of them are lefts—you can count on a feeling of good fellowship and cooperation deriving from a genuine affection for Old Tim to straighten things out. Up to now this has all ended with a good-natured joshing of Old Tim, which Tim has grown to depend upon and enjoy, but the shoe-changers are making genuine trouble this year at Happy Knoll. Furthermore it seems that

ONE OF THIS COUNTRY'S premier novelists of manners, John Marquand was born in Wilmington, Delaware, in 1893 and lived most of his life in Curzon's Mill, Massachusetts. After graduating in 1915 from Harvard, where he majored in chemistry, Marquand worked briefly for the *Boston Transcript* before serving in the U.S. Army. His novels, many of them satiric depictions of upper-crust society in New England, and particularly Boston, included *Women and Thomas Harrow, Point of No Return,* and *The Late George Apley,* for which he won the Pulitzer Prize for fiction in 1938. *Life at Happy Knoll,* from which the following is excerpted, is Marquand's look at the life and times of a fictional country club in mid-20th-century America, told in the form of sometimes heated correspondence among several disgruntled members. First appearing in serial form in *Sports Illustrated* in 1955, *Life at Happy Knoll* is one of the last published works of the author, who died in 1960.

the shower-and-change group has also been growing more aggressive. The locker benches are becoming more and more filled with moist towels, moist undergarments and loose ice cubes, so that shoe-changers find it difficult to remove their footwear. We had hoped, as you well remember, that the generous gift to the locker room by H. S. Fosbroke of an attractive alcove with dark oak dressing stalls—officially known as the Fosbroke Alcove, and now called, I regret to say, the Fosbroke Boudoir—would obviate this difficulty. The shoe-changers, we had hoped, would all use the Fosbroke Alcove, which is much nearer the men's bar and would thus be separated from the more vociferous showerers. It has not worked out this way. It seems that the shoe-changers prefer benches in front of their lockers, as always. They insist that they are paying a high price for the use of these and several have insisted that the showerers and dressers use the Fosbroke Alcove and that a table be placed there with ice and set-ups. It would be no trouble, this element says, for the showerers to bring their bottles and flasks to the table, no matter what their nudity.

Superficially, this would seem like a worthwhile suggestion and it has always been my opinion that the bringing of private bottles into the locker room should be discouraged, since this practice cuts into the bar receipts; but there has been great objection to this move. It seems that most of the opposition centers around Old Ned who, you know, has been removed from the men's bar to the locker room this season. It gives Ned great happiness to circulate with trays of ice and soda, this being an activity which keeps him in touch simultaneously with his old friends in the bar and with his new friends near the showers, and there is no doubt that Old Ned is once

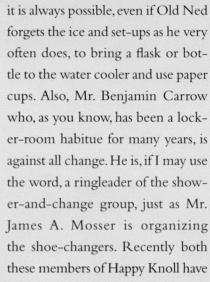

OLD TIM

more beginning to make himself indispensable. In an older day, when only glasses were available, the Fosbroke contingent might have moved to the Alcove, but with the two newly installed water coolers, this action is no longer necessary because it is always possible, even if Old Ned forgets the ice and set-ups as he very often does, to bring a flask or bottle to the water cooler and use paper cups. Also, Mr. Benjamin Carrow who, as you know, has been a locker-room habitue for many years, is against all change. He is, if I may use the word, a ringleader of the shower-and-change group, just as Mr. James A. Mosser is organizing the shoe-changers. Recently both these members of Happy Knoll have written communications to the Board of Governors, which throws this controversy fully into focus, and I am sending you copies for your information and guidance.

Sincerely,
Roger Horlick

Letter from Mr. James A. Mosser to the Board of Governors of the Happy Knoll Country Club.

GENTLEMEN:

By way of introduction I beg to state that for the last twenty-two years I have been both an active and an appreciative member of the Happy Knoll Country Club. This longish period of membership dates from my first arrival in this community when I purchased for Mrs. Mosser, then but recently a bride, our present home on Wedgewood Lane directly after I was made a junior partner in the New York law firm of Caulkins, Bryan and Russell of which there now seems a prospect that I may become a senior partner if I can keep my health and memory together for another decade. It was for this purpose that I first joined the Happy Knoll Country Club and why, in spite of certain difficulties and grievances, I have persisted, often against Mrs. Mosser's advice, in retaining my membership. I have always been a believer in that old motto —and I believe my Latin is correct —MENS SANA IN CORPORE SANO. After the daily exigencies of a law firm in downtown New York, I have found that relaxation is necessary. Because of our Northern climate and the fact that Mrs. Mosser does not enjoy a winter golfing vacation, bridge is my hobby until the grass grows green upon the course at Happy Knoll. When this fortunate event arrives, Mrs. Mosser notwithstanding, I am able to counterbalance cares of the office by resorting to the still greater worries of golf.

Frankly, in spite of the tutorial money which I have paid to our professional, Mr. Muldoon, I can not see that my game has improved perceptibly over the decades; but this, honestly, is not the point. The point is that I still hope it may improve, and therefore I play at the Happy Knoll Country Club on two weekday afternoons and on Saturday and Sunday mornings invariably, whether Mrs. Mosser may approve of it or not. For twenty-two years I have rented locker number 67 which stands nearest the aisle of Alcove C. I have never dominated this area. I have made but little noise. I have watched the personnel around me during my locker room life undergo considerable change. I am sorry to say that in recent years the change is growing more rapid and is declining toward the worse.

Each year more members appear to consider the alcoves between the steel lockers not as a dressing space for which they were intended, but rather as

OLD NED

informal lounging rooms in which they can sit indefinitely in a semidraped condition, retailing loud anecdotes of their last eighteen holes or settling the interminable details of their complicated gambling debts. This tendency has immeasurably increased since Old Ned has been moved to the locker room from the bar to assist Tim, the regular attendant. I do not mean to imply that Tim does not need assistance. On the contrary, the increasing noise in the locker room throws him in a state of greater, if possible, than normal confusion; but the addition of Ned only makes confusion worse confounded because both Ned and Tim are so naturally gregarious that all they do is to stand listening and often joining in the conversation. The latter is easy for, though I have never fallen a victim to the charm of these two senile and incompetent employees, they are individually popular among the more heavy drinking groups.

I am the last person, I hope, to object to conviviality, but I do object to sodden bath towels, to paper cups and odd shoes and garments being strewn everywhere for weeks on end. During this season I have never seen Old Tim once pick up any of these articles. Indeed the only time I have seen him bend over was to grab for an abandoned fifty-cent piece, and to my amazement his reflexes were quicker than those of Old Ned. It may be that my instinctive liking for order makes me somewhat of a stickler, but still I should be glad to put up with everything except for the occasions when I cannot get to my locker or open it because of the large number of moist individuals who loll in front of it and who actually seem to resent my intrusion.

I shall not name names or criticize any one member of Happy Knoll, but I will say this—that the sight of a middle-aged Happy Knoll member in the nude grows less aesthetic to me year by year. Balanced diet, I am convinced, does not interest many. At any rate, their physical bulk is continually between me and my shoes when I am able to find the latter. There used to be a time when persons would hear if I said "Excuse me," but now under the ministrations of Old Ned they are too preoccupied to hear or to move in any direction. In fact, I frequently feel as though I were among bodies falling into hell as depicted on the bas-reliefs of a medieval cathedral. Is this sort of thing sport, gentlemen? Is this for what Happy Knoll was intended?

These questions, I admit, are purely rhetorical. I have been told again and again that if I don't want a shower bath and a drink I should change my shoes in the Fosbroke Alcove, but how am I to do so? Would Old Tim ever find my shoes if I left them there? Would he ever return them to my locker? The answer is, he would not. The only way to keep clothing and equipment safe at Happy Knoll is to put them firmly under lock and key, as are mine in locker 67. I am sorry to spoil the fun in front of locker 67, but I must get to it sometimes and it is not my fault that a certain Happy Knoll member collided with my key while it was in the lock and scratched his torso severely while demonstrating the follow-through he made on the difficult 10th. If there has been any complaint to the Board of Governors regarding this incident, I, too, must complain that there are other danger factors in the locker room besides keys. Only the day before yesterday, when arriving from the links, I stepped upon a number of ice cubes that had been accidentally dropped in the corridor by Old Ned. These became impaled upon my golfing spikes so that I slid a considerable distance, finally lost my balance and fell. This accident only caused our club nudists merriment instead of concern. In fact, Old Ned was too convulsed to be able to help me up and the injuries I suffered are today more serious than any key scratch.

This letter, gentlemen, is not a complaint; rather it is an invitation. Why does not your committee drop into the locker room at six o'clock some afternoon, or even at seven or eight, and hear some poorly told off-color stories, see some horrible physiques and slip on some ice yourselves? If you did, perhaps you would agree with me that any change, however insignificant, would be for the better.

Respectfully yours,

James A. Mosser

~

Letter from Mr. Benjamin Carrow to the Board of Governors of the Happy Knoll Country Club.

GENTLEMEN:

I do not like to indulge in personalities, especially as concerns members of so fine a country club as Happy Knoll, but maybe in this case I should, since I understand that Mr. James A. Mosser—who rents locker 67 in good old Alcove C—is writing you a complaint about what he calls "disorders" in the locker room. It gives me pleasure to state that neither I nor any of the gang have anything against this Mosser character personally—only he is a fussy, skinny old guy, like so many of these lawyers who argue over income taxes and never have any clean fun and lose all their sense of humor, if they were ever born with any. None of the gang has anything against him—we are only sorry he doesn't want to fit in with the group; and believe me, we have one of the swellest crowds in the locker room this summer that you gentlemen have ever seen, a whole lot too swell for any sorehead to go and ruin. Come to think of it, I have a right to be just as sore at Mosser as Mosser is at any of the gang. I ripped myself clean across the back last week because he left his key jutting out of his locker in Alcove C, an injury which made me lose my first match in the Four Ball.

Nevertheless, I don't complain, even though Muldoon himself assured me I would have won if I had gone through the ball instead of wincing on impact, from the pain the scar gave me. *C'est la guerre* has always been my motto, if you will excuse my French. Neither I nor any of the gang has any gripes about Mosser. He is the one who is public griper No. 1, and his reason seems to me mighty trivial. Frankly, gentlemen, all it was: he stepped with his spiked shoes on some ice cubes that had fallen in the alley outside of Alcove C and then did just a simple pratfall.

THE ICE-CUBE INCIDENT

It may have been the fault of our crowd that we laughed, as did Old Ned and Old Tim who were present at the time, hustling a few bourbons on the rocks. But what were we to do instead? Cry? And who can avoid laughing at those things? Remember the old vaudeville days? I still think a good bump on the rear furnishes the best sure-fire entertainment in the world. Anyway, he did not hurt himself, or if he did, it is only because he eats too much wheat germ and too much saccharine in his coffee and nothing else. Anyway the ice cubes were definitely not, as he intimated, put there for him to step upon, on purpose. The locker room gang may play jokes like that on ourselves, but never on outsiders. Why, frequently ice cubes get slithering around the locker room by accident, and twice on leaving the showers to get back to the bourbon in good old Alcove C I have stepped on them myself, barefoot. And in this connection, let me tell you, just for the laugh, the good line Old Ned got off the last time I did so. He said, It isn't everybody who is able to slide on ice in summer. Honestly, gentlemen, you cannot beat Old Ned. He is a jewel, and all the gang

would be glad to die for him. You never did a wiser thing than move him from the bar, where his talents were wasted serving the quarrelsome stuffed shirts who seem to congregate in that place.

Anyway, this letter is not intended only to explain that you mustn't mind anything that Mosser says about what he calls "conditions" in the locker room. This epistle also comes from the whole gang to convey to you gentlemen our congratulations. The Happy Knoll locker room is, in my opinion, the finest locker room I have ever seen anywhere —and I've seen plenty in my day, beginning at Princeton where I used to do the 100-yard dash (I've put on weight since then). There is, in my opinion, a real philosophy behind locker rooms, and you gentlemen have had the vision to catch it. There aren't many places left in this tough world where a gang can get together with a little Turkish toweling around its middle and relax and indulge in a good old gabfest. Well, we've got it here at Happy Knoll, and those two old princes, Ned and Tim, give just the right atmosphere. Get out of a hot shower and Ned always has the bourbon ready and it's like college days again. I'm fifty years young now every time I play a round of golf. Gentlemen, don't change anything in the locker room, and with my congratulations I want to offer you an invitation. Come down and join us sometime around fivish, sixish or even sevenish, and we'll show you what a good time really is. It's about time we had a testimonial party for the Board of Governors.

Very respectfully yours,
Ben Carrow

VI. FOR THE

The first Massachusetts Amateur Championship, conducted at Myopia Hunt Club in 1903, the year of the MGA's founding, drew 38 entrants. A hundred years later, entrants for the Amateur routinely exceed 1,000, and a dozen sectional qualifying sites around the state are now the norm for this event alone. As the MGA has grown, the success of its early Amateur and, beginning in 1905, Open championships led to an array of other state champion- ships, which now total 11 (all but the Open for amateurs). As an indication of the undying spirit of competition in Massachusetts, the competitions conducted by the MGA now require some 75 golf courses every year to handle the fields. The individuals whose names have entered the MGA's roll of champions have indeed earned their mark in golf history.

RECORD

THE CHAMPIONSHIPS OF THE MASSACHUSETTS GOLF ASSOCIATION

Brae Burn Country Club, West Newton, Massachusetts

Massachusetts Amateur Championship

The oldest and most venerated event conducted by the MGA, the state amateur annually crowns the best amateur player in the state. Unique in its appeal and format, this event challenges competitors with grueling rounds of stroke and match play over the course of several days. Arthur G. Lockwood was the inaugural champion in 1903 and now shares his name on the championship trophy with such golf legends as Francis Ouimet, Jesse Guilford, Frederick Wright and Ted Bishop.

YEAR	CHAMPION	AFFILIATION	SITE
1903	Arthur G. Lockwood	Allston	Myopia
1904	Andrew Carnegie II	Essex	Essex
1905	Arthur G. Lockwood	Allston	The Country Club
1906	Arthur G. Lockwood	Allston	Brae Burn
1907	John G. Anderson	Woodland	Woodland
1908	T. R. Fuller	Commonwealth	Wollaston
1909	Percival Gilbert	Brae Burn	Oakley
1910	H. W. Stucklen	Brae Burn	Brae Burn
1911	John G. Anderson	Brae Burn	Essex
1912	Heinie Schmidt	Worcester	Brae Burn
1913	Francis D. Ouimet	Woodland	Wollaston
1914	Francis D. Ouimet	Woodland	Brae Burn
1915	Francis D. Ouimet	Woodland	Woodland
1916	Jesse P. Guilford	Woodland	Wollaston
1917–18	Not held		
1919	Francis D. Ouimet	Woodland	Winchester
1920	Frederick J. Wright, Jr.	Albemarle	The Country Club
1921	Jesse P. Guilford	Woodland	Worcester
1922	Francis D. Ouimet	Woodland	Kernwood
1923	Karl E. Mosser	Brae Burn	Brae Burn
1924	Jesse P. Guilford	Brae Burn	Woodland
1925	Francis D. Ouimet	Woodland	The Country Club
1926	Frederick J. Wright, Jr.	Albemarle	Brae Burn
1927	Edward E. Lowery	Norfolk	Charles River
1928	Frederick J. Wright, Jr.	Albemarle	Essex
1929	Frederick J. Wright, Jr.	Albemarle	Belmont Springs
1930	Frederick J. Wright, Jr.	Albemarle	Salem
1931	Frederick J. Wright, Jr.	Albemarle	Winchester
1932	Edward P. Kirouac	Walpole	Kernwood
1933	Joseph P. Lynch	Albemarle	Worcester
1934	William O. Blaney	Brae Burn	The Country Club
1935	Edward S. Stimpson	Brae Burn	Brae Burn
1936	Clark Hodder	Framingham	Charles River
1937	David Whiteside	New Bedford	Winchester
1938	Frederick J. Wright, Jr.	Trapelo	Essex
1939	Ted Adams	South Shore	Tedesco
1940	Ted Bishop	Woodland	Salem
1941	Leo J. Martin	Trapelo	Longmeadow
1942–45	Not held		
1946	Ted Bishop	Norfolk	Charles River
1947	John Chew	Bear Hill	Commonwealth
1948	Edward Martin	Winchester	Worcester

A New Hampshire native, Jesse Guilford was known as "The Siege Gun" for his prodigious drives (up to 280 yards in the hickory-shaft era), but he was just as skilled in the short game. He won three state amateurs, two state opens and the 1921 U.S. Amateur in a career that spanned six decades.

Framingham's Bill Mallon was a two-time winner of both the Massachusetts Amateur and the New England Amateur in the early 1970s. After moderate success as a touring professional, Mallon returned home to win three consecutive New England Opens in 1976–1978, then gave up competitive golf to become a physician specializing in sports medicine.

1949	Robert W. Knowles, Jr.	The C'ntry Club	The Country Club
1950	Richard D. Chapman	Oyster Harbors	Brae Burn
1951	Edward Martin	Winchester	Vesper
1952	Tom Mahan, Jr.	United Shoe	Winchester
1953	Ernie Doherty	Shaker Glen	Salem
1954	Rupert Daniels	Bear Hill	Pittsfield
1955	Ed Connell	Thorny Lea	Myopia
1956	Charles Volpone	Ould Newbury	Belmont
1957	David Sullivan	Charles River	Longmeadow
1958	William G. Harding	Dedham	Kittansett
1959	John Tosca, Jr.	Thorny Lea	Taconic
1960	Pat Granese	United Shoe	Tedesco
1961	Ted Bishop	Pine Brook	Oak Hill
1962	Joe Carr	Wachusett	Salem
1963	Bruce Dobie	Hillcrest	Vesper
1964	William Foley	Wollaston	Worcester
1965	Ted Carangelo	Tedesco	Woodland
1966	Warren Tibbetts	Vesper	Charles River
1967	Barrie Bruce	Colonial	The Country Club
1968	Mike Ohanian	Oakley	Nashawtuc
1969	Peter Drooker	Pine Brook	Brae Burn
1970	John Tosca, Jr.	Thorny Lea	Essex
1971	Tracy Mehr	Amherst	Taconic
1972	Gary Burnett	Longmeadow	Longmeadow
1973	Bill Mallon	Framingham	Belmont
1974	Bill Mallon	Framingham	Pleasant Valley
1975	Bruce Douglass	Thorny Lea	Winchester
1976	Bruce Douglass	Thorny Lea	The Country Club
1977	Gary Burnett	Longmeadow	Weston
1978	Dave Brilliant	Belmont	Kittansett

1979	Ed Polchlopek	Hampden	Vesper
1980	Jim McDermott	Fall River	Salem
1981	Steven Tasho	Thorny Lea	Taconic
1982	James Hallet	Bass River	Tedesco
1983	James Hallet	Bass River	Woodland
1984	Jim McDermott	Fall River	Pittsfield
1985	Steven Tasho	Thorny Lea	Myopia
1986	Fran Quinn, Jr.	Pleasant Valley	Winchester
1987	Kevin Johnson	Halifax	The Country Club
1988	Kevin Johnson	Halifax	Thorny Lea
1989	Jim McDermott	Fall River	Worcester
1990	Ray Wright	Framingham	Kittansett
1991	John Salamone	Framingham	Brae Burn
1992	Trevor Gliwski	Taconic	Longmeadow
1993	Flynt Lincoln	Longmeadow	Essex
1994	Douglas Preston	Oak Hill	Charles River
1995	Ed Fletcher	Bay Pointe	Concord
1996	James Driscoll	Charles River	Myopia
1997	Jim Salinetti	Stockbridge	Weston
1998	James Driscoll	Charles River	Belmont
1999	Jim Salinetti	Stockbridge	Kittansett
2000	Jim Salinetti	Stockbridge	Worcester
2001	Brendan Hester	Pleasant Valley	The Orchards
2002			Winchester

Centennial Championship Site:
The Country Club, July 14–18, 2003

Waiting to tee off in the 1988 Massachusetts Amateur at Thorny Lea Golf Club are (left to right) Kevin Johnson of the Country Club of Halifax, Jim McDermott of the Fall River Country Club and Steve Tasho of Thorny Lea. Among them the three players would capture a total of seven state amateur championships in the 1980s.

In 1995, at the age of 17, Brookline High School graduate James Driscoll won the Western Junior and reached the final of the U.S. Junior Amateur. Subsequently, before turning professional, he won two Massachusetts Amateurs, in 1996 and 1998, and reached the final of the U.S. Amateur in 2000.

Massachusetts Open Championship

This event is the only one of its kind on the MGA championship slate, welcoming both amateur and professional golfers to compete against each other. Inaugurated in 1905 by Donald Ross' victory at Vesper Country Club, the state open has provided some of the most defining moments in Massachusetts golf history. Notable champions of past years include Walter Hagen, Francis Ouimet, Gene Sarazen, Byron Nelson and Bob Toski.

YEAR	CHAMPION	AFFILIATION	SITE
1905	Donald J. Ross	Oakley	Vesper
1906	Alex Ross	Brae Burn	Wollaston
1907	Alex Ross	Brae Burn	Brae Burn
1908	Alex Ross	Brae Burn	The Country Club
1909	Alex Ross	Brae Burn	Woodland
1910	Alex Ross	Brae Burn	Essex
1911	Donald J. Ross	Essex	The Country Club
1912	Alex Ross	Brae Burn	Oakley
1913	Tom McNamara	Boston	Brae Burn
1914	Mike Brady	Wollaston	Belmont Spring
1915	Walter Hagen	Rochester	The Country Club
1916	Mike Brady	Oakley	Brae Burn
1917–18	Not held		
1919	Jesse P. Guilford	Woodland	Worcester
1920	George L. Bowden	Commonwealth	Commonwealth
1921	Louis Tellier	Brae Burn	Essex
1922	George Kerrigan	White Beeches	Springfield
1923	Mike Brady	Detroit	Tedesco
1924	Willie Ogg	Worcester	Kernwood
1925	Tom Lally	San Antonio	Charles River
1926	Donald Vinton	Plymouth	Worcester
1927	Johnny Farrell	Quaker Ridge	Sandy Burr
1928	Leo Diegel	New York	Wollaston
1929	Jesse P. Guilford	Woodland	Vesper
1930	Joe Turnesa	New York	Brae Burn
1931	Wiffy Cox	New York	Worcester
1932	Francis Ouimet	Woodland	Oyster Harbors
1933	Ted Turner	North Adams	Belmont Spring
1934	Roy Bronsdon	Oyster Harbors	Oyster Harbors
1935	Gene Sarazen	E. Brookfield	Oak Hill
1936	Harold McSpaden	Winchester	Oak Hill
1937	Harold McSpaden	Winchester	Oyster Harbors
1938	Harold McSpaden	Winchester	Oyster Harbors
1939	Byron Nelson	Reading	Worcester
1940	Horton Smith	Chicopee	Oyster Harbors
1941	Harold McSpaden	Winchester	Oyster Harbors
1942	Ben Loving	Longmeadow	Oyster Harbors
1943–45	Not held		
1946	Ellsworth Vines	Chicago	Longmeadow
1947	Gene Kunes	Englewood	Belmont
1948	Jerry Gianferante	Longmeadow	Oak Hill

Brae Burn professional Alex Ross, brother of Donald Ross, dominated the Massachusetts Open during its first decade, winning six times. In his crowning achievement in the 1907 U.S. Open at the Philadelphia Cricket Club, Ross shot four rounds in the 70s to defeat Woodland Golf Club's Gil Nicholls for the national championship by two strokes.

The 1958 state open champion, Bob Toski of Haydenville, won six professional tournaments over a 12-month period in 1953-54, including the $50,000 World Championship at Tam O'Shanter in Chicago, before embarking on a long and distinguished career as a golf instructor.

1949	Edward Burke	New Haven	Wachusett		1978	Curt Madson	Unattached	Spring Valley
1950	John Thoren	Myopia	South Shore		1979	Jay Dolan	Hillcrest	Brae Burn
1951	Julius Boros	Mid Pines	Salem		1980	Paul Moran	Mount Snow	Essex
1952	Everett Stuart	Nantucket	Charles River		1981	Bob Menne	Nashawtuc	Nashawtuc
1953	Jim Browning	Weston	Worcester		1982	Dana Quigley	Crestwood	Longmeadow
1954	Don Hoenig	Wachusett	Wachusett		1983	Dana Quigley	Crestwood	Charles River
1955	John Thoren	Myopia	Coonamesset		1984	Dana Quigley	Crestwood	Wollaston
1956	Ed Oliver	Norfolk	Coonamesset		1985	James Hallet	Bass River	Wellesley
1957	Bob Crowley	Pine Brook	Coonamesset		1986	Kevin Johnson	Halifax	New Seabury
1958	Bob Toski	Northampton	Hyannisport		1987	Steve Jurgenson	Woodland	Weston
1959	George Kinsman	Unicorn	Hyannisport		1988	Jeff Lewis	Cummaquid	Spring Valley
1960	Bill Ezinicki	Hillview	Pittsfield		1989	Andy Morse	Blue Hill	Oak Hill
1961	Don Hoenig	Pleasant Valley	Tedesco		1990	Fran Quinn, Jr.	Pleasant Valley	Vesper
1962	Bob Crowley	Pine Brook	Belmont		1991	John Elliot	Mount Snow	Salem
1963	Bill Flynn	Thomson	Kernwood		1992	Andy Morse	Blue Hill	Taconic
1964	Bill Ezinicki	New Seabury	Pleasant Valley		1993	Pat Bates	Bass Rocks	Tedesco
1965	Jim Browning	Weston	Winchester		1994	Peter Morgan	River Hills	Woodland
1966	Bob Crowley	Pine Brook	Weston		1995	Geoffrey Sisk	Marshfield	Wollaston
1967	Paul Harney	Pleasant Valley	New Seabury		1996	Jeff Leonard	Hunters Green	Winchester
1968	Paul Harney	Pleasant Valley	International		1997	Geoffrey Sisk	Marshfield	Crumpin-Fox
1969	Paul Harney	Pleasant Valley	Spring Valley		1998	Rodney Butcher	Potowomut	Oak Hill
1970	Paul Harney	Pleasant Valley	Salem		1999	Kevin Quinn	Charles River	Wellesley
1971	Charles Volpone	Nashawtuc	Vesper		2000	James Gilleon	Black Bear	Pittsfield
1972	Charles Volpone	Nashawtuc	Tedesco		2001	Rich Parker	Fore-U DR	Mount Pleasant
1973	Bob Crowley	Pine Brook	Kernwood		2002			Longmeadow
1974	Dick Hanscom	Charles River	Woodland					
1975	Dick Hanscom	Charles River	Charles River					
1976	Paul Barkhouse	Ferncroft	Worcester					
1977	Paul Harney	Pleasant Valley	New Seabury					

Centennial Championship Site:
Tedesco Country Club, June 14–18, 2003

Dana Quigley's regional record, the best of any New England professional in the 1980s and 1990s, included three consecutive Massachusetts Open titles. MGA president Harry B. McCracken gave Quigley the winner's check at the 1984 state open at Wollaston Golf Club.

Charlie Volpone, who at 19 defeated the redoubtable Fred Wright to win the 1956 Massachusetts Amateur, went on to win two consecutive state opens as a professional, in 1971-72; he also won state open titles in Vermont, New Hampshire and Maine.

Bob Crowley, longtime head professional at Pine Brook Country Club in Weston, won three Massachusetts Opens over a 16-year span, including the 1973 state open at Kernwood Country Club in Salem, where he is pictured. The winningest club professional in New England in the post-World War II era, Crowley also captured the Maine, Vermont and New Hampshire state opens.

Massachusetts Junior Amateur Championship

Celebrating the future of the amateur game, this event crowns the best junior players in the state. In 1961, the event expanded to honor the best junior and junior-junior player and since that time has further grown to recognize three age groups (Junior, Pre-Junior & Boys divisions) within this category. Many former junior amateur players have gone on to successful amateur and professional careers in the Commonwealth and beyond.

YEAR	CHAMPION	AFFILIATION	SITE
1914	Raymond Ouimet	Brookline H.S.	Oakley
1915	Frederick J. Wright, Jr.	Watertown H.S.	Albemarle
1916	Frederick J. Wright, Jr.	Watertown H.S.	Woodland
1917	Not held		
1918	N.T. Lovell	Newton H.S.	Albemarle
1919	Edward E. Lowery	Newton H.S.	The Country Club
1920	Edward E. Lowery	Newton H.S.	Oakley
1921	Edward H. Learnard	Newton	Bellevue
1922	Clark Hodder	Commonwealth	Commonwealth
1923	Joseph M. Batchelder	Wenham	Wollaston
1924	Marshal W. Forrest	Vesper	Belmont Spring
1925	Ralph Munro	United Shoe	Tedesco
1926	James Conroy	Scarboro	Woodland
1927	Joseph P. Lynch	Albemarle	Pine Brook
1928	Charles S. Eaton	Winchester	Unicorn
1929	W. H. Donnelly, Jr.	Woodland	Brae Burn
1930	Wilfred Crossley	Norfolk	Belmont Spring
1931	W. H. Donnelly, Jr.	Woodland	Sandy Burr
1932	Richard Ruggles	Stoney Brae	Wollaston
1933	Edward H. Peterson	Oakley	Blue Hill
1934	Patrick Hegarty	Riverside	Woodland
1935	Gerald Anderson	Green Hill	Cohasset
1936	Stanley Taylor	Oyster Harbors	Unicorn
1937	John McNiff	Salem	Belmont
1938	Robert Adams	South Shore	Salem
1939	Edward O. Tabor, Jr.	Vesper	Blue Hill
1940	Ed Franzeim	Bellevue	Wollaston
1941	James Danahy	Blue Hill	Belmont
1942 -45	Not held		
1946	Robert Woodward	Bellevue	Furnace Brook
1947	John Nies, Jr.	United Shoe	Worcester
1948	Robert Zirkel	Winchester	Winchester
1949	Leo Grace	Commonwealth	Woodland
1950	William McCarthy	Furnace Brook	Wollaston
1951	Joe Tosca, Jr.	Thorny Lea	Charles River
1952	Ralph Milley	Meadow Brook	Commonwealth
1953	Ronnie Mattson	Wilbraham	United Shoe
1954	Ralph Haddad	Walpole	Commonwealth
1955	Ronnie Mattson	Wilbraham	Commonwealth
1956	Jay Dolan	Hillcrest	Wachusett
1957	Roland LaMontagne	Thorny Lea	Wollaston
1958	Burton Page	Colonial	Brookline

Above: MGA president Lionel MacDuff of Salem Country Club presented trophies at the conclusion of the 1973 Junior Amateur at Cohasset Golf Club to champion Joe Miller (right) of Longmeadow Country Club and Randy Millen of Pine Oaks Golf Club in South Easton, winner in the junior-junior division. **Right:** 1974 junior champion Marc Hetnik of Putterham Meadows Golf Club in Brookline.

1959	Robert Kirouac	Sharon	Wachusett
1960	Robert O'Connor	Unicorn	Charles River
1961	Robert Barclay	Salem	Winchester
1962	Robert Barclay	Salem	Brookline
1963	William Carroll	Longmeadow	Wachusett
1964	James Catalano	Needham	Wellesley
1965	Richard Bliss	Westboro	Dedham
1966	Dennis Perrone	Berkshire Hills	Glen Ellen
1967	Doug Johnson	Norton	Framingham
1968	Arthur E. Burke, III	Greenfield	Putterham
1969	Arthur E. Burke, III	Greenfield	Concord
1970	Robert Reni	Framingham	Oakley
1971	Rick Karbowski	Pleasant Valley	Chestnut Hill
1972	Rick Karbowski	Pleasant Valley	The Country Club
1973	Joe Miller	Longmeadow GC	Cohasset
1974	Marc Hetnik	Putterham	Wellesley
1975	Paul Littlejohn	Braintree	Duxbury
1976	Greg Orlik	Hickory Ridge	Hatherly
1977	Joseph Lynch	New Seabury	Thorny Lea
1978	Steve Minelli	Plymouth	Framingham
1979	Ken Whalley	Colonial	Hickory Ridge
1980	Terry O'Hara	Pleasant Valley	Oakley
1981	Michael Stone	Allendale	Wollaston
1982	Walter Les	Ludlow	Weston
1983	Artie Wilson	Sharon	Dedham
1984	Kevin Johnson	Halifax	Cohasset
1985	Mike Zmetrovitch	Haverhill	Kernwood
1986	Paul Bastien	Dennis Pines	Hatherly
1987	Craig Mazzini	Plymouth	Putterham

1988	Steven Bergamesca	Duxbury	Plymouth
1989	Robert Prophett	Pocasset	Indian Ridge
1990	Marc Spencer	Haverhill	Dedham
1991	Eric McPhail	Sandy Burr	Haverhill
1992	Ryan Pelis	Pine Grove	Green Hill
1993	James Driscoll	Charles River	Kernwood
1994	Justin Peters	Pembroke	The Orchards
1995	James Donnelly, IV	Beverly	Cummaquid
1996	Nathaniel Hoopes	Kittansett	Bass Rocks
1997	Ned Yetten	Indian Ridge	Walpole
1998	Michael Carbone	Dennis Pines	Oakley
1999	Brent Wanner	Dennis Pines	Woods Hole
2000	Ben Spitz	Rockland	Dedham
2001	Steven Alminas	Elmcrest	Quashnet Valley
2002			New Bedford

Centennial Championship Site:
Duxbury Yacht Club, August 4–6, 2003

Duxbury Yacht Club, host of the Massachusetts Junior Amateur in the MGA's centennial year of 2003.

Massachusetts Senior Amateur Championship

Honoring the best senior golfer in the state, this event is open to all amateur players who are 55 years of age or older. A competitive handicap index is established each year as competitors vie for this special title over a two-day period. As of 2001, John Nies, Jr., stood as the only individual who held both a Junior (1947) and Senior (1994) title.

YEAR	CHAMPION	AFFILIATION	SITE
1961	William O. Blaney	Brae Burn	Brae Burn
1962	Bruce Coffin	Salem	Charles River
1963	John C. Mercer	Oak Hill	Oak Hill
1964	David McLelland, Jr.	Taconic	Salem
1965	Max Hoffman	Pine Brook	Charles River
1966	Tim Holland	Wenham	Pine Brook
1967	Tim Holland	Wenham	Worcester
1968	Tim Holland	Wenham	Vesper
1969	Ted Bishop	Woodland	Tedesco
1970	Chester T. Birch	Eastward Ho!	Oyster Harbors/ New Seabury
1971	Larry Stepenuck	Andover	Kittansett
1972	Gerry Anderson	Worcester	Wellesley
1973	Leon Bishop	Thorny Lea	New Seabury
1974	Frank Geremonte	Meadow Brook	Haverhill
1975	Warren Tibbetts	Vesper	International
1976	John Frithsen	Bass Rocks	Eastward Ho!
1977	John Frithsen	Bass Rocks	Pittsfield
1978	Bill Anthony	Oyster Harbors	Oyster Harbors
1979	Ed Barry	Charles River	New Bedford
1980	Fran Hannaway	Salem	Wianno Club
1981	Ed Barry	Charles River	Hyannisport
1982	Frank Sendrowski	Marlboro	Hickory Ridge
1983	Tony Ciociolo	Worcester	Cummaquid
1984	John Frithsen	Bass Rocks	Eastward Ho!
1985	Fordie Pitts, Jr.	Wollaston	Wellesley
1986	Dick Crosby	Meadow Brook	Woods Hole
1987	John Gargalianos	Salem	Oakley
1988	Mel Cowe	Plymouth	Ocean Edge
1989	Fordie Pitts, Jr.	Wollaston	Pocasset
1990	Ed Myers	Oak Ridge	Crumpin-Fox
1991	Skip Duprey	Cummaquid	Hatherly
1992	George O'Rourke	Braintree	Pittsfield
1993	Paul Kelly	Woodland	Segregansett
1994	John Nies, Jr.	Essex	Cohasset
1995	Arthur Schwartz	Stockbridge	Stockbridge
1996	Jim Holbrook	Indian Ridge	Tedesco
1997	Jim Holbrook	Indian Ridge	Springfield
1998	Ed Fletcher	Bay Pointe	Eastward Ho!
1999	Donald Zargoren	New Seabury	Hatherly
2000	Ed Fletcher	Quashet Valley	Haverhill
2001	Ed Fletcher	Quashet Valley	Essex
2002			Woodland

Centennial Championship Site:
Brae Burn Country Club, September 22–23, 2003

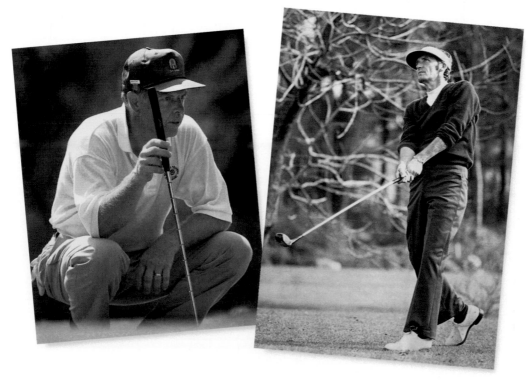

Far left: When two-time state senior amateur champion Ed Fletcher won the Massachusetts State Amateur in 1995, two months shy of his 54th birthday, he became the oldest state amateur champion in the long history of the event, replacing Ted Bishop, who won in 1961 at the age of 48. **Left:** 1985 state senior amateur champion Fordie Pitts, Jr., also gained victories in the Massachusetts Father and Son, the Massachusetts Father and Daughter and the Massachusetts Senior Four-Ball.

Other MGA Championships

Massachusetts Father and Son Championship

The best father and son pairs in the state compete annually at this popular MGA event. The Father and Son Championship pits the winners of the Father and Son Gross Championship from each MGA member club against each other in an 18-hole foursomes stroke play format.

Year	Champion	Affiliation	Site
1977	Addison and Flynt Lincoln	Longmeadow	Essex
1978	Addison and Flynt Lincoln	Longmeadow	Worcester
1979	Terry O'Hara and Terry, Jr.	Pleasant Valley	Cohasset
1980	Donald and Peter Jepsen	Riverside	Belmont
1981	Henry and John Thompson	Concord	Wellesley
1982	Donald and Peter Jepson	Riverside	Marshfield
1983	Bud and Ken Hollingsworth	Bass River	Kernwood
1984	Fordie Pitts and Fordie, Jr.	Scituate	Essex
1985	Joe and Craig Mazzini	Plymouth	Duxbury
1986	Fordie Pitts and Fordie, Jr.	Scituate	Pittsfield
1987	Joseph and Jason Cook	Brockton	Cohasset
1988	Fordie Pitts and Fordie, Jr.	Scituate	Marshfield
1989	Joseph and Jason Cook	Brockton	Foxborough
1990	Fordie Pitts and Fordie, Jr.	Scituate	Pocasset
1991	Tom and Tim Martin	Woodland	Cohasset
1992	Don and Ron Laverdiere	Hickory Ridge	Thomson
1993	Ted and Jack Kenerson	Brae Burn	Norton
1994	George and John Dixon	Vesper	Brae Burn
1995	Joseph and Jason Cook	Brockton	Foxborough
1996	James and Jason Ruschioni	Oak Hill	Thorny Lea
1997	Dick and Jim Salinetti	Stockbridge	Ludlow
1998	Joseph and Jason Cook	Brockton	Dedham
1999	Dick and Jim Salinetti	Stockbridge	Blue Hill
2000	Dick and Jim Salinetti	Stockbridge	Cohasset
2001	Michael and Andrew Oleksak	Crestview	Fall River
2002			Bass Rocks

Centennial Championship Site: Stockbridge Country Club, Stockbridge Golf Club, August 25, 2003

Massachusetts Father and Daughter Championship

Open to any father and daughter team who are both members at an MGA member club. (The WGAM hosts the counterpart event every year—the Mother and Daughter Championship.) Format consists of one round of 18-hole stroke play; a father is permitted to play one round with one daughter in the championship.

Year	Champion	Affiliation	Site
1981	Fordie and Mary Lou Pitts	Scituate	Wellesley
1982	Tom and Kathy Rourke	Ferncroft	Marshfield
1983	Al and Robin Auger	Beverly	Concord
1984	Mel and Beth O'Kelly	Marshfield	Beverly
1985	Mel and Beth O'Kelly	Marshfield	Dedham
1986	Mel and Beth O'Kelly	Marshfield	Pembroke
1987	Fordie and Mary Lou Pitts	Scituate	Foxboro
1988	Fordie and Karen Pitts	Scituate	Dedham
1989	Mel and Beth O'Kelly	Marshfield	Hatherly
1990	David DeCarolis and Amy Miller	Oak Hill	Bay Pointe
1991	Fordie and Karen Pitts	Scituate	Franklin
1992	Not held		
1993	Tom Rourke and Kathy Natale	Ferncroft	Bass Rocks
1994	Not held		
1995	Paul and Merry Chiampa	Longmeadow CC	Wahconah
1996	Fordie and Karen Pitts	Scituate	Hatherly
1997	Fordie and Karen Pitts	Scituate	Marlboro
1998	Tom Rourke and Kathy Natale	Ferncroft	Tatnuck
1999	Gary and Melanie Curtin	Presidents	Bellevue
2000	Brian and Liz Callery	The Ridge Club	Whitinsville
2001	David DeCarolis and Amy Miller	Oak Hill	Highland
2002			Wilbraham

Centennial Championship Site: Concord Country Club, August 21, 2003

Mel and Beth O'Kelly, playing out of Marshfield Country Club, won four Father and Daughter titles in the 1980s.

Oyster Harbors Club in Osterville, host of the Massachusetts Four-Ball Championship in the MGA's centennial year of 2003.

Massachusetts Four-Ball Championship

Injecting a team element into an individualized sport, this event honors the best two-person teams of amateur golfers in the state. Since its inception in 1981, the event has celebrated some of the best amateur teams in the region and embraced the spirit of teamwork. Champions of the past have been brothers, friends and even father and son pairs.

Year	Champions	Site
1981	Walter Sharis and Warren Nelson	Concord
1982	James Hallet and Rick Edwards	Haverhill
1983	James Hallet and Rick Edwards	Indian Ridge
1984	Burton Page and Mike O'Keefe	Halifax
1985	Burton Page and Ken Whalley	Fall River
1986	Jon Fasick and Carter Fasick	Woodland
1987	Joe Keller and Charles Volpone	Haverhill
1988	Steven Tasho and Bruce Chalas	Stow Acres
1989	Alistair Catto and Dean Godek	Hyannisport
1990	Ed Gunderson and Kevin Heffron	The Orchards
1991	Jon Fasick and Carter Fasick	Hyannisport/Wianno
1992	Patrick Grant and Jerry Daly	Marshfield/Duxbury
1993	Joe Keller and Charles Volpone	Stow Acres
1994	Steven Tasho and Bruce Chalas	Stow Acres
1995	Cy Kilgore and Bill Jenks	Stow Acres
1996	James and Jason Ruschioni	Stow Acres
1997	Jon Fasick and Carter Fasick	Stow Acres
1998	Jon Fasick and Carter Fasick	Stow Acres
1999	Alistair Catto and Dean Godek	Franklin
2000	Charles Tryder and Joe Maher	Walpole
2001	James and Jason Ruschioni	Stow Acres
2002		The International

Centennial Championship Site:
Oyster Harbors Country Club, May 19–20, 2003

Massachusetts Public Links Championship

Created to honor the spirit of public golf in 1982, this event is limited to competitors who are bona fide public course players who do not hold membership at any course from which the general public is excluded or at any private club maintaining its own course. Traditionally, the competition takes place over a two-day period and players are not limited by a handicap index requirement.

Year	Champion	Affiliation	Site
1982	Don Reycroft	Ponkapoag	Leo J. Martin
1983	Ralph Johnson	Halifax	George Wright
1984	Harvey Ortof	Colonial	George Wright
1985	Harvey Ortof	Colonial	George Wright
1986	Dave Curley	Monoosnock	George Wright
1987	Thomas Rooney	Ponkapoag	George Wright
1988	Bob Bradley	Ponkapoag	George Wright
1989	Steve St. Amand	Olde Salem	George Wright
1990	Steve St. Amand	Olde Salem	George Wright
1991	Alistair Catto	The Orchards	George Wright
1992	Bill Jenks	Ponkapoag	George Wright
1993	Steve St. Amand	Olde Salem	George Wright
1994	Jon Fasick	New England	Poquoy Brook
1995	Daniel Hyde	Newton Comm.	Maplegate
1996	Keith Allcock	Norton	Wachusett
1997	Kevin Murphy	Bradford	Shaker Hills
1998	Eric McPhail	Sandy Burr	Olde Barnstable Fairgrounds
1999	Kevin Hanlon	Foxborough	Westover
2000	Josh Hillman	Greenfield	Franklin Park
2001	Eric McPhail	Sandy Burr	Chicopee
2002			New England

Centennial Championship Site:
Crumpin-Fox Club, August 18–19, 2003

Don Reycroft of Ponkapoag Golf Course in Canton captured the inaugural Massachusetts Public Links Championship in 1982. He is seen here with Ray Bump, MGA president in 1986-87; Bump was the driving force behind the creation of the publinx competition.

Massachusetts Mid-Amateur Championship

Players who are slightly past their prime can find respite in this event which is open to amateur golfers who are 30 years of age or older. The inaugural event held in 1984 at New Seabury marked the first time that golfers of common age could compete without going head to head with some of the younger collegiate stars. A competitive handicap index is established each year to maintain the high level of competition among the field.

YEAR	CHAMPION	AFFILIATION	SITE
1984	Peter Drooker	Pine Brook	New Seabury
1985	James Ruschioni	Oak Hill	New Seabury
1986	Joseph Keller	Oyster Harbors	New Seabury /Quashnet Valley
1987	Joseph Keller	Oyster Harbors	New Seabury /Quashnet Valley
1988	Paul Murphy	Charles River	New Seabury /Quashnet Valley
1989	Robert Bradley	Ponkapoag	New Seabury /Willowbend
1990	Jon Fasick	New England	New Seabury /Willowbend
1991	James Ruschioni	Oak Hill	New Seabury /Cape Cod
1992	Joseph Keller	Oyster Harbors	New Seabury /Willowbend
1993	Dick Stimets	Oyster Harbors	New Seabury /Willowbend
1994	Kevin Carey	Dennis Pines	New Seabury /Cape Cod
1995	Kevin Carey	Dennis Pines	New Seabury /The Ridge Club
1996	Robert Bradley	Ponkapoag	Stockbridge /Wyantenuck
1997	James Ruschioni	Oak Hill	Duxbury /Marshfield
1998	Steven Tasho	Thorny Lea	Concord /Nashawtuc
1999	Frank Vana, Jr.	Marlborough	Longmeadow
2000	Frank Vana, Jr.	Marlborough	Sterling
2001	Frank Vana, Jr.	Marlborough	Crestview
2002			Walpole

Centennial Championship Site:
Myopia Hunt Club, September 29–30, 2003

Right: **Jim Ruschioni of Oak Hill Country Club in Fitchburg was one of the state's dominant amateur players in the 1990s, qualifying for match play in the state amateur 10 times, twice finishing as runner-up. He won the Massachusetts Mid-Amateur in 1991 and 1997 and also prevailed in the Father and Son and the Four-Ball championships with son Jason.**

Massachusetts Senior Four-Ball Championship

The second youngest MGA championship event, the Senior Four-Ball began in 1997 and is open to two-person teams of amateur golfers who are 55 years of age or older. The senior field is limited each year and a competitive handicap index is established in order to create a competitive, team environment on the course.

YEAR	CHAMPIONS	SITE
1997	Fordie Pitts, Jr. and Ed Fletcher	Oak Hill
1998	Fordie Pitts, Jr. and Ed Fletcher	Oak Hill
1999	Peter Grogan and Jim Holbrook	Haverhill
2000	Fred Walker and Bob Coffey	Berkshire Hills
2001	Jack Maher and Ed Fletcher	Sterling
2002		Cummaquid

Centennial Championship Site:
Worcester Country Club, August 11–12, 2003

Massachusetts Net Team Championship

The youngest MGA championship event on the schedule, the Net Team made its debut at the turn of the 20th century at The Kittansett Club. Created for the mid-handicap golfer, this event is open to two-person teams of amateur golfers who hold membership in the same MGA club.

YEAR	CHAMPION	SITE
2000	Bruce Feno and Ken Sylvia	Kittansett
2001	Roger Prevey and William Preite	Stockbridge
2002		Hyannisport

Centennial Championship Site:
Weston Golf Club, October 2, 2003

Massachusetts Women's Amateur Championship

Known as the Association Championship, this competition is conducted by the Women's Golf Association of Massachusetts. The current format for entrants is an 18-hole stroke play qualifying round, followed by match play in two flights of 32.

Year	Champion	Affiliation	Site
1900	Grace Keyes	Concord	Oakley
1901	Margaret Curtis	Oakley	The Country Club
1902	Molly B. Adams	Wollaston	Wollaston
1903	Fanny C. Osgood	The Country Club	Oakley
1904	Fanny C. Osgood	The Country Club	Wollaston
1905	Pauline Mackay	Oakley	Brae Burn
1906	Pauline Mackay	Oakley	Woodland
1907	Margaret Curtis	The Country Club	The Country Club
1908	Margaret Curtis	The Country Club	Brae Burn
1909	Molly B. Adams	Wollaston	Oakley
1910	Fanny C. Osgood	The Country Club	Wollaston
1911	Fanny C. Osgood	The Country Club	Oakley
1912	Martha L. Roope	Brae Burn	Wollaston
1913	Fanny C. Osgood	The Country Club	Oakley
1914	Margaret Curtis	The Country Club	Woodland
1915	Vera Ramsey	Salem	Brae Burn
1916	Vera Ramsey	Salem	The Country Club
1917	Katherine H. Jackson	Oakley	Woodland
1918	Not held		
1919	Florence K. Daley	Oakley	Brae Burn
1920	Harriot Curtis	Essex	Belmont Springs
1921	Glenna Collett	Metacomet	Winchester
1922	Dorothy C. Hurd		Brae Burn
1923	Katherine E. Belcher	Winchester	Worcester
1924	K. Belcher Stone	Oakley	The Country Club
1925	Edith N. Baker	Oakley	Weston
1926	Madeline Waxman	Kernwood	Kernwood
1927	Edith N. Baker	Oakley	Woodland
1928	Edith N. Baker	Oakley	Weston
1929	Edith N. Baker	Oakley	Charles River
1930	Dorothy Richards	Weston	Salem
1931	Rosamund Vahey	Oakley	Brae Burn
1932	Edith N. Baker	Oakley	Andover
1933	Mary Parkinson	Dedham	Charles River
1934	Rosamund Vahey	Oakley	Winchester
1935	Rosamund Vahey	Oakley	Brae Burn
1936	Dorothy H. Whittemore	Brae Burn	Salem
1937	Deborah Verry	Tatnuck	The Country Club
1938	Dorothy H. Beard	Charles River	Belmont
1939	Dorothy H. Beard	Charles River	Weston
1940	Deborah Verry	Tatnuck	Worcester
1941	Mary Grew	Dedham	Winchester
1942	Dorothy H. Beard	Charles River	Brae Burn
1943	Not held		
-45			

Belmont Country Club, host of the WGAM's 100th staging of the state women's amateur championship in 2003.

1946	Nancy Black	Marshfield	Charles River
1947	Nancy Black	Marshfield	Belmont
1948	Florence McClusky	Worcester	Weston
1949	Ruth Woodward	Fall River	Salem
1950	Ann C. Boros	Marshfield	Brae Burn
1951	Laddie Homer	Brae Burn	Charles River
1952	Ann Nicolls	Weston	The Country Club
1953	Florence McClusky	Worcester	Winchester
1954	Joanne Goodwin	Plymouth	Essex
1955	Theodora Rooney	Charles River	Pine Brook
1956	Joanne Goodwin	Dartmouth	Salem
1957	Beatrice Bower	Essex	Belmont
1958	Joanne Goodwin	Haverhill	Worcester
1959	Dana Lombard	Weston	Brae Burn
1960	Gene McAuliffe	Charles River	Concord
1961	Joanne Goodwin	Haverhill	Charles River
1962	Florence McClusky	Worcester	Kernwood
1963	Ann Sampson	Haverhill	Haverhill
1964	Dana Lombard	Weston	Marshfield
1965	Florence McClusky	Worcester	The Country Club
1966	Florence McClusky	Worcester	Winchester
1967	Dana Lombard	Weston	Brae Burn
1968	Dana Lombard	Weston	Nashawtuc
1969	Patricia O'Brien	Pittsfield	Dedham
1970	Barbara Thorner	Tedesco	Tedesco
1971	Patricia O'Brien	Pittsfield	Charles River
1972	Pat Bradley	Indian Ridge	Worcester
1973	Noreen Friel	Andover	Pine Brook
1974	Debbie Simourian	Woodland	Brae Burn
1975	Jeanne-Marie Boylan	Charles River	Weston
1976	Jeanne-Marie Boylan	Charles River	Winchester
1977	Debbie Jamgochian	Woodland	Belmont
1978	Jeanne-Marie Boylan	Hatherly	Concord
1979	Sally Quinlan	Dennis Pines	Salem
1980	Noreen Uihlein	New Bedford	Duxbury
1981	Noreen Uihlein	New Bedford	Charles River
1982	Muffy Marlio	Kittansett	Dedham
1983	Muffy Marlio	Kittansett	Tedesco
1984	Karen Plamondon	Crystal Springs	Kittansett
1985	Loren Milhench	Kittansett	Wollaston
1986	Loren Milhench	Kittansett	Walpole
1987	Marion Maney	New Seabury	Wellesley
1988	Anne Marie Tobin	Bellevue	Brae Burn
1989	Carri Wood	Bass River	Longmeadow
1990	Natalie Galligan	Brae Burn	The Country Club
1991	Anne Marie Tobin	Bellevue	Essex
1992	Anne Marie Tobin	Bellevue	Myopia
1993	Anne Marie Tobin	Bellevue	Mount Pleasant
1994	Anne Marie Tobin	Bellevue	Oak Hill
1995	Anne Marie Tobin	Bellevue	The Orchards
1996	Mary Gale	Tatnuck	Belmont
1997	Karen Richardson	Haverhill	Concord
1998	Tracy Welch	Winchester	Kernwood
1999	Laura Torrisi	Sterling	Oak Hill
2000	Anne Marie Tobin	Bellevue	Oakley
2001	Laura Torrisi	Stow Acres	Dedham
2002			Wyantenuck

Oakley Country Club's Rosamund Vahey was one of the dominant women amateurs in Massachusetts in the 1930s, winning the Association Championship three times.

Joanne Goodwin, described in the press as "a petite precisionist from Plymouth," won her first Association Championship in 1954 at the age of 18, and added three more titles over the years.

The Massachusetts Connection

National Championships Conducted in Massachusetts

Year	Championship	Winner	Site
1897	U.S. Women's Amateur	Beatrix Hoyt	Essex
1898	U.S. Open	Fred Herd	Myopia
1901	U.S. Open	Willie Anderson	Myopia
1902	U.S. Women's Amateur	Genevieve Hecker	The Country Club
1905	U.S. Open	Willie Anderson	Myopia
1906	U.S. Women's Amateur	Harriot Curtis	Brae Burn
1908	U.S. Open	Fred McLeod	Myopia
1910	U.S. Amateur	William Fownes	The Country Club
1912	U.S. Women's Amateur	Margaret Curtis	Essex
1913	U.S. Open	Francis D. Ouimet	The Country Club
1916	U.S. Women's Amateur	Alexa Sterling	Belmont Springs
1919	U.S. Open	Walter Hagen	Brae Burn
1922	U.S. Amateur	Jess Sweetser	The Country Club
1925	U.S. Open	William Macfarlane	Worcester
1928	U.S. Amateur	Robert Tyre Jones, Jr.	Brae Burn
1932	U.S. Women's Amateur	Virginia Van Wie	Salem
1934	U.S. Amateur	Lawson Little	The Country Club
1941	U.S. Women's Amateur	Elizabeth Hicks	The Country Club
1953	U.S. Girls Junior	Mildred Meyerson	The Country Club
1954	U.S. Women's Open	Babe Zaharias	Salem
1956	PGA Championship	Jack Burke	Blue Hill
1956	U.S. Junior	Harlan Stevenson	Taconic
1957	U.S. Amateur	Hillman Robbins	The Country Club
1960	U.S. Women's Open	Betsy Rawls	Worcester
1960	U.S. Senior Amateur	Michael Cestone	Oyster Harbors
1963	U.S. Women's Amateur	Anne Sander	Taconic
1963	U.S. Open	Julius Boros	The Country Club
1967	LPGA Championship	Kathy Whitworth	Pleasant Valley
1968	LPGA Championship	Sandra Post	Pleasant Valley
1968	U.S. Junior	Eddie Pearce	The Country Club
1970	LPGA Championship	Shirley Englehorn	Pleasant Valley
1971	LPGA Championship	Kathy Whitworth	Pleasant Valley
1972	LPGA Championship	Kathy Ahern	Pleasant Valley
1973	LPGA Championship	Mary Mills	Pleasant Valley
1974	LPGA Championship	Sandra Haynie	Pleasant Valley
1975	U.S. Women's Amateur	Beth Daniels	Brae Burn
1975	U.S. Girls Junior	Dayana Benson	Dedham
1977	U.S. Senior Amateur	Dale Morey	Salem
1982	U.S. Amateur	Jay Sigel	The Country Club
1984	U.S. Women's Open	Hollis Stacy	Salem
1987	U.S. Girls Junior	Michelle McGann	The Orchards
1988	U.S. Open	Curtis Strange	The Country Club
1992	U.S. Junior	Tiger Woods	Wollaston
1995	U.S. Women's Amateur	Kelli Kuehne	The Country Club
1995	U.S. Women's Mid-Amateur	Ellen Port	Essex
1995	U.S. Girls Junior	Marcy Newton	Longmeadow
1995	U.S. Amateur Public Links	Chris Wollmann	Stow Acres
1996	U.S. Senior Amateur	Gordon Brewer	Taconic
1997	U.S. Women's Amateur	Silvia Cavalleri	Brae Burn
2001	U.S. Senior Open	Bruce Fleisher	Salem
2003	U.S. Men's State Team		Charles River
2003	U.S. Women's State Team		Wellesley

Top: **A formidable opponent in match play, Newport native Lawson Little won the U.S. Amateur at The Country Club in September of 1934 and completed there the first of his two successive "Little Slams" in the British and U.S. Amateurs of 1934 and 1935. After turning professional, Little won the U.S. Open at the Canterbury Golf Club in Cleveland, Ohio, in 1940.** *Middle:* **The 1963 U.S. Open at The Country Club was decided in a three-way playoff among, from left, eventual champion Julius Boros, Arnold Palmer and Jacky Cupit.** *Above:* **Texan Jack Burke won the 1956 PGA Championship at Blue Hill Country Club in Canton, defeating Ted Kroll in the final, 3 and 2. It was the only time during the 20th century that the PGA Championship was played in Massachusetts.**

National Championships
Won by Massachusetts Players

Year	Championship	Winner
1905	U.S. Women's Amateur	Pauline McKay
1906	U.S. Women's Amateur	Harriot Curtis
1907	U.S. Open	Alex Ross
1907	U.S. Women's Amateur	Margaret Curtis
1908	U.S. Women's Amateur	Katherine Harley
1911	U.S. Women's Amateur	Margaret Curtis
1912	U.S. Women's Amateur	Margaret Curtis
1913	U.S. Open	Francis D. Ouimet
1914	U.S. Amateur	Francis D. Ouimet
1914	U.S. Women's Amateur	Katherine Harley
1921	U.S. Amateur	Jesse Guilford
1931	U.S. Amateur	Francis D. Ouimet
1946	U.S. Amateur	Ted Bishop
1947	U.S. Public Links	Wilfred Crossley
1956	U.S. Senior	Fred Wright
1981	U.S. Women's Open	Pat Bradley
1987	U.S. Public Links	Kevin Johnson
1992	U.S. Women's Mid-Amateur	Marion Maney-McInemey

International Competitions
Conducted in Massachusetts

Year	Event	Winner	Site
1927	Ryder Cup	United States	Worcester
1932	Walker Cup	United States	The Country Club
1938	Curtis Cup	United States	Essex
1953	Walker Cup	United States	Kittansett
1958	Curtis Cup	Great Britain & Ireland	Brae Burn
1970	Curtis Cup	United States	Brae Burn
1973	Walker Cup	United States	The Country Club
1999	Ryder Cup	United States	The Country Club

Right: The Massachusetts Junior Amateur champion in 1930, Wilfred Crossley of Dedham defeated Avery Beck, 6 and 5, in the final of the 1947 U.S. Amateur Public Links Championship, played at Meadowbrook Golf Club in Minneapolis.
Below: Charles River Country Club, site of the USGA's Men's State Team Championship in 2003.

"The stupendous Fourth Estate..."
—*Thomas Carlyle*

Herb Wind in a characteristic posture, covering the 1963 U.S. Open at The Country Club in Brookline for *The New Yorker*.

THE MEN AND WOMEN who nurtured and advanced the structure of the game of golf and the men and women who played it for pleasure or profit in Massachusetts owe a debt of appreciation to those writers who specialized in the sport and helped by carrying the word to the public through their various publications—starting with Charles Bramwell of the *Boston Herald* who covered the game George Wright and his friends played at Franklin Park on December 10, 1890. We here express that appreciation to:

John G. Anderson, *Boston Evening Transcript*

Roger Barry, *Patriot Ledger*

Ben Bowker, *Boston Evening Transcript*

Fred Burnham, *Haverhill Gazette*

Ralph Clifford, *Boston Traveler*

Fred Cole, *Lawrence Eagle*

Joe Concannon, *Boston Globe*

Geoff Converse, *Cape Cod Times*

Russ Conway, *Lawrence Eagle Tribune*

Nick Del Ninno, *Boston Traveler*

Kitte Desmond, *Boston Globe*

William Doyle, *Worcester Telegram*

Rob Duca, *Cape Cod Times*

John English, *Boston Herald*

Gerry Finn, *Springfield Union*

Tom Fitzgerald, *Boston Globe*

John M. Flynn, *Berkshire Eagle*

A. Linde Fowler, *Boston Evening Transcript*

Tim Geary, *Fall River Herald News*

Joe Gordon, *Boston Herald*

Tom Gorman, *Dedham Transcript News*

Owen Griffith, *Cape Cod Times*

Bill Grimes, *Boston American*

Paul Harber, *Boston Globe*

Russ Held, *Springfield Union*

Gerry Hern, *Boston Post*

Ron Hobson, *Patriot Ledger*

Paul Johnson, *Worcester Telegram*

George Kelleher, *Springfield Union*

Steve Kelly, *Springfield Republican*

Fred Knight, *Boston Traveler*

Lee Lahey, *Berkshire Eagle*

Henry Landress, *Worcester Telegram*

Gary Larrabee, *Salem Evening News*

Joe Looney, *Boston Herald*

E. Terry MacGovern, *Berkshire Courier*

Jim McCabe, *Boston Globe*

Bob McDonough, *Berkshire Eagle*

Jack McCarthy, *Boston Herald*

George McGuane, *Lowell Sun*

D. J. McGuiness, *Boston Globe*

Jack Mahoney, *Boston Herald*

Harry Molter, *Christian Science Monitor*

W. E. Mullins, *Boston Herald*

Tim Murphy, *Worcester Telegram*

Jack O'Leary, *Boston Herald*

Larry Paton, *Boston Herald*

Bob Pryor, *Marlboro Enterprise*

Jim Regan, *Springfield Union*

Matt Rillovick, *Lynn Item*

Ernie Roberts, *Boston Globe*

Tony Romano, *Salem Evening News*

Frank Ryan, *Boston Traveler*

Walter Ryan, *Haverhill Gazette*

Arthur Sampson, *Boston Herald*

Frank Stoddard, *Brockton Enterprise*

Ed Toole, *Springfield Union*

John Veracka, *Marlboro Enterprise*

W. A. Whitcomb, *Boston Globe*

Bob White, *Boston Post*

Herbert Warren Wind, *The New Yorker*

SEGREGANSETT COUNTRY CLUB
...TON, M

"Eastward Ho!" Golf Links
...AM, MASSACHUSE

VESPER
Vesper Country Club
M. G. A. RATING

BASS RIVER GOLF CLUB
South Yarmouth, Massachusetts

...NTY ADAMS COUNTRY CLUB
NORTH ADAMS
Score Card

...hasset Golf Club
...ohasset Mass.
CONASSET GOLF CLUB

ALBEMARLE GOLF CLUB
...TON, MASS.

Observe Rules and Ethics of Golf
SWAMPSCOTT COUNTRY CLUB
TEDESCO

San...

South Shore Country Club
Hingham

Country Club of Greenfield

Marshfield Country Club

Please Replace All Divots
CAC

Belmont Country Club
BELMONT, MASS.

ANDOVER COUNTRY CLUB
ANDOVER MASSACHUSETTS

...OLF CLUB
...BRIDGE
...SETTS

DIVOTS—It is...

MILTON